Dia Center for the Arts
Discussions in Contemporary Culture
Number 10

VISUAL DISPLAY

Culture Beyond Appearances

Edited by Lynne Cooke and Peter Wollen

Bay Press Seattle 1995

Printed in the United States of America.
First Printing 1995

Library of Congress Number 89-650815
ISSN 1047-6806
ISBN 0-941920-32-1   1000864675

Bay Press
115 West Denny Way
Seattle, WA 98119
206.284.1218 (fax)

Design by Bethany Johns with Kathleen Oginski,
Bethany Johns Design, New York.

Typeset in Joanna, Bank Gothic and Meta.

Cover image: Cary Wolinsky, *Wookey Hole*.

VISUAL DISPLAY

Culture Beyond Appearances

TABLE OF CONTENTS

A NOTE ON THE SERIES

Since 1987, Dia has presented the Discussions in Contemporary Culture series to provide a setting for multidisciplinary groups of scholars to consider and debate timely cultural topics. In that same year, Dia opened an exhibition facility dedicated to the presentation of large-scale, long-term exhibitions of site-specific contemporary art. The conference "Visual Display," held in May 1993, was thus apropos of Dia's commitment to the critical understanding of our own exhibition endeavors. While the participants discussed many different forms of visual display—including religious, museological, economic, medical, and filmic—the discussions that ensued provided informative structures for examining not only the displays themselves but the historical and social contexts from which they came. Two years in the making, this book, the tenth in the series, documents the proceedings of the conference.

Lynne Cooke, Dia's Curator, and Peter Wollen, as editors of this volume, drew from their distinguished experience in formulating the ideas that shaped the conference and this book. We would like to extend our warmest thanks to them, as well as all of the panelists for their contributions, and to David Freedberg and Giuliana Bruno for acting as moderators at the conference. The lion's share of the work in preparing the book for publication was, however, done by Karen Kelly, Dia's Director of Publications, with the editorial expertise of Susan Bell. She was assisted in every aspect of managing the book's production by Franklin Sirmans, Publications Assistant, who also devoted himself to finding the photographs that help to illuminate the written contributions. We are, as always, grateful to them for their skillful, expert guidance. In addition, we are indebted to Anastasia Aukeman and Kristin M. Jones, who read and reread the galleys. For their good humor and resilience during the frantic weeks of organization prior to the conference, thanks to Sara Tucker, Laura Fields, Steven Evans, Michelle Marozik, and the entire staff at Dia.

With her elegant design, Bethany Johns has given a complementary shape to the book's content. We thank her for her continued commitment to this series of books. She was assisted by Kathleen Oginski, whose patience and care is gratefully acknowledged. For their abiding support, we are also indebted to Kim Barnett, Sally Brunsman, and Paula Ladenburg at Bay Press.

Public programs at Dia are supported in part by a generous grant from the Lila Acheson Wallace Theatre Fund at Community Funds, Inc. Additional funding was provided by the members of the Dia Art Council, the major annual support group of Dia Center for the Arts, and the Dia Art Circle.   **Michael Govan, Director**

Eliot Elisofon, *Hat Windows*, 1938.

Peter Wollen

INTRODUCTION

Visual display is the other side of the spectacle: the side of production rather than consumption or reception, the designer rather than the viewer, the agent rather than the patient. It is related to exhibitionism rather than scopophilia. In his notorious seminar on Edgar Allan Poe's *The Purloined Letter*, Jacques Lacan demonstrated how display might, on occasion, be the best method of concealment—provided, of course, the precaution has been taken of transforming the superficial appearance of the hidden object. Whereas the dull, empirical, Marie Bonaparte–like, seeing-is-believing police chief overlooks and misses the incriminating letter (the signifier on display) for which he is searching, the uncannily brilliant Dupin, figure of the Lacanian psychoanalyst himself, able to understand a logic that is coded, immediately sees the signifier displayed in full view, just as he desires.

Writing a few years later, Guy Debord, the theorist of the spectacle, noted how, in modern times, an excess of display has the effect of concealing the truth of the society that produces it, providing the viewer with an unending stream of images that might be best understood, not simply as detached from a real world of things, as Debord implied, but as working to efface any trace of the symbolic, condemning the viewer to a world in which we can see everything but understand nothing—allowing us, as viewer-victims, in Debord's phrase, only "a random 'choice of ephemera.'" In Edward Ball's paper in this volume, written from the point of view of a technician working within the world of the spectacle, the tensions inherent in media display are themselves displayed: tensions built into the rift between scene and image, participant and onlooker. The world of the spectacle is an imaginary world, offering transient and illusory satisfactions, while thereby denying access through the signifier to cure or truth.

Display, however, when its flow is arrested, can still have a revelatory power, provided it is seen, not in terms of the image, but in terms of the symptom. In fact, it is only through display that truth is revealed—not, of course, directly, but obliquely and *en travesti*. It is through modes of display that regimes of all sorts reveal the truths they mean to conceal. Above all, it is necessary to place the myriad contemporary forms of display in a historical context. The main effect of the interminable transience of modern spectacle, as Debord noted, is to efface history and historical understanding. Each historic period has its own rhetorical mode of display, because each has different truths to conceal.

Stephen Bann, in "Shrines, Curiosities, and the Rhetoric of Display," reveals how the passage from shrine to cabinet to museum takes place along a single axis—the axis of rhetoric. At different historical periods, the mode of display reflects the priority of the holy, the marvelous, and the antique, and in each case, the power of display depends, not simply on the object displayed, but also on the rhetoric of the display itself. The return of a baroque rhetoric— that of the *Wunderkammer*—in the contemporary Museum of Jurassic Technology, delineated by Ralph Rugoff, or of a Shandy-esque rhetoric as in Daniel Spoerri's *Musée sentimental*, evoked here by Jean-Hubert Martin, can be seen, not simply as a reappropriation of past historical modes of display, but as a critical refunctioning of their rhetoric. History is reconstructed in Spoerri's work through objects that arouse idiosyncratic personal feelings; in the Museum of Jurassic Technology through objects designed to provoke idiosyncratic scientific, or quasi-scientific rumination.

Moreover, the Museum of Jurassic Technology reminds us that science has its own rhetoric of exhibition. Lisa Cartwright and Ludmilla Jordanova each concentrate specifically on medicine as the site of scientific display— a site necessarily founded on the human body itself, both gendered and socially stratified. Supposedly, of course, medical display is designed on sci- entific principles as a pragmatic aid for health-care professionals. In reality, however, it too depends upon a rhetoric that can be read as producing not only information about disease, but also about its own institutional and epistemic pathology. The sciences, more than any other human institution, seek to be presented as ordered, rational, and developing in a dynamic and appropriate way, yet the rhetoric of medical-imaging produces narratives of success and maps of conquest, which reinsert science into the imaginary universe of the soap opera and imperial saga.

Death, it goes without saying, is the secret truth of medical practice, and it is death that reappears in displaced form in sites as apparently different as Peale's Museum in Baltimore and Madame Tussaud's in London, where uncanny similarity throws the rhetoric of each into a sharp, new light. As detailed by Susan Stewart and Marina Warner, the obsession in the museum with history is always, necessarily, an obsession with death. The waxwork display links many of the themes of the conference since wax is used, for example, for the creation of incorruptible relics in shrines in the Middle Ages and after, for the visual display of human anatomy in Baroque medical displays, for the representation of history and popular memory in post-Revolutionary France, for sexual fetishism in twentieth-century art—as witness the works of Oskar Kokoschka, Hans Bellmer, or Cindy Sherman. Marina Warner notes that beneath all these forms of embalming and simulation, religious, political, medical, or aesthetic, lurks a single myth, that of Sleeping Beauty.

In "Visual Stories," Ann Reynolds discusses both the discourse of pedagogy as developed by Alfred Parr in relation to an ensemble of taxidermy (next of kin to waxworks), artifacts, and graphics that constituted the rhetorical collection of the modern museum. Underlying Parr's approach to portray display was a belief in the value of visual aids in education, ranging from life-size models to stylized diagrams. At the deepest level, Parr saw his educational task as instilling the idea of nature as a balanced system, a concept that had its implicit political parallel in the idea of society as a balanced whole.

In "Envisioning Capital," on the visual display techniques used to portray political economy, equally a mix of techniques ranging from photographs to diagrams, Susan Buck-Morss approaches the same area of inquiry from the other side. She focuses on the ways in which political economy envisions and presents itself as a rational, balanced system through its rhetoric of presentation when, in fact, it is irrational and, indeed, ill-understood. The pedagogic imperative, in both cases, tends toward the production of a rational model of visual display to contain the contradictions and excesses of nature and capital. Thus, by the deployment of illustrative and diagrammatic material, capital presents itself as a coherent system that can be grasped in a glance, rather than as a complex process with its mechanism concealed by commodity fetishism. Its self-display is symptomatic of a hidden pathology. The apparent rationality of such display merely conceals a world of fetishistic derealization.

Politics explicitly enter the picture in the contrasting discussions of Nazism considered in Eric Santner's discussion of the discourse of nationalism and the Holocaust and in my own account of the historical connections between the Dadaist display techniques pioneered at the Cabaret Voltaire during the 1914–18 war and the complementary and connected displays of the idealized human body at the 1936 Berlin Olympics and its counterpart, the contemporary exhibition "Degenerate Art." Eric Santner notes that the unassimilable excess of the Nazi regime of racial purity was exhibited and framed as representation in the House of German Art, whereas the concentration camps were concealed and kept secret. The discourse of purity—and the rejection of modernity in the sense of technological civilization—also formed a common thread between Dadaism, which sought purity in a return to primal forms, and Nazism, which, at least in one of its moments, focused the imperative of purity on a myth of German origins in a mythical Arcadia.

In Hollywood science fiction, on the other hand, as Scott Bukatman describes, the most advanced technology is used to figure not the past but an imaginary counter-Arcadian world of even more advanced technology. The technologically driven goal of instrumental reason is displayed in the most technologically driven of the arts—the cinema. Cinema had its origin in a technology developed to reproduce the experience of perceiving the overwhelmingly fantastic as though it were real. As Bukatman points out, rapture can replace terror in these representations of the sublime. Here the technology of visual display teeters on the edge of the sacred, providing a new rhetoric of celestial visions. The special effects of Douglas Trumbull return, far beyond the Burkean or Kantian sublime of Romanticism, to encounter the special effects of the cathedral clergy who controlled the representation of the sacred in medieval England, artificers who created forms of visual display calculated to strike the pilgrim with awe. In each case, a complex rhetoric had to be developed, alongside a state-of-the-art technology. If today this technology threatens to overwhelm history, solace can be taken in the opportunity rhetoric always offers for decipherment and unmasking. The secret life of the spectacle can never be entirely occluded by its mesmeric force. We can learn how to approach it with skepticism, to locate it within history, to decipher its signs, to deflect its imaginary power.

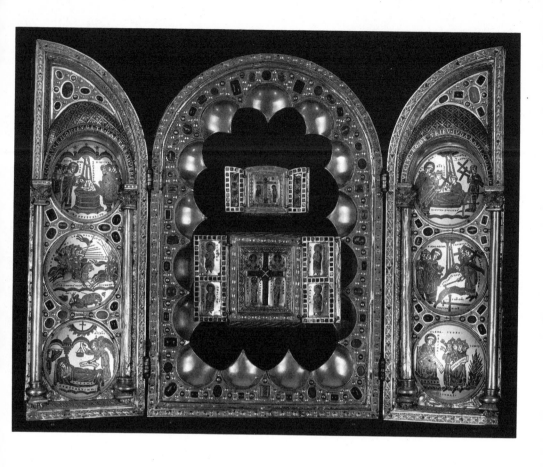

Stavelot Triptych, c. 1150, The Pierpont Morgan Library, New York.

Stephen Bann

SHRINES, CURIOSITIES, AND THE RHETORIC OF DISPLAY

It has become customary in the last few years to look at the genealogical
links between contemporary museum practice and what can be taken as its
direct ancestor, the cabinet of curiosities of the sixteenth and seventeenth
centuries. Indeed, now that the institution of the museum is frequently
shown to be afflicted with a kind of Hegelian death wish, the precedent of
the cabinet of curiosities can seem to be a highly relevant model; it shares the
contemporary museum's intimate concern with particulars—eccentric in its
coverage and modest in scale. What I want to do certainly takes for granted
the relevance and interest of the cabinet of curiosities for contemporary concepts of visual display. But I propose to examine the question from the other
side, as it were. I want to look, however briefly, at a form of visual display
that anticipates the cabinet of curiosities in the same way—or at least in an
analogous way—that the cabinet of curiosities anticipates the contemporary
museum. We can formulate some of the issues of visual display more adequately if we take into account that the regime of curiosity itself was tributary
to certain established ways of disposing objects and communicating through
them, even if the very precondition of curiosity signaled a shift in the world-
view, or the epistemic matrix, that had underwritten the earlier regime.

What then were these forms of display that held a central place in the pre-
Renaissance culture of Europe? They were the amazingly elaborate and costly
arrangements for showing the relics of saints and other cultic objects to the
faithful pilgrims who traveled hundreds and sometimes thousands of miles to
gain sight of them—a custom that began in the early Middle Ages, accelerated
remarkably after the twelfth century, and was halved in midtide by the onset
of the Reformation. While the tradition of pilgrimage in the Catholic countries
was not obliterated, many of the major shrines and the well-established lines
of communication throughout Europe and the Middle East were interrupted.

What can this practice of pilgrimage tell us, then, about visual display?
Over the past few years, this phenomenon and its implications for the estab-

lishment of symbolic relationships in space have been studied.[1] But I wonder if enough attention has been paid to the most fundamental of questions: how did the objects of cult themselves communicate to the faithful? What role did visuality and the technical conditions of display fulfill in the onlooker's experience?

It can be said from the start that the proposition offered the onlooker was not a simple, unilateral one. The splendid Stavelot Triptych in the Pierpont Morgan Library neatly demonstrates a general point about visual display in medieval art. On the one hand, through the six Mosan enamel roundels that occupy its open wings, it tells the story of the History of the True Cross. Specific episodes were selected from the famous account of Jacopus de Voragine that involved the Emperor Constantine, the Empress Helena, and many others in the amazing adventures of the piece of wood that supported the crucified Christ. On the other hand, because of the Byzantine relics placed at the center of the display, the triptych offers not the story of the Cross, but the Cross itself, in the form of a relic. Inaccessible to view in its tiny recessed compartment, this fragment of the True Cross is nonetheless accessible to the imagination through the immediacy of the enameled cruci- fixion image and the hieratic poses of the attendant saints. An antithesis emerges here, successfully reconciled through the form of the triptych: the metaphysics of presence, underlying the relic's display, are antithetical to the powerful rhetoric of storytelling that propels the cycles of the History of the True Cross as far ahead as Piero della Francesca and Adam Elsheimer. On the one hand, the fragmentary object is built up synecdochically into a sacred prototype; on the other, the object becomes an endlessly transformed and transforming agent within a historical narrative that incorporates all of time from the death of Adam to the Christian Empire of Constantine.

A quite separate act of imaginative reconstruction is needed to visualize a wider context, the entire environment of the pilgrimage church. At the beginning of his book *Word and Image*, Norman Bryson has an interesting passage where he considers the stained glass windows in the apse and choir aisles of Canterbury Cathedral. For him, the splendor of the gemlike color cannot obviate the fact that these windows reveal the transcendence of Scripture, that is, of the Word. "The status of the window is that of a relay or a place of transit through which the eye must pass to reach its goal,

Choir of Canterbury Cathedral, built 1175–84.

which is the Word."[2] This results in a situation that Bryson goes on to describe as "the supremacy of the *discursive* over the *figural*."[3] We can anticipate, in these luminous projections of all manner of sacred texts, the future immolation of the *signifier* in Western art before its transcendental *signified*. With the irresistable rise of the theory and practice of perspective from the Renaissance onwards, the Word will become predominant: color and form will be valued not in their own right, but only insofar as they enable and facilitate the telling of a sacred tale.

But, as the Stavelot Triptych teaches us, the visual display of a shrine does not work simply in one register. A reconstructed plan of Canterbury Cathedral shows us that the glass-glazing scheme, impressive though it was in its own right, took place as only one aspect of the development of the building around the shrine; the building that was to give Canterbury its status as one of the great focuses of European pilgrimage. If we are to think of the windows — which survive as the programming for the sacred texts — as integrally involved in the system of presentation, then we must also think of the shrines of St. Thomas à Becket, and the other local saints such as Alphège and Dunstan, as equally involved.

Remarkably little concrete evidence has survived that would enable us to visualize this display. The shrine of Becket itself was pictured only once, as far as we can tell. It is depicted in one of the stained glass windows representing the saint's miracles, manifesting itself to a sick man in a dream. But there survives from Saint Augustine's, the other great abbey of Canterbury, a medieval drawing of the arrangement of shrines around the high altar; it conveys well the era's taste for richness and redundancy in the display of shrines, relics, and sacred books. The individual shrines bear texts relating to their original dedications, sometimes to local saints such as Saint Mildred — whose body is recorded as having been moved subsequently to another location, and sometimes to more generally revered saints such as the protomartyr Stephen and Lawrence. In the place of greatest honor, it would seem, around the relics of Saint Ethelbert, are the "books sent by [Pope] Gregory to Augustine," founder of the English Church; the books are juxtaposed with two reliquaries representing truncated limbs, which have been a (mildly disconcerting) feature of displays of Christian relics from the Middle Ages up to the present day.

In one sense, the Saint Augustine drawing further demonstrates Bryson's point about the supremacy of the "discursive" over the "figural." These altars and sacred objects are, almost obsessively, labeled and dated. And yet, no one is pretending, of course, that the sketch in any way conveys the full experience of the location. Suppose we provide one of the types of objects depicted, one syntagmatically absorbed in a series of such objects whose common feature was a high level of intricate craftmanship and a brilliant responsiveness to the ambient light. We can appreciate that the effect of this gleaming gold object—though detached from the sketch and from its own origins—must have been extraordinary. Many existing churches, particularly in Southern Europe have, to a certain extent, retained this effect. But our contemporary visual culture, so different from the medieval one, so satiated with electronically produced effects, makes it extremely difficult for us to recapture the specificity of the experience of a centuries-old sacred object.

Drawing depicting the High Altar of St. Augustine's, Canterbury Cathedral, Canterbury, England.

The canonical text most useful for understanding the aesthetic system of the great pilgrimage displays is Abbot Suger's treatise on the Abbey of Saint-Denis, titled *Sancti Dionysii liber de rebus in administratione sua gestis*. Louis Marin gives a striking commentary on Suger's work in his study posthumously published in 1993, titled *Des pouvoirs de l'image*. Here is how he glosses Suger's well-known passages describing the spectacle of one of the altars in the abbey church:

> …[W]e should note that the precious material, whether it be gold or gems, is never conceived, and never accumulated, with a view to forming what could properly be called a treasure or a reserve of riches, but is devoted to the *ornatus*, to adornment, decor, dressing, to the ostentation of liturgical objects and sacramental instruments. In other words, the rare and precious material is first and foremost the vehicle and vector of the power of a sacred

object which, though not yet an image, is destined to exercise that power through vision. The material—gold and precious stones—clothe the object in light, and reflect or make manifest the transcendent, invisible, and all-powerful nature of visibility.[4]

It is possible to learn from Marin's careful distinction between the notion of an inert "treasure"—a mere accumulation of "riches"—and the operational effect of precious material as a "vehicle of power," a certain lesson in contemporary museology. No doubt, power is a concept rarely absent from the museological discourse of our times. Another extract from Marin's commentary shows precisely how the representation of power can be enabled to attest to the power of representation:

> It is no less remarkable…that a part of this gold and these precious stones
> is derived from the gold rings and precious stones of kings, princes, counts,
> archbishops, and bishops, which is to say, from the signs and insignia of
> their temporal and spiritual power—a power that finds itself, by way of its
> "signifiers," transferred to the altar, the crucifix, the reliquaries of Saint-
> Denis; these [rings and stones] have thus become "signifiers" of another
> form of power…that of the light manifested in the sacred objects. More than
> a displacement of powers, we have here a transmutation of power [*puissance*]
> that, by virtue of empowering the relics of saints' bodies…turns the bodies
> in which it is realized and the buildings in which it operates into foyers of
> grace; and by its "extraterritorality," turns the church and sacred place into
> asylums of forgiveness.[5]

Marin is describing a system in which "power" circulates in a series of "transmutations." The power of the monarch becomes the power of light to express the identity of those splendid objects to the maximum degree, and ultimately the power of the sacred place itself which, following this "transmutation," becomes an "asylum"—an enclosure offering a refuge from the real political power of the monarch with which we began. But is there any reason to suppose that this implicit ideology of Abbot Suger, brilliantly glossed by Marin, was anything more than a pious hope? As mentioned, it is not easy to find sources that describe the actual functioning of the pilgrimage circuits. There is one famous account, Erasmus's *Peregrinatio Religionis Ergo*. This has traditionally been seen, quite rightly, as a text that satirizes the whole business of pilgrimage, exposing it to such ridicule that it is often suggested that Henry VIII might have taken heart from it when he decided to destroy the shrine of Becket in Canterbury Cathedral. Erasmus does indeed bring reason to bear on the apparent irrationality of the cult of relics: one of the two participants in his dialogue says of the "True Cross" that it "is exhibited publicly and privately in so many places that if the fragments were joined together they'd seem a full load for a freighter."[6] But his satirical tone does not prevent him from having extremely valuable things to say about the ritual whose value he is questioning. Erasmus probably visited the shrine of Becket between 1512 and 1514, three centuries after Suger's texts were written. But his description suggests a process of "transmutation," as Marin puts it, which may still have worked for less skeptical observers. In particular, it conveys a crucial point. The visual display of such a great pilgrimage shrine was conducted, one might say stage-managed, by a guide and demonstrator. No less than the prior, the head of the monastic foundation, displayed the shrine of Becket, in a fashion that Erasmus's dialogue makes luminously plain:

> ...He opened for us the chest in which the rest of the holy man's body is said to lie.
> Men[edemus]: You saw the bones?
> Ogyg[ius]: No, that's not permitted, nor would it be possible without the use of ladders. But within the wooden chest is a golden chest; when this is drawn up by ropes, it reveals inestimable treasure.
> Men.: What do I hear?
> Ogyg.: The cheapest part was gold. Everything shone and dazzled with rare and surpassingly large jewels, some bigger than a goose egg. Some monks stood about reverently. When the cover was removed, we all adored. The prior pointed out each jewel by touching it with a white rod, adding its French name, its worth, and the name of the donor. The principal ones were gifts from kings.[7]

To be a pilgrim at Canterbury was to take part in a performance. The prior in his role as master of ceremonies did not single out individual modes of representation featured in the building—for instance, the stained glass—but animated a whole sequence of interrelating and interfused modes. Thus, when the shrine of Becket—the focus of the performance—was abruptly removed, and the foundation itself dissolved, the building simply lost its *raison d'être*. Accounts from the rest of the sixteenth century demonstrate the incapacity of the reforming archbishops to find a suitable use for the vast medieval church, and it is only in the seventeenth century that it becomes the object of a kind of aesthetic recuperation. The new statutes granted by King Charles I in the 1620s refer to the duty of the dean and chapter to take care of the fabric of the cathedral, or the *fabrica illa pulcherrima*. Toward the end of the seventeenth century, a sequence of paintings was done of the choir, which portray real and intended improvements to the church's fittings—a new high altar and an organ—while still indicating the presence of the iron screens (mentioned by Erasmus) necessary to regulate the flow of pilgrims in the pre-Reformation period.

These descriptions of Canterbury refer to a double experience of iconoclastic fervor, the first at the time of the Reformation when Henry VIII destroyed the shrine of Becket in 1538, and the second during the civil war in the mid-seventeenth century when the cathedral was subjected to a further furious onslaught of zealots who suspected the dean and chapter of reintroducing Papist practices.[8] It is not so much the motives for iconoclasm but the recuperative strategies, which were the response to iconoclasm, that are revealing in significant ways. Ronald Paulson has gone so far as to suggest in his recent book *Breaking and Remaking* (1989) that the "aesthetic practice" of English poets and artists in the period from 1700 to 1820 was dominated by the need to make long-term restitution for the iconoclasm of the fairly distant past. The short-term restitutive process, nonetheless integral to a long-term historical sequence, can be equally important. The cabinet of curiosities, for example, might be seen in the light of the medieval practice described above. It is not a resumption or revival of the earlier practice, but in some sense a restitution and recuperation.

The convention of display (and the fact that any display requires a displayer) creates, thus, a dynamic link between two very different phenomena: medieval religious iconography and the Renaissance cabinet of curiosities. The two practices are linked by the practice of restitution, as Paulson discusses in *Breaking and Remaking*. It can also be helpful in the understanding of an object's and an era's recuperation to utilize the concept of mourning, as expounded by Freud in a short piece written during World War I. Through the work of mourning, according to Freud, the libido will slowly release its hold on the objects that are lost, and fix on new ones in turn. The curiosity, and the museological activity associated with it, is among other things a work of mourning.

Before introducing the specific example of John Bargrave's cabinet, a little more needs to be explored about curiosity as a cultural phenomenon, within a distinct historical conjuncture. In the above translation of the Erasmus dialogue, there is a rather spectacular anachronism. The dialogue refers to the East Anglian village of Walsingham, the other shrine visited by Erasmus. "The village has scarcely any means of support apart from the tourist trade," says Ogygius. "Tourism" is the term that the translator has found for the more neutral phrase, *commeantium frequentia*, the frequency of people coming and going.[9] Right at the beginning of the dialogue, Menedemus opines that his friend has a special motive for going on a pilgrimage: "Out of curiosity, I dare

De Seve inv.   *Babel Sculp.*

George-Louis Leclerc, Comte de Buffon, *Cabinet du Roy*, 1749.

say." But Ogygius replies: "On the contrary, out of devotion."[10] The original Latin has: *Animi gratia, ut arbitror. / Imo religionis causa.* Ogygius is going not to gratify his "mind," but for a religious purpose. It is important to note that Erasmus would in fact have had no notion of "curiosity" in the rather specialized sense in which the term came to be known in the course of the sixteenth century. In particular, he would not have been aware of the particular practice of collecting that gave rise to the cabinets of curiosities. I make this point very precisely because in fact Erasmus did nonetheless collect objects, many of which after his death in Basel in 1536 entered the possession of his friend Bonifacius Amerbach. But it was to be Bonifacius's son, Basilius Amerbach (1533–1591), who absorbed these objects into his own remarkable cabinet in the second part of the century—a collection whose immense historical importance can be measured by the fact that it was bought by the city of Basel in 1661, and so formed the nucleus of the first public collection of works of art in the world.

Curiosity, therefore, is a term that indicates a historically and culturally specific attitude to the collection and display of objects, and would have had no meaning before 1550. To use the striking phrase of Krzysztof Pomian, who has done more than anyone else to revive interest in the phenomenon, it "enjoyed a temporary spell in power, an interim rule between those of theology and science."[11] Pomian's thesis holds true, while, at the same time, it is tempting to look more deeply into the precise position curiosity occupied between "theology" and "science." There is ample evidence in Pomian's own essays of its antinomy to the method of the physical sciences, which asserted their own "rule" in the course of the seventeenth century. For the scientific temper of a scholar like Bacon or Descartes, the habit of "curiosity" was offensive because it attached itself almost obsessively to the individual object, rather than using classes of objects to arrive at general conclusions which would have the force of law. Curiosity in sum was inimical to inductive reasoning. But Pomian presupposes a no less significant process of conflict and differentiation that must have taken place at the beginning of the "rule" of curiosity. Erasmus's opposition between *animi gratia* and *religio* is not sufficiently rich. *Animi gratia*, an aspect of curiosity, did not by any means remain in the mind. Attachment to objects—we might reasonably say, the cult of objects—was an inseparable feature of curiosity, and so was a particular style of display. The more we look at John Bargrave's cabinet, the more the despoiled cathedral church of Canterbury resonates, though, again, not as a revival in any sense, but a recuperation, or an act of mourning for what is lost.

John Bargrave was born in 1610, the second son of a soldier of Kentish yeoman stock who had married a London heiress, acquired a coat of arms, and built a fine country house in a village adjacent to Canterbury in the years of John's childhood. John's father was also closely connected by kinship to the network of Kentish families who, in the century following the Reformation, consolidated their hold on the office that had succeeded that of the prior: the dean, or chief member of the cathedral chapter. Dean Boys had married John Bargrave's aunt; he was commemorated at his death in 1625 by a sumptuous monument showing him awaiting the Resurrection in his well-stocked library. He was directly succeeded by John's uncle, Isaac Bargrave, who retained his office until the early days of the Civil War, and aroused the enmity of the Puritans by his liturgical, musical, and artistic innovations.

Bargrave was therefore intimately aware, as he grew up, of the attempts led by members of his family to reinvest the *fabrica illa pulcherrima* with the powerful aesthetic qualities it had abruptly lost when the ox-carts of Henry VIII removed all vestiges of the shrine of Thomas Becket. He was also aware of the growing hostility, amounting to paranoia, in the Puritan community, which took any opportunity to condemn the apparent resacralization of images and objects. When the King's mother-in-law, Marie de Médicis, visited Canterbury in 1641, and asked to be shown round the cathedral, she was reportedly shown the only object that still bore the martyr's name, "Arch-Bishop Thomas Becket's stone." Writing a few years later, the Puritan Richard Culmer, who was shortly to distinguish himself by smashing many of the medieval stained glass windows in the nave, commented: "some say she kist it, as thousands of Papists have done before her, and it was then said to her, looke on the crack in that stone, that mouth calls to heaven for vengeance on those that shed this holy Martyr's blood..."[12]

The political and ecclesiastical debates of the early seventeenth century had revived, phantasmatically, the memory of the cathedral as a place of pilgrimage, and provoked a kind of violent regression to the terms of the Reformation conflict. Culmer claimed in the very title of the tract that "the

Canterburian cathedral" was "in an Abbey-like, corrupt and rotten condition which calls for a speedy Reformation or Dissolution." But by 1644, the date of Culmer's attack, Dean Isaac Bargrave was already dead as a consequence of the Parliament's oppressive action, and his nephew John was expelled from his fellowship at a Cambridge college. It was at this juncture that John, balked of his expected clerical career, began to travel abroad and became, in effect, a collector of curiosities.

Three separate stages in Bargrave's career as a collector may seem obvious enough, but acquire a special resonance in view of the medieval prelude to his endeavors. First of all, there is the time of collecting. Between 1647 and 1660, the year of the Restoration of the Stuart monarchy, John Bargrave made four lengthy trips to Rome and Naples, taking in large parts of France and Central Europe on his outward and return journeys. In the course of these peregrinations, he accumulated a large stock of objects, which he stored in the leather pouches still conserved to this day with the collection. His mode of traveling and accumulating placed severe restrictions on the size of the objects: Bargrave could only carry (and indeed could only afford) small antique statuettes and other such vestiges of Roman civilization. When he was offered the whole mummified body of a child by the obliging Franciscans of Toulouse, he would "out of curiosity" (as he wrote later) have been delighted to accept it, but had to settle instead for the prudent substitute of "the finger of a Frenchman."[13] When confronted with the imposing spectacle of the broken giant obelisk in the Circus of Maxentius, which his compatriot the Earl of Arundel had tried hard to purchase and export to England, Bargrave simply annexed a fragment: "I took another stone, and with it broke off of the butt end of it this piece and as much more, and had this polished."[14] Bargrave was well aware that his "neighbour and friendly acquaintance," the great Bernini, later re-erected this great object in the celebrated fountain of the Piazza Navona. His bit, however, remains separate. It transcends the status of a fragment only to the extent that it is, as he puts it, "almost like a heart,"[15] and it is by no means the only heart-shaped object in the collection.

These brief quotations from Bargrave are taken from the extensive manuscript catalogue of his cabinet of curiosities, left to accompany it after his death in 1680, when the whole collection became the property of the dean

Joseph Cornell, *Sans titre (Boîte à compartiments)*, c. 1950–53.

and chapter of Canterbury Cathedral. Bargrave's words anticipate the third stage of his career as a collector: the afterlife of the collection. If the leather pouches represent the time of collecting, the cabinet represents the collection's afterlife—a cabinet made specially by the dean and chapter to accommodate the surplus of objects that were now entrusted to their care. The word BARGRAVEANA inscribed upon it exactly conveys the objectification of the collection: it has become identifiable by a neologism, created from the collector's name, and described exhaustively in the itemized catalogue.

But between the time of collecting and the afterlife of the collection, there exists a second stage: the time of display. The time of collecting is an accumulation of small-scale and fragmentary objects; it is a work of mourning. Deprived of the splendid surroundings of his youth, and lamenting the vanished ideology of his Kentish family connections, Bargrave strove to reinvest his spiritual and emotional self in new objects, which could perhaps achieve a limited form of transcendence. The small portrait he commissioned in Rome in 1650, installed beneath the Bargrave arms, represents him with his hand on his heart: the gesture is a performative enactment, a manifestation of self, to which the selection and fashioning of heart-shaped stones supplied a further dimension.

The time of display, by contrast, is the period of two decades when Bargrave returned to Canterbury, a canon of the foundation and prebendary of the same stall that his uncle had occupied. Bargrave commissioned his own cabinets, installed them in his study, and fulfilled his reputation as a collector, or "virtuoso," by receiving visitors, as he did the diarist John Evelyn on May 13, 1672. What went on? What did he say to them? Or, rather, how did he perform for them? We can begin to answer this critical question by reading back from Bargrave's catalogue, which was, we may suppose, the condensed version of Bargrave's curatorial notes—his individual *anamnesis* and his way of narrativizing the objects of the collection. We can imagine the cabinets, open and not closed—since he tells us that the two portraits were intended to hang by ribbons from the outside of them. We can imagine this little theater being set up before its audience, and Bargrave launching into an animated description that would simultaneously tell the story of an object's acquisition and venture into speculations on its scientific origin:

This I met with amongst the Rhaetian Alps. One would wonder that nature should so counterfeit art. There is no man but [that] seeth it but would veryly believe that by tools and art it had binn put into that figure. I remember that the Montecolian man that sold it me told me that he ventured his life to clamber the rocks to gett it. Where it grew I cannot say; but where it was, it was covered, he said, with long sedgy grass growing about it, under the dripp of an higher rock, where the snow continually melteth and droppeth; and so all the mountayn chrystall is increased an extra by an external addition, and groweth not from any rock.[16]

Like the prior who "pointed out each jewel by touching it with a white rod," Bargrave specifies an object and tells its history. The power of the object depends, however, not on its being caught up in a series of prestigious relays, working through the audience's vision to establish transcendence. Pomian's evocation of "an interim rule between those of theology and science" needs to be modified, however slightly, if we consider that "curiosity" functions here precisely as a bridge between the two regimes, or (to use the grammatical term) a shifter. In Bryson's terms, the medieval stained glass window is "a place of transit which the eye must pass to reach its goal, which is the Word." For Bargrave, though, the window of his study, opening on the apse of the cathedral, is a means of demonstrating the efficacy of his "optick instruments," bought in Germany. They transform the display room into an emblem of the acquisition of knowledge through the light of reason, the camera obscura: "With this instrument you may see the jackdaws fly about Bell Harry steeple, when the sun shines, in any room of your house that hath a window that way."[17]

Titian Ramsay Peale II, The Long Room, Interior of Front Room in Peale's Museum, 1822.

Susan Stewart

DEATH AND LIFE, IN THAT ORDER, IN THE WORKS OF CHARLES WILLSON PEALE

Any collection promises totality. The appearance of that totality is made possible by the face-to-face experience of display, the all-at-onceness under which the collection might be apprehended by an observer. This display, of course, marks the defeat of time, the triumph over the particularity of contexts in which the collected objects first appeared. In display, collected objects are gathered through dual processes of temporal diremption and the imposition of frame. The arrested life of the displayed collection finds its unity in memory and narrative. From the toys of the dead in Egyptian tombs to the moving statues of Daedalus described in The Meno and De Anima to the terror of infinite motion in the red shoes or the mechanical toy that will not stop, the reversed and anticipatory gesture to the situation of stasis in display is the dream of animation under which the collection's total world speaks or comes to life—and all-at-onceness becomes extension, movement, consequence, and reciprocity.[1] This dream of animation has thereby a kind of social/political claim, for it posits the collection as an intervention, or act of significance, and it compels the consciousness of the observer to enter into the consciousness of the collector—the opaqueness and fixity of the collection on display is transformed into the utopian republic of the fantasy where individual desire finds its fellow dreamer and recognizes itself.

This study explores the interrelations of display, arrested life, the attribution or erasure of cause and context, and absolute or totalized knowledge—the completion that is key for the collection and for the recollection it promises. Although the given qualities of such animated objects allow them to endure beyond flux and history, this very transcendence and permanence also links them to the world of the dead, to the end of organic growth and the onset of inaccessibility to the living. It is not surprising that mechanical toys and objects such as those I've mentioned express a repetition and infinite action that the everyday world finds impossible: mechanisms do not tire or feel, they simply work or don't work. As part of the general inversion that the world of the dead represents, the inanimate comes to life in the service of the awakened dead. The theme of animation is itself a kind of allegory of memory and of the role willed memory plays in reawakening the obdurate material world, given the passage of time. Further, I am interested in the link between the collection and the portrait as devices for recollection—gestures of *countenance* designed to stay oblivion.[2] But rather than continuing in such general terms, let us focus on a particular historical moment, the end of the Enlightenment, and a set of aesthetic practices—the painting and collecting activities of Charles Willson Peale—where these issues appear, to continue our metaphor, with some vividness. Further, Peale's practices take place in a context of changing religious and political thought, which provides a suggestive supplement to any universal theory of collecting.

Charles Willson Peale was born on the eastern shore of Maryland in 1741, the son of a schoolteacher who had been a convicted felon in England. The family moved to various small Maryland towns until they settled in Annapolis when Peale was nine. Apprenticed as a saddler when young, Peale practiced various professions throughout his long life: repairer of bells, watches, and saddles, sculptor, miniature painter, portrait painter, Revolutionary soldier, propagandist and civic official, mezzotint engraver, museum keeper, zoologist and botanist, and inventor of such mechanisms as a portable steam bath, a fan chair, a velocipede, a physiognotrace for making silhouettes, a polygraph for making multiple copies of documents, a windmill, a stove, a bridge, and false teeth. He studied painting in London with Benjamin West for two years. When he returned he moved his family to Philadelphia; there at the height of the Revolution he served as both a soldier and a maker of banners and posters for the war effort.[3]

Most established artists of the eighteenth century had a painting room gallery for displaying works for sale or works in the artist's personal collection. In Peale's case this exhibition gallery eventually became the first American museum, embracing both cultural and natural history. During the War for Independence, Peale expanded his display gallery into an exhibition of portraits of Revolutionary heroes. Beginning with his first portrait of Washington in 1772, Peale had established by 1782 a tall and long skylighted chamber for showing full-length and bust-sized portraits. Here he arranged the portraits high on the wall in order to represent the primates, while those lower forms of life he had collected filled the cases and the floor below. A watercolor, delineated by Peale and painted in 1822 by his son, Titian Ramsay Peale II, shows the Long Room of the museum from the time it was located in the Statehouse in Philadelphia. Cases of birds line the left wall with the portraits hanging above. At the right are cases displaying insects, minerals, and fossils. On the cases rest busts of Washington, Benjamin Rush, and others. What cannot be seen here are the additional rooms and the table for exhibiting experiments with electricity and perpetual motion.

In addition to the vertical, hierarchical arrangement by principles of evolution, the materials were also organized according to what Peale knew of the Linnaean system. Peale explained that:

> an extensive collection should be found, the various inhabitants of every element, not only of the animal, but also specimens of the vegetable tribe, — and all the brilliant and precious stones, down to the common grit, — all the minerals in their virgin state. — Petrifaction's [sic] of the human body, of which two instances are known, and through that immense variety which should grace every well stored Museum. Here should be seen no duplicates, and only the varieties of each species, all placed in the most conspicuous point of light, to be seen to advantage, without being handled.[4]

He proposes that the "gentle intelligent Oran Outang," lacking speech, should be placed nearer to the monkey tribe than to that of humans and that the flying squirrel, ostrich, cassowary, and bat will provide the connecting links between quadrupeds and birds. Further, Peale was an innovator in museum display techniques. Finding that ordinary taxidermy did not produce a lifelike effect, he stretched skins over wooden cores he had carved to indicate musculature,[5] and he offered painted backgrounds of the proper context for each specimen. The museum displayed both live and dead animals. When a live grizzly on display escaped and ran through the hall, Peale was forced to shoot him.[6]

By 1794, his collections had grown so enormous that the museum had to be moved to Philosophical Hall. Following Rousseauist principles of nature as the proper teacher of mankind and his deeply held Deist beliefs in a non-intervening God, Peale saw his enterprise as a "School of Wisdom" designed to teach the public to follow the example of nature. Clearly, Peale's painting and collecting activity served the interests of postwar American society: his portraits memorialized the heroes and patrons of the war, while his collections of cultural and natural objects provided a synopsis of the New World in miniature, linking recent historical events to the grand context of Nature and providing evidence of a Natural providence legitimating those events. To this extent, Peale's collecting activity parallels that of such Renaissance antiquaries as John Leyland and William Camden, who provided a secular and nationalist narrative for England designed to supplant previous forms of religious authority. Yet if we turn to the particular details of Peale's aesthetic practices at large—his paintings and inventions as well as his collections— we find other interpretations possible that are linked to the psychological history of Peale himself and the religious and intellectual climate of his day.

Peale's Deism and rationalism can be discerned in the very names he gave to his children. He refused to give them family names or Biblical names; rather, he chose names for them from his copy of Matthew Pilkington's *Dictionary of Painters*: Raphaelle, Angelica Kauffman, Rembrandt, Titian, Rubens, and Sybilla after, obviously, the Sybils. And later he expanded to Franklin (after Benjamin), Aldrovand (after Ulisse Aldrovandi, the Renaissance museum keeper of Bologna), and Linnaeus. Moreover, he recorded their births, not in the traditional family Bible, but on the flyleaf of his Pilkington. Like Washington, Jefferson, and Franklin, Peale was attracted to British Deism, with its tenet of God as inventor and first cause without any justification for institutional religion and clericism, its interpretation of Christianity as a moral system akin to civic virtue, and its picture of nature as regular and predictable.[7] Yet there are two aspects of Deism as it was debated in Britain and the United States of particular relevance here. As a legacy of Newtonian physics (and before Hume's *Treatise* of 1739, with its critique of causality, gained popular currency), Deism held the external world to be material and composed of objects now moving, now at rest. Rest is their natural state, not motion; when such objects move, it is because an active force is moving them. Motion that seems to be initiated by purely material objects is simply transmitted motion, like billiard balls colliding with one another. Genuine autokinesis is found only in humans and animals. This motion is initiated by the will, and the *feeling* of causing motion is enough to give evidence that one causes it. If all motion originates in the will, then the motion studied by scientists must also originate in the will — eventually one must reach a first cause of motion, which is God.[8] Moreover, in Deism there was an ongoing conflict regarding life after death. Throughout the eighteenth century, some Deists contended that this world is the only world, while others believed in some afterlife in which moral virtue would be rewarded. Many argued with Calvinist notions of election, yet Franklin, for example, came at the end of his life to hold that the soul was immortal.[9] What remain central tenets of Deist thought are the denial of miracles, the denial of supernatural revelation, and the denial of any special redemptive interposition of God in history. These central theological arguments are of much consequence in the formal choices Peale made in his art: the material, knowable world can be organized by an empirical and reasoned science; human will is the source of all motion in the physical world and human motion is by divine agency; death is a material fact and the categories "life" and "death" are mutually exclusive; Biblical and mythological narrative cannot represent reality.

Peale's only true apprenticeship as a painter came during his stay with West in London in 1767 and 1768. But this influence is remarkable for its absence in Peale's ensuing work. Peale never chose to imitate the style of history painting and mythological painting practiced by West once West was unable to commission religious paintings from the Church of England.[10] This fact might be best explored by turning to an anomaly in Peale's oeuvre, his copy of West's painting Elisha Restoring the Shunamite's Son. The work was one of the first he completed upon arriving at West's London studio; he made a small (16-by-24–inch) watercolor copy of this Biblical composition and later took the copy with him when he returned to Maryland, eventually including the work in his exhibition galleries. The Biblical story of 2 Kings 4:8–37 provides the background for the work. It tells of a wealthy, childless woman who provides the prophet Elisha with food and rest; in return Elisha predicts the birth of a son to her. The prediction comes true, but the child later dies and when Elisha's servant Gehazi tries to revive the child, he fails. Elisha himself arrives and, putting his mouth on the boy's mouth, his eyes on the boy's eyes and his hands on his hands, miraculously makes the flesh of the child become warm. The child sneezes seven times and opens his eyes. West, and Peale after him, have shown the scene of revival. The mother is seen from

Charles Willson Peale, *Elisha Restoring the Shunamite's Son*, 1767.

behind as she bends over the child; the child's limbs are still limp and complete the triangular composition, with both mother and child held within the trajectory of the prophet's open hands. Gehazi is recognizable, holding the staff that failed to revive the boy, to the right.

Peale made very few copies of paintings during his career, and this is the only original painting of West's that he copied during his apprenticeship.[11] He preferred to paint "from life," and this tenet clearly is allied to his Deism, with its rejection of bibliolatry and textual evidence, and its turn to nature and the authority of sensory experience. In a copy of *Emile* owned by one of his heirs, Peale himself probably underlined a passage urging teachers never to substitute representation for reality, or shadow for substance, but to teach only from actual objects.[12] This tenet meant that, despite some rare exceptions, he always painted from life once his career began. Further, Peale's museum would be based upon the actual sample and not a replica or model. Yet just as Peale had subjected himself to West's prior technical authority in the copy of *Elisha*, so had he chosen as his model a subject that would have been an anathema to his beliefs—that is, the evidence of miracles and divine interposition.

This early copy/painting, so distant from Peale's religious and aesthetic principles, might be contrasted to Peale's painting *Rachel Weeping*, which he worked on intermittently from 1772 to 1776.[13] In contrast to the distanced miracle of the Elisha painting, this work stems directly from an immediate and personal tragic experience. Infant mortality was unfortunately common in the eighteenth century, and Charles and Rachel Peale lost their first four children in infancy. This picture records the death of the fourth of these children, Margaret, who was killed by the smallpox epidemic in Annapolis in 1772. Moved by a request from Rachel that he create a memorial portrait of the child, Peale first painted the infant alone, arms and chin bound down by white satin ribbons, as it is seen in the foreground. Between 1772 and 1776 he worked on the picture several times, adding his wife and a table of medicines in order to symbolize their futile attempts to save the child's life. Although this is one of the few noncommissioned, and therefore personal, works in Peale's collection, he nevertheless hung it in his painting room. Because Rachel could not bear to look at it, he eventually placed it behind a green curtain and for a time added a note: "Before you draw this curtain/ Consider whether you will affect a Mother or Father who has lost a child."[14] The story of Peale's painting is the opposite of West's. It is an account of the stubborn material truth of death itself. Rachel holds herself in a gesture of containment and the one source of eruption from such stillness—the tears that seem to bead on the surface of the paint, become material there and in the Biblical title later given the picture by members of the family.

This picture is only the first instance of Peale's working through, in his painting and collecting practices, an anxiety regarding death—as all anxieties do, of course, in the sense that anxieties appear around the impossibility of, or refusal of, an empirical or experienced reference. For Peale, the creation of new knowledge was a stay against death. And taxonomy, the organization of knowledge, served as an antidote to surplus meaning and emotion. His practices thereby mirror the famous passage in Freud's 1916 essay on mourning and transience where Freud writes:

> We only see that libido clings to its objects and will not renounce those that are lost even when a substitute lies ready to hand. Such then is mourning...
> when it has renounced everything that has been lost, then it has consumed

itself, and our libido is once more free...to replace the lost objects....It is to be hoped that the same will be true of the losses caused by this war....We shall build up again all that war has destroyed.[15]

In common with his contemporaries, Peale lived in an environment of infant mortality, epidemic, and war. But the question for him becomes the meaning of suffering if divine interposition is not possible, and the meaning of nature's lessons when such lessons are unnatural and even monstrous. *Rachel Weeping* is a painting about the limit of nature and about the limit of science's capacity to intervene in nature. The other side of the Rousseauist doctrine of natural virtue is nature's indifference, ambivalence, and capacity for anachronism and disorder. The material representation of death helps to recollect the referent and bring it to the attention of knowledge.

Of all the facts science could provide, one that continued to escape verifiability and which was the center of much scientific debate at the time was the fact of death. Peale's family doctor during his Philadelphia years, Benjamin Rush, for example, had in his library two pamphlets on the problem of suspended animation. The first, "An Essay on Vital Suspension: Being an Attempt to Investigate and to Ascertain Those Diseases, in which the Principles of Life are Apparently Extinguished, by a Medical Practitioner," printed in London in 1741, explains that the best way to investigate the nature of death is to consider the "inherent properties of life." When this project of delineating properties results only in ambiguity, the doctor concludes that "all bodies in nature are *aut viva aut mortua*, there being no intermediate state." He also concludes that it must be a work of supernatural human art to recall to vital existence that which is dead.

After the expression of further doubts and hesitations, the physician suggests that stimulants be applied to denudated muscle and if any contraction follows, life remains. "It is proof of the temerity and imbecility of human judgement that we have too many instances on record, wherein even the most skillful physicians have erred in the decisions they have pronounced, respecting the extinction of life, this should incite the practitioner never to be deterred."[16] A later pamphlet by David Hosack, a New York physician, "An Enquiry into the Causes of Suspended Animation from Drowning with the Means of Restoring Life," recommends the application of heat to the

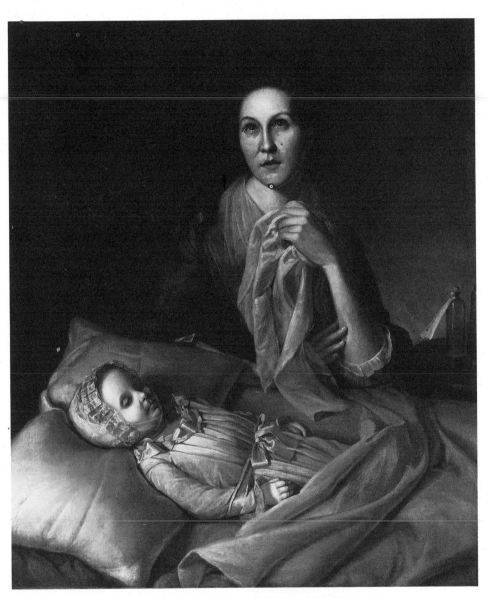

Charles Willson Peale, *Rachel Weeping*, 1772–76.

body's system much in the style of Elisha reviving the Shunamite's son.[17]

Given the ambivalent status of signs of life and death and their capacity for misrepresentation, eighteenth-century folkloric practices accompanying death are of particular relevance. Often in the house of the dead, clocks were stopped at the hour of decease, mirrors were turned to the wall, and black cloth was thrown over pictures and over any beehives in the garden.[18] These gestures of stopping time and stopping the motion of representation can be connected to the imperative of viewing the corpse. Death is signified in these instances by a halting of motion, a stilling of context and multiplication and by attention to the empirical reality of sense impression regardless of the physician's doubts about the validity of such impressions. In *Rachel Weeping* the mother's gaze does not enter the frame of the picture of the dead child. By placing the work behind a curtain, Peale permanently continued the mourning practice, and by showing the child and mother withheld from gesture and motion, he painted the end of human will and autokinesis. This presentation, in fact, continues, for the viewer of Peale's exhibition gallery, the experience of display and burial—the mourner's experience of viewing. When Rachel herself died in April of 1790 (either from a lung disorder or from the complications of her eleventh pregnancy), Peale refused to have her buried for three or four days because of his fears about premature burial. Her death was made much more difficult for Peale by the concurrent death of his friend Benjamin Franklin.

A year and a half later Peale added a relevant set of remarks to his initial address to the Board of Visitors appointed for his new museum. He explained that he planned to follow the Linnaean system and then added a rather startling point. Explaining that "good and faithful painting" can make the likeness of man available to posterity, he said that nevertheless he would like to find a way to use "powerful antisepticks" to preserve the remains of great men, thereby keeping their bodies from becoming "the food of worms" and making them available for reverence and memory. He continued that he was sorry he "did not preserve the remains of Benjamin Franklin in this way."[19] Lillian Miller adds a note to the Peale papers that:

> although [Peale] never exhibited embalmed people in the museum, his
> proposal was serious and follows from two central tenets: that as a species in

the order of natural history, human beings should be treated like other species, and that moral values could be transmitted to posterity by the physical representations of exemplary men. For Peale death was an event in the economy of nature and no special sanctity was attached to the corpse.[20]

Despite Miller's statement regarding the typicality of Peale's Enlightenment attitude toward death, there remains in his work a persistent theme of anxiety concerning the death of children and the possibility of war as a cause of human extinction. Although natural death is reconcilable to Enlightenment values, the death of a child is in a profound sense unnatural, a death that most radically arrests the progress of time. In March 1806 Peale attempted to obtain an embalmed child from a New York church.[21] Peale's request for the child's corpse comes many years after the death of his first child, but echoes another moment of trauma in his life. In the chaotic aftermath of the Revolutionary defeat at the Battle of Trenton, Peale had not been able to recognize his brother James. He wrote in a letter to Thomas Jefferson, "I thought it the most hellish scene I have ever beheld." When a man walked out of the line of soldiers toward Peale, "He had lost all his clothes. He was in an old, dirty, blanket jacket, his beard long and his face so full of sores he could not clean it, which disfigured him in such a manner that he was not known to me at first sight." What war had destroyed here—clothes and face—are those qualities of person making portraiture intelligible.[22] Furthermore, the disfigurement of countenance, of the lineaments of the total person, which Peale had so carefully learned to represent in his portraits, presents a severe blow to totality and to the possibility of knowledge and recollection, which was key to all of Peale's aesthetic and epistemological values.

After the war and a brief period of public service, Peale suffered a kind of nervous breakdown—the symptoms were an inability to move and an inability to remember—specifically, Peale's memory loss centered around the order and number of his children and the status of death. Toward the close of 1782, he decided to hang the painting of *Rachel Weeping* in his gallery behind the curtain with the message beginning "Draw not this curtain." He added a poem that he said was anonymous, but that also appeared on the last page of his letterbook for 1782–95. The poem warns that the death is "no more than moulded clay," but that the display might evoke an excessive response in anyone viewing the mother's unceasing mourning:

> Draw not the Curtain, if a Tear
> just trembling in a Parent's eye
> Can fill your awful soul with fear,
> or cause your tender Breast to sigh
>
> A child lays dead before your eyes
> and seems no more than moulded clay
> While the affected Mother crys
> and constant mourns from day to day.[23]

A month or so later Peale experienced a breakdown, writing on January 15, 1783, that for more than two years he had been in a kind of lethargy marked by dramatic memory loss: "some short time past," he wrote, "I was sitting by the fireside musing within myself when a thought struck my fancy, i.e. how many children have I. Four, I answers as if it were by Instinct, four! Let me see if I am right and looking round (and) began to name them as they appeared before me, as my not seeing Raphaelle, I was puzzled for a some moments to make out my number." He then recounts another instance occurring just the day before when he "chanced to be looking at the picture of my mother-in-law" and he instantly remembered her person, but could not recollect whether she were dead or not and the circumstances of her will.[24]

It is significant that it is the painting that induces in this latter case the ambiguity of the mother-in-law's life or death. The painting is a kind of presence, a bringing to mind if not to sense, but what kind of presence is it? One of the ways in which a painter can explore the cognitive boundary between displaying death and displaying life is through various devices of trompe l'oeil—the kind of fool-the-eye that suspended animation, or an exaggeration of the conventions of realistic art, can bring about. Trompe l'oeil, itself a kind of material and secular miracle of animation, appealed to Peale in various ways throughout his career and later became the device used by Raphaelle, his most troubled child, in his paintings. Following eighteenth-century aesthetic conventions, the older Peale ranked the various forms of

Charles Willson Peale, *Staircase Group: Rafaelle and Titian Ramsay Peale I*, 1795.

nature morte, which he referred to as "deceptions," low in his hierarchy of painting because they teach no moral values. Yet he saw such work as potentially crowd-pleasing or, more charitably perhaps, as being attractive to afficionadi of painterly technique. The painting most often called *Staircase Group: Raphaelle and Titian Ramsay Peale I* was finished for the "Columbianum, or American Academy of Painting, Sculpture, Architecture, and Engraving" at the Philadelphia Statehouse in 1795. It shows Peale's two sons in life-size, climbing a winding stairway. The deception was designed to fool the viewer into believing in its reality. Peale insisted that the picture be hung in a doorway rather than on the wall and he had an actual step built into the room at the base of the painted step. According to Rembrandt Peale, George Washington, on a later visit to the museum, bowed politely to the figures, for he thought they were "living persons."[25] As early as 1787, Peale had placed a life-sized wax figure of himself in his museum as a way of fooling the public into assuming his presence there. And there are other accounts of Peale traveling through Maryland in a carriage harnessed simultaneously with living horses and stuffed fawns, as well as several other taxidermic specimens. This project, he reported in his *Autobiography*, "excited much curiosity along the road."[26]

Peale's "deceptions" may be seen in classic psychoanalytic terms as "derealizations." They serve, like all derealizations, as means of defense, keeping the irreducible fact of a boundary between life and death at bay. The second characteristic of derealizations—their dependence on the past, on the ego's store of memories and earlier painful experiences—is also evident here. The theme of animations centers around issues of the preservation of meaning in the face of its traumatic disturbance.[27] As Peale recovers from his postwar breakdown, his first project is an effort to create an exhibition of moving pictures.

Peale decided to invent a spectacle similar to Philippe de Loutherbourg's miniature theater of sound and light in London. He created six pictures, which he advertised in 1785 as "perspective views, with changeable effects, of nature delineated in motion." He chose scenes of dawn rising over a rural landscape, night sinking on Market Street in Philadelphia, a Roman temple battered by a thunderstorm that ended in a rainbow, a view of Satan's fiery palace as described by Milton, and a historical painting of the Revolutionary

War's sea battle between the *Bonhomme Richard* and the *Serapis*.[28]

In such works, Peale experimented with light, painting, sculpture, and the use of natural objects. Carved waves were worked by cranks, while real spray spurted out of concealed pipes. Painted transparencies were passed across one another before candles in order to produce airy effects. Foreground objects were either flat cut-outs or three-dimensional props, and Peale sustained the phantasmagoric mood with music he played on a specially built organ. He soon discovered, however, that the public wanted perpetually new works—all of which cost a great deal in time, labor, and materials. In a letter to Benjamin West in 1788, Peale told him that for two or three years he had studied and labored to create this exhibition of moving pictures; consequently he had "injured his health and straitened his circumstances."[29]

It was at this time that he turned fully toward his project of a museum, or, as he called it, a world in miniature. He began by building a landscape out of turf, trees, a thicket, and a pond situated on the gallery floor. On the mound he placed those birds that commonly walk on the ground, as well as a stuffed bear, deer, leopard, tiger, wildcat, fox, raccoon, rabbit, and squirrel. The boughs of the trees were loaded with birds, and the thicket was full of snakes. On the banks of the pond he placed shells, turtles, frogs, lizards, and watersnakes, while in the water stuffed fishes swam between the legs of stuffed waterfowl. A hole in the mound displayed minerals and rare earths.

Peale's two major sources for his collection were gifts, largely of curiosities or items that were in some way souvenirs of historical events and famous persons, and those items he and his sons gathered as they traveled in search of specimens. In his search for varieties of every species, with no duplicates, he promulgated Linnaeus' system in the interest of universal laws.[30] Although he would later imagine, as his own dynasty grew, his museum's world as one of paired specimens for reproduction, his wish that there be "no duplicates" is connected to the concepts of uniqueness, individuality, and character, which inform his portraiture: the republic of the New World was to be built from the singular actions of singular individuals.

Peale's *Discourse Introductory to a Course of Lectures* (1800) is perhaps the fullest statement of his philosophy of collecting. He links himself in a great chain of largely unrecognized founders of national museums, from the Alexandrian Library and repository of Ptolemy Philadelphus (a kind of historical pun on his own name and location) to contemporary British and European museums. By 1800 Peale's collections were overflowing Philosophical Hall, and Raphaelle and Rembrandt's museum in Baltimore, begun in 1797, had already failed. Peale's *Discourse* is in fact a somewhat hysterical document, full of elevated scientific claims and sudden plunges toward dark lyrical effects. In recounting the history of museums, he includes a dirge to Aldrovandi before he goes on to tell of the British Museum and how hard it is for the public to view it. A recurring theme of the document is the idea that science is a cure for war. Peale tells how "the chiefs of several nations of Indians," who before had been bitter enemies, met by chance when visiting the museum and were inspired to resolve their differences.[31] But most jarringly, as Peale presents his philosophical and political rationale for the museum, he weaves into the lecture the story of the death of his son Titian in 1798. Titian Ramsay Peale the First's death occurred in September of that year and two months later Raphaelle Peale's first child died in infancy. In 1799 Charles Peale named a son by his second wife after Titian. Thus he connects the rebirth of the museum with the rebirth of his son. The lecture includes the performance of two musical interludes with words written by Rembrandt Peale. The first is called the "Beauties of Creation" and suggests:

> Mark the beauties of Creation,
> Mark the harmony that reigns!
> Each, supported in its station,
> Age to age unchang'd remains.

The second is an "Ode on the Death of Titian Peale":

> His early loss let Science mourn
> Responsive with our frequent sighs,—
> Sweet flower of genius! That had borne
> The fairest fruit beneath the skies![32]

Again, taxonomy is seen as an antidote to emotion and surplus meaning. Charles Peale attached a note to his lecture explaining:

This early devoted and much lamented youth, died with the Yellow Fever in New York in 1798. It might be excused if the fondness of a parent indulged in the eulogium of his son; yet the testimony of numerous friends and acquaintances confirm his worth...and the plans which he had commenced, to the prosecution of which his whole soul was devoted, far beyond his years, raised the greatest expectation of his becoming the Linnaeus of America...[33]

In ensuing years, as the yellow fever made periodic reappearances, Peale advertised the museum in the *Philadelphia Repository and Weekly Register* as a place where lost children could be kept until called for.[34]

In 1801 Peale heard of the discovery of huge bones by a farmer near Newburgh, New York. He and Rembrandt traveled quickly to the farm,

Charles Willson Peale, *The Exhumation of the Mastodon*, 1806.

examined the bones and purchased rights to dig further in the marlpit where they had been found.[35] Cuvier had published the mastodon as an example of an extinct species. The discovery of this specimen was dramatic evidence that species could become extinct over geological time.[36] The American Philosophical Society gave the Peales a loan to conduct the excavation and the family eventually put together two mastodon skeletons, which went on to a wide and varied career as exhibitions, from P. T. Barnum to the American Museum of Natural History in New York to Peale's Museum in Baltimore, where one set is currently on display. In 1807 Peale wrote to Benjamin West of his progress in painting a picture of the site: "Although I have introduced upwards of 50 figures, yet the number of spectators in fine weather amounted to hundreds. Eighteen of my figures are portraits, having taken

Charles Willson Peale, *Noah and His Ark*, 1819.

the advantage of taking most of this number of my family..."[37]

This picture is in fact a kind of summa of Peale's career, offering a counterpoint to a copy he made in 1819 of Charles Catton's picture of *Noah's Ark*—
just as the realism of *Rachel Weeping* was in counterpoint to the copy of
Elisha Restoring the Shunamite's Son. The copy of Catton's *Noah* and the picture
of the exhumation provide a number of insights into the relations between
mourning and taxonomy, memory and animation. As Peale continued to add
to the canvas of the exhumation through 1808 he delineated more and more
family members and friends to be included in the glory of his momentous
discovery. Just as Noah's sons, in the face of extinction, would help their
father gather members of each species and begin a new world, so would
Peale's aesthetic dynasty continue his scientific project. Rembrandt's 1803
pamphlet on the mastodon proclaims, "The bones exist—the animals do
not!" He goes on to explain that science has awakened this literally buried
fact of "stupendous creation."[38] Science's triumph over death is quite literally
demonstrated as Peale includes in his painting both the living and the dead.
The painting dramatizes a critical moment in the excavation when a violent
thunderstorm threatened to flood the pit and end the search. The painting
forms both a complement to, and inversion of, the Noah's Ark theme. Here
the dead—extinct species and those of Peale's family and friends who are
gone—are awakened and brought back into the light. Yet flooding threatens,
just as it did in the picture of the Ark, and the family is once again the focus
for regeneration and recollection. Of the Noah's Ark painting, Peale wrote
that he admired very much the innocence of the venerable old man, the sweet
idea of parental love, the peacock and other birds whose lines of beauty are
so richly tinted. "I can only say," he wrote, "that it is a Museum in itself and
a subject in the line of the fine arts and that although I have never liked the
copying of pictures, yet should I wish to make a copy of it."[39]

Of course it has long been a convention of the conversation piece, a
genre Peale knew well and often practiced, to evoke mourning in a scene by
including allusions to, or representations of, the dead in a picture of the living. Mario Praz has pointed out that these conventions frequently rely on
portraits accompanied by busts, as is the case in Peale's play on such conventions in his *Peale Family Group*, which he worked on from 1770–1773 and again
in 1809.[40] Here the family gathered around a scene where Charles, stopping

at his easel with face lowered from view, and James, pointing with a small stick, are giving their brother St. George advice, as St. George tries to draw a portrait of their mother holding Charles's daughter Eleanor. The family is flanked by busts of Benjamin West, Peale himself, and his early patron Edmund Jennings, and by an oil sketch of the muses on the easel: those customarily in the place of the dead are, in fact, living immortals. And the children, who in such conversation pieces are usually those who receive whatever lessons the dead have to teach, here are infants who died in their first year. This quality of death pushed forward is emphasized by the placement of the still life in the foreground of the picture and by the nonreciprocity of the gazes depicted. One of Peale's last additions to the painting was the dog, Argus, placed in the foreground. At the same time, Peale painted out the words *Concordis Anima* (harmony embodied), which had once before been written there. Peale wrote in 1808 to Rembrandt that he had erased these words because "the design was sufficient to explain the theme."[41]

But we can also see that it is time that erased the truth of the legend.

Charles Willson Peale, *Peale Family Group*, 1773–1809.

Once more the lesson nature has to teach is an unnatural one. When the picture was finished only Charles and James Peale (d. 1831) remained alive from the scene. And we cannot help but remember that the dog is named "bright-eyed" after the giant who was put to death by Hermes and whose eyes were then placed in a peacock's tail. Nature's lesson is the production and reproduction of nature, not the production of order and sequence; and nature calls for vigilant observation, not the construction of moral aphorisms.[42]

Further, Peale recognized that he was himself pressed to complete works such as Peale Family Group in preparation for death.[43] Among his last works are his 1822 portrait of James studying a portrait miniature by lamplight and his self-portrait of the same year, The Artist in His Museum. Peale had been asked by the museum trustees to paint a life-sized, full-length portrait of himself. Peale wrote to Rembrandt on July 23, 1822: "I think it is important that I should not only make it a lasting ornament to my art as a painter, but also that the design should be expressive that I bring forth into public view the beauties of nature and art, the rise and progress of the Museum."[44] Peale holds back the curtain so that the collections might be seen, and places in the foreground the giant mastodon jaw and tibia—the mounted skeleton can be discerned to the right just above the set-aside palette. A Quaker woman holds up her hands in astonishment at the mastodon, while a father talks with his son, who is holding an open book, and another figure looks at the birds. At eighty-one, Peale conducts here an experiment with the relation between artificial and natural light, the latter coming from behind in the museum and the former coming from a mirror which reflects a secondary light onto his head. The light of painting thus turns back from the foreground of the picture, the light of nature moves forward from the back with Peale outlined by their interrelation. Yet the curtain reminds us of the collected and staged qualities of this nature, and as well of the curtain hiding a scene of death and extinction in Rachel Weeping. And the life-sized "deception" of Peale's figure appears realistically on the most artificial side of the curtain.[45]

This work does little to resolve for us the status of the animated taxonomy and does perhaps even less to define the boundary where life ends and art begins. There are few pictures of knowledge farther from Platonism than the Enlightenment's skeptical empiricism on the one hand, and psychoanalytic concepts of latency and the unconscious on the other. Yet in the case of Peale

Charles Willson Peale, *The Artist in His Museum*, 1822.

we see the limit of Enlightenment taxonomy at the threshold of inarticulate emotion. Peale frequently referred to himself as a "memorialist," meaning by this that he was painting the dead in the service of a future memory. Further, just as Freud's theory of mourning is developed around the traumatic consequences of war, so does Peale develop his museum as an antidote to war's losses and as a gesture against disorder and the extinction of knowledge. In this nexus of motion and emotion, arrested life and animation, loss and memory which Peale has left for us, we can begin to recollect, with both a sense of difference and a sense of urgency, a central issue regarding representation.

Installation view of Daniel Spoerri's *Musée sentimental* of Cologne, 1979.

Jean-Hubert Martin

THE "MUSÉE SENTIMENTAL" OF DANIEL SPOERRI

The phenomenon of museums or exhibitions conceived by artists appeared in the seventies and continues today. Different from artists' collections, they are often temporary and gather heterogeneous objects from various categories and fields. Artists' museums and museum shows tend to create a microcosmic space where each element transmits a global view by relaying a single story.

A variety of artists have "curated" in very different manners; nevertheless, an overriding approach seems to propose art as unsequestered from life, and as only an element of a larger, anthropological whole. The Beuys Block, installed in 1970, is still visible at the Hessisches Landesmuseum in Darmstadt. It is both a concentration of Joseph Beuys's work and a synthetical vision of the artist's relationship with the world. Beuys gathered manufactured objects with symbolic character—animal substances in different shapes, and energy-transforming apparatus—and installed them in vitrines. Later, in 1972, Marcel Broodthaers installed an experimental exhibition around the theme of the eagle, what he termed his own Museum of Modern Art, at the Düsseldorf Kunsthalle. In his short text about the exhibition, Broodthaers insisted on the blindness of the public, on the importance of the symbol of authority exemplified by the symbolic power of the eagle, and on the artist as the author of a definition who takes any object for his own purpose. The exhibition gathered dozens of different types of eagles, from many cultures and in all materials. They were classified in the corresponding catalogue in alphabetical order according to places of origin. Each eagle was accompanied by a label, "This is not a work of art." Like Beuys, Broodthaers perceived display as symbolic and outside the realm of traditional visual art.

In the 1992 Documenta exhibition, Claes Oldenburg exhibited his Mouse Museum, which now belongs in the collection of the Ludwig Museum in Cologne. He had been working on this idea since the mid-sixties. The vitrines in the Mouse Museum house 385 tiny objects, many manufactured objects of

Joseph Beuys during the installation of Vitrine 1
of *Beuys Block* at the Haus der Kunst, Munich, 1968.

consumer culture—toys and miniatures—but also three-dimensional sketches of sculptures and fake "natural" elements, like plants and food, transposed in synthetic material. Oldenburg's museum is a whole world of fakes and pastiches in reduction, portraying, in the end, the flatness and uniformity of our environment.

The banality of daily life was also the focus of a diverse collection of objects gathered by Christian Boltanski in Paris in 1974: "Inventory of Objects Having Belonged to a Lady of Bois-Colombes." But, here, the accent was clearly morbid, as all the objects, shown in large vitrines, were a reminder of the death of their owner. Boltanski, like Beuys, succeeded in using vitrines, like those found in an ethnographic museum, to emphasize the melancholic, funereal characteristics of objects.

In Bern, Switzerland, Bertrand Lavier presented *The Painting of the Martin from 1604 to 1984*, which established "Martin" as the most common name in Western culture through an analysis of Western painting. Works of several nations were represented over four centuries. One could also find various genres represented—history and battle painting, still life, landscape, abstraction, comic strip, and conceptual art. Reproducing the traditional chronological scheme would have brought back the usual museum appearance and erased the originality of the enterprise, so Lavier chose a classification system according to the alphabetical order of first names.

In 1990, Joseph Kosuth curated an exhibition called "Of the Unsayable Devoted to Wittgenstein." The works shown came mostly from living artists. The exhibition design was innovative and stimulating: a Wittgenstein quotation ran along the walls, and the works were installed with a freedom that the conventions of hanging have made us forget. Kosuth used the whole surface of the walls, from floor to ceiling. Some works were juxtaposed to provoke unexpected formal comparisons, and others were brought together for meaningful conceptual encounters. Because many works were ready-made objects, he found a subtle balance, avoiding an odds-and-ends effect and creating visual and mental associations to open up the way for imaginative ways of seeing.

Many more artists have created their own museums, including Richard Hamilton in the fifties, Andy Warhol at the Rhode Island School of Design in Providence in 1970, and the shops of Ben, Raymond Hains, or Jean Michel Alberola. The following analysis of one in particular, Daniel Spoerri's *musée sentimental* (sentimental museum), demands first an account of the background of the artist. Daniel Spoerri was born in Rumania in 1930. His father, who was Jewish but who had converted to Protestantism, was killed by the Nazis, a circumstance that forced the family to move to Switzerland, where Daniel grew up.

He started his career dancing in the Bern Opera and became the star dancer of the company. But, interested in many varied activities, he was also an artist, cook, poet, screenplay registrar, choreographer, publisher, curator, and dilettante. Personifying the type of ideology that emerged in the sixties — "Art in life and life in art" — he became a major figure of the Fluxus and

Claes Oldenburg, *Mouse Museum*, 1977,
as installed at the Whitney Museum of American Art in 1978.

New Realist movements. When he arrived in Paris in 1959, he was publishing multiples under the name of MAT—*Multiplication d'art transformable* (Multiplication of Transformable Art). He was especially fascinated by Yves Klein, whom he referred to as "the last real artist," and Jean Tinguely, who always remained a close friend.

The combination of Spoerri's experience with theater direction, concrete poetry, and his contact with the Parisian neo-Dada artists led him to the *tableau piège* (snare picture) in 1960. Freezing a situation at a given moment, Spoerri glued all the objects of a room exactly where he found them. At the Gallery Köpke in Copenhagen, in 1961, the artist froze the whole apartment of Robert Filliou, who had just been thrown out of Denmark.

Spoerri then created a grocery store with all sorts of food packages stamped "Attention—work of art." Each item was sold at the same price as it would cost in a normal store. Thus, compared to Rauschenberg or Johns, to whom he is artistically related but whose references are still high art in structure and materials, Spoerri's position was more radically Duchampian, relying on the subject itself to make the art. The problem raised by this type of artistic activity is how to continue and further develop his practice.

Daniel Spoerri understood immediately that it was possible to get trapped making conceptual work based on found objects. So, in 1961, he decided to forego the process of actually freezing objects into position; instead he presented a map of the *tableau piège* with the place of each object carefully drawn in what he termed the anecdotal topography of chance. The objects dematerialized into his precise descriptions of them, providing a unique analysis of our relationships with them.

The result of Spoerri's reflections on the object resulted in the creation of the *musée sentimental*, the first realization of which took place at the Centre Georges Pompidou in Paris in 1977. Spoerri was asked to realize both a museum of fetish and a museum shop, *la boutique aberrant* (the aberrant boutique), within the frame of an enormous welded metal sculpture by Tinguely in the entrance hall to the museum. The *boutique aberrant* sold all sorts of objects that had been collected by Spoerri from artists. Upon his request, they gave old tools, brushes, palettes, unfinished works, and, in general, anything lying around in the corners of their studios. The fetishistic spirit, usually applied to the dead, was here applied to the living. These relics of the heroic activities of contemporary artists were then sold to benefit Amnesty International.

Beside this little fetish museum was the *musée sentimental*. It was designed as a long black corridor with vitrines of different sizes and shapes inserted into the wall. Most of the objects in the vitrines related to French history and culture, including things like Vincent Van Gogh's furniture from his home in Auvers-sur-Oise, René Magritte's bowler hat, Arthur Rimbaud's suitcase, and three little toy horses owned by Marcel Duchamp when he was a child. One of Spoerri's most cherished objects in this first *musée sentimental* was Ingres's violin. The nineteenth-century painter played violin and devoted much time to music, a fact that became so well known that it led to a common expression in the French language: *un violin d'Ingres* refers to a hobby. Spoerri was interested in these connections between language and objects. The object in this case was the form given to a concept, derived from the activity implied by the object.

One object, Constantin Brancusi's nail cutter, had been stolen by Spoerri from the artist's studio after his death in 1960. It was shown with a hand-written label telling of its introduction into the *musée sentimental*. He considered the nail cutter as a trace not only of Brancusi, but also of the impasse Ronsin, the dead-end street where both Tinguely and Brancusi had their studios. This fetish was a memory of the place and of the time, and, like any fetish, it activated a mental process. The nail cutter was also symbolic in its use as an ordinary object, separating dead parts of the body from living ones. For Spoerri, it became a symbolic image of rupture. The death of Brancusi, the separation from the impasse Ronsin, meant for him initiation and beginning in art. These objects are then connected to the world of death; they remind and revive the invisible past through visual stimulation.

The second *musée sentimental* was exhibited on a much larger scale in the Kunstverein Cologne in 1979. The project started with an invitation to Spoerri to teach at the art school in Cologne, which was signed by Karl Marx, painter and the director of the school. Spoerri agreed and had an idea to start his new job with an homage to Karl Marx, by collecting a "dinner of homonyms." Through the phone book, he found and invited Engels, Kant, Hegel, Goethe, Faust, Wagner, Strauss, Bach, Dürer, Holbein, Cranach, Julius Caesar, Hamlet, and Frankenstein. Besides the joke, the question, similar to the one raised by the stamp "Attention—work of art"

Eros, as installed in Spoerri's *musée sentimental* of Cologne, 1979.
The arrangement of objects included panty hose, black lace, and a leather muzzle.

put on simple objects, was that of the determination or the influence imposed on people by naming.

Spoerri considered his class at the art school to be his collaborators in the production of Cologne's *musée sentimental*. He saw this project as an enlargement of his snare pictures, an idea he had already discussed with his New Realist friends, like Tinguely who had tried to push him in the early sixties to freeze a whole village with all its objects. Spoerri had not been interested by this simplified and naive enlargement process, but, in Cologne the extension of the snare picture led to the idea of imaging the personality and characteristic identity of the city.

Instead of relying on chance, as in the *musée sentimental* of Paris, Spoerri and his students tried to describe the city of Cologne with key words, which helped to define its specificity. They ended up with 120 sections ranking from the particular, like former German chancellor Konrad Adenauer or Surrealist Max Ernst, to the general, like Eros or Animal. Many sections included several objects. Each student was put in charge of one or several sections and had to do research and write the text for the catalogue. The work was supervised by Daniel Spoerri and Marie-Louise Plessen, a historian who had also helped him on the Paris project. The exhibition's catalogue was titled Entwurf zu einem Lexikon von Reliquien und Relikten aus zwei Jahrtausenden Köln incognito (Essay for a lexicon of relics and sacred remains as well as remnants from two millenaries, Cologne incognito).

An example of a meaningful object Spoerri was looking for was a pair of boots brought in by a student. Coated in a thick solid crust of the mud that often covers the streets of Cologne in February, the boots were evocative of the carnival held that month. One of the only items for which Spoerri wrote a text for the catalogue was his favorite: during the war, when the cathedral was bombed, a piece of its leaded roof fell and hung from a spire. The piece of lead was taken down from the place where it had been since the war and became one of the features of the exhibition. Without this provenance, the piece of lead in itself was of no interest at all.

Other objects included an early picture Max Ernst painted when he was a child, an Indian feather headdress which Adenauer got as a present during a trip to the United States, and also his scissors. Spoerri wanted to show the leather jacket of the first drug addict killed by an overdose in Cologne. The

Top: Max Ernst, *Picture of A Young Boy*, c. 1912.
Bottom: Native American adornments from
the collection of Konrad Adenauer. As installed in
Spoerri's *musée sentimental* of Cologne, 1979.

students were absolutely against it. Daniel Spoerri argued that the family of Adenauer was probably not pleased that his souvenir was next to the souvenirs of a whore and, so there was no reason to leave aside the myths of their own generation. The fight escalated to the point where the organizers considered canceling the show.

The egalitarian attitude the organizers took, avoiding hierarchy in their decision making, is well established with the three Ursulas in the show. The first was the famous patron saint of Cologne and her famous relic-shrine. The second was the funeral epitaph of Ursula Maria Columba Von Groote, who is supposed to have been a mistress of Casanova. The third was Ursula Gerdes, the first tenant of the then newly built Eros Center.

The director of the Kunsthalle wrote in the catalogue's introduction that this exhibition had no piece made by the artist. In fact, there was one: *Der Vater Rhein* (Father Rhine) is a precious silver piece only used for Cologne's official dinners. Spoerri placed the piece of silver on a bed of sugar and 300 butcher's knives. This presentation became then the illustration of the Latin expression *Dulce et decorum est pro patria mori* — "It is sweet and beautiful to die o'r the fatherland." Exemplified here is his interest in the connections between linguistic and visual levels.

The third version was the *Musée sentimental de Prusse*, which took place in the Berlin Museum in 1981. Bigger than the one in Cologne, including 178 key words, it was curated by both Marie-Louise Plessen and Daniel Spoerri. The opposition of extremes — like trivial and precious, sacred and obscene, banal and meaningful — was less obvious than in the previous one.

Der Vater Rhein (Father Rhine), as installed in Spoerri's *musée sentimental* of Cologne, 1979. "Father Rhine" is a German legend, which implies that all life comes from the Rhine River.

Pickelhauben (spiked helmets) worn during the reign of Friedrich Wilhelm I of Prussia, as installed in Spoerri's *musée sentimental* of Prussia, Berlin Museum, 1981.

A predominance of objects with an aristocratic and military provenance perhaps could not be avoided; they validated the Prussian image as part of the
collective imagination. Alphabetical order, nevertheless, brought unexpected
associations between objects.

Prussian military helmets, after which other countries (ironically those
who later took over Prussia) modeled their own helmets, were shown. Some
surprising semantic changes caused by World War I were visible; for example,
the cigarettes Ma petite (my small one in French) became Meine Kleine (in
German) at the beginning of the war. Also represented were the famous giant
soldiers called *Lange Kerls* (the large guys), who guarded the life of Friedrich
Wilhelm I at the beginning of the eighteenth century; some objects belonging to witches; the bronze statue of Friedrich Wilhelm II on horseback; and
a figure from one of the numerous panopticum of the nineteenth century,
showing the effects of a tight corset. The Queen of Prussia, Louise, known
for her beauty and political finesse, was represented by several items, most
notably by her death mask that had been overpainted by the artist Arnulf
Rainer. Artistic intervention was a novelty in this version of the *musée sentimental*. The Swiss artist Bernhard Lüginbühl made an enormous knife, and Martin
Schwarz was asked to remake a Caspar David Friedrich painting that had

burned during the war—he repainted it, showing the results of the fire.

Another Spoerri collection was recently installed in the Chateau d'Oiron in France. This castle, built by a dignitary during the Renaissance, belongs to a group of castles in the Loire Valley. The original decoration has been preserved in three rooms, most notably in a unique fifty-meter-long painting gallery by the Fontainebleau school, but the castle was empty of furniture. Through inventories and the quality of the existing decor, it is clear that the castle housed an important art collection. There is also reason to believe, according to recent studies about collecting during the sixteenth and seventeenth centuries, that there was a cabinet of curiosities. This cabinet was used as a basis to build up a new contemporary collection. Most of the works were commissioned, and many of the sixty artists worked directly in the spaces of the castle. The first stage of this collection opened to the public at the end of June 1993.

Daniel Spoerri, with his interest in history and his scholarly knowledge of cabinets of curiosities, was a choice artist to work in the Chateau d'Oiron. In 1983–84, he acquired a collection made by a countess of Wendelstadt, Germany, in the 1870s. All the forty-eight objects in it were labeled as presents from friends, who

Objects belonging to witches, including garlic and onions to protect against evil spirits, a pouch of linseed for dreaming, a bunch of elder leaves to protect against tumors, peas to protect against warts, herbs, lard, and various other magic formulas. Installed by Lili Fischer in Spoerri's *musée sentimental* of Prussia, Berlin Museum, 1981.

had described and testified as to their origins and histories. The objects themselves are insignificant: pieces of wood, cloth, and wallpaper. But, contained
in a box labeled "Mama W," they are personalized souvenirs and carry emotional power—an Indian arrowhead found in Elinwood, North America;
necklaces made with little locks worn by women in Nijui-Novgorod, Russia;
wallpaper from a room in the house of a Mr. Simon where Napoleon III
met with Bismarck; a little part of the coffin of Juliet brought from Verona
by Wendelstadt in 1868. Mama W's collection is a decadent form of the
Renaissance's cabinet of curiosities, considered by Daniel Spoerri as the
prototype for the musée sentimental. To emphasize the opposition between
their ephemerality and their emotional value, Spoerri mounted these objects
in rich and heavy frames.

Le musée sentimental de Napoléon was never realized, but it seems appropriate
to mention it here. Napoleon's myth is, of course, still very alive in France.
Spoerri's collection includes about a dozen of Napoleon's hats—all truly
made for him by his hatter, but many of them never worn by the emperor.

The purpose of the methodology used in conceiving the musée sentimental
was to abolish hierarchies and normal, given categories. Memory and history,
for Spoerri, sit in strong opposition to each other. Combining passion, imagination, fantasies, and facts, memory is thus the result of human experience,
whereby time is dilated and chronology doesn't count, only heritage and
inner beliefs. On the contrary, history is a vision of the past with forged and
codified rules. From a distance and with supposed scientific rigor, history
shapes human experience by subjecting it to an analysis that attempts to separate the true from the false. Sometimes in historical museums, one might
find a few odd relics or fetishes well known through cultural mythology in
the corner of a vitrine. Thus, both memory and history might be represented
in museums, but their separation is rarely clear.

And, as cultural mythologies shift, objects can lose their historical signification. A good example of historical devaluation of an object is the bezoar,
a mineral formed on a swallowed object in the stomach of animals, such
as cows and horses. Praised and very expensive during the Renaissance,
they were thought to possess magical powers and were considered by some
authors as the origins of stone and, therefore, of the earth. They were found
in cabinets of curiosities of the courts of Northern Europe mounted on

Soccer ball from the final game of the
German Soccer league in 1978, as installed in
Spoerri's *musée sentimental* of Cologne, 1979.

very refined goldsmith pedestals. But today a few veterinary museums are the only museums where bezoars are found; other museums have discarded them, or put them in storage, and when found in the slaughterhouses, they are thrown away.

Yet the *musée sentimental* also reconciles history and memory, science and myth, and is therefore open to a wide scope of curiosities. It combines rational thinking with sensitivity, negating the typical Western attitude since the eighteenth century that separates art from science. As in the cabinets of curiosities of the Renaissance, in this form Spoerri expresses a need to rebuild a microcosm based on the memory of a community.

In terms of art, the *musée sentimental* raises the question of the fundamental role of the artist, his social and critical responsibility, and his link to history. Where many artists try desperately to create meaning for a community out of the invisible or the supernatural, Spoerri simply juxtaposed objects that already possessed communal meaning and power, given by history and not by the individual decision of an artist. Unextravagant in the exhibition design, he used normal museological display, hanging, lighting, and vitrines for the objects to be protected and seen in good light on eye level.

During this century, the definition of art as a completely autonomous field has proven obsolete. By the same token, the equation that art is life and vice versa, as defined in the sixties, could not last long. Perhaps most valuable to remember is, as Filliou, a close friend of Daniel Spoerri, has said, that art is what makes life more interesting than art.

The Delani and Sonnabend Hall, Madelena Delani Gallery,
Museum of Jurassic Technology, Los Angeles, California.

Ralph Rugoff

BEYOND BELIEF:
THE MUSEUM AS METAPHOR

The Museum of Jurassic Technology is situated between Los Angeles's east and west sides, sandwiched between a realty office and a now-defunct forensic laboratory. Modest in scale though not in ambition, it calls itself "an ethnographic and natural history museum of the lower Jurassic," designed to serve both the academic community and the general public.

Its exhibition spaces, cluttered with traditional glass-and-wood vitrines, form a dimly lit maze. Displays feature preserved insects, animal skeletons, dioramas, mineralogical specimens, and various science and technology exhibits —some obsolete, like the Boules of Conundrum, a brass mechanism for producing man-made gems, others covering more recent material such as "Life in the Extreme Ultraviolet" and "Post-Plasmatic Visualization." Many of these displays utilize up-to-date viewer-activated and audiovisual technologies, but under the direction of founder David Wilson, the museum has taken great pains to create the impression of having nineteenth-century roots.

Presentations are reassuringly meticulous. Fact-filled wall labels offer scholarly, step-by-step explanations for even the oddest natural phenomena, enacting the museum's mission of guiding viewers "from familiar objects toward the unfamiliar." In those exhibits that feature an audio component, the narrator speaks in a tone familiar from countless educational films: pedantic, slightly pompous, void of ambiguity. Occasionally you come across blank wall spaces and empty vitrines occupied by signs reading: "Exhibit temporarily removed for study," indicating that the curatorial and research staffs are on the ball.

On the surface of it, this isn't a museum with which you could fall in love. Yet as you make your way through its dimly lit halls, a vaguely disturbing thought arises—like a faint scratching at a back window of the mind. While this is supposedly a Museum of Jurassic Technology, there are few displays that actually make reference to either the geographic Jurassic (the area of the lower Nile) or the prehistoric time period. Most exhibits seem to deal with science or natural history, but a significant number venture outside this sphere in presenting fruit-stone carvings, fifteenth-century battle maps, and engravings of the Tower of Babel. An animated model of Noah's Ark and several references to a higher power—the introductory slide show ends with the line "Glory to Him, who endureth forever"—stir up suspicions that this may not, after all, be a secular institution.

Taken together, these observations lead to an irrevocable conclusion: the museum isn't what it says it is. If not an outright impostor, at the very least it has to be considered an unreliable narrator. Of course, this quality of being hard to pin down, of suggesting there's more than meets the eye here, is essential to seduction. More than one romance has begun on exactly this kind of shaky ground, and such is the terrain on which my own relationship with this institution blossomed.

The Delani and Sonnabend Hall, located in the rear of the MJT, is its most lyrical installation, and may even be a type of love story, though one where the protagonists never meet. Through a series of exhibits and listening stations, it chronicles the lives and work of two individuals from the early twentieth century: Madalena Delani, a classical singer afflicted with what may have been Korsakoff Syndrome (which impairs short-term memory), and Geoffrey Sonnabend, supposedly a professor of neurophysiology at Northwestern University.

Skipping over the wealth of biographical detail provided in the exhibit, I will cut to the chase: in 1936 Delani gives a concert in a Brazilian spa resort near the giant Iguaçu Falls. Sonnabend is also at the spa, convalescing from a breakdown suffered after an unsuccessful research project on the memory pathways of carp. After attending Delani's recital of romantic lieder, the professor from Illinois spends a sleepless night, during which he devises a novel theory of memory. He spends the next eight years elaborating this theory, finally publishing his findings in a three-volume tome titled *Obliscence, Theories of Forgetting, and the Problem of Matter*, which is synopsized in the museum's Hall of Obliscence.

Departing from previous research in the field, Sonnabend maintained that forgetting, rather than remembering, is the inevitable outcome of all experience. In other words, we are all amnesiacs, and what we know as "memory" is nothing more than an imaginative act scaffolded around decaying fragments of lived experience. Memory, Sonnabend wrote, is only

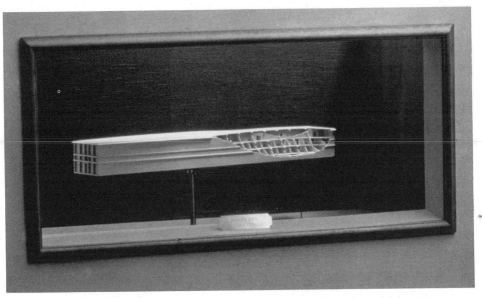

Noah's Ark, scale model, Museum of Jurassic Technology, Los Angeles, California.

a confabulation designed to "buffer us against the intolerable knowledge of the irreversible passage of time and the irretrievability of its moments and events." Did Delani's singing, which one critic reportedly described as "steeped in a haunting sense of loss," somehow inspire Sonnabend's theory? Was her plaintive vocal expression due to her lost connection to the past? In a darkened chamber of reliquaries that is the exhibit's most poetic installation, the singer's biography is recounted by a voice-over narration that drops hints along these lines.

To the accompaniment of Delani's singing, the viewer is led through a rise-and-fall career biography that underscores the limits of documentary reconstruction. Wall-mounted photographs showing the singer at progressive stages of her career are illuminated at appropriate moments, but quite unlike the visuals we expect from historical documentaries, the information they provide is negligible. Similarly, the personal effects displayed in vitrines —concert programs, opera gloves, sheet music—add little to our understanding of Delani's fate. The viewer is left to mull over a grim coda that has the irony of an O'Henry twist: after giving the concert at the Iguaçu Falls, the singer returned to Buenos Aires the next day and was killed in a car crash. The concert Sonnabend heard was her last.

Is this a true story? You can never be sure at the MJT, where a number of exhibits—such as a display devoted to a South American bat that uses radar to fly through solid walls—strain credulity. Even when the suspicion arises that fact and fiction have been deftly intermingled, it remains difficult to delineate their respective borders. By making use of information that lies on the edges of our cultural literacy—things we've heard of but don't necessarily know much about, such as bat radar, ultraviolet rays, or the Jurassic itself—the museum draws us into a shadowy zone where exhibits slip from the factual to the metaphorical with disarming fluency. It is this fluency which makes the seduction irresistible.

*   .*   *

It's difficult to characterize an exhibit like the Delani and Sonnabend Hall. On one level, it's a rumination on twists of fate, and the convergence of inexplicable lines of influence. On another, the lugubrious Delani exhibit, which concludes with a glowing photograph of the forgotten singer's headstone, could be a memorial to memory itself.

But for a history museum to pay serious attention to a theory that holds all knowledge of the past as an illusion—clearly this is a loaded proposition. In fact it's hard not to see the Delani and Sonnabend Hall as a commentary on the larger institution, calling attention to the aura of unreality surrounding its own recreations (such as Sonnabend's attic study). It might also be a dig at museums in general, which—as repositories of cultural memory built around "decaying fragments of experience"—conform to Sonnabend's theory of memory as imaginative reconstruction.

In the end, there's no way of knowing how to read this material. Like other smitten lovers, I have visited and revisited the museum only to find myself seduced again. I look for clues wherever I can, even in the museum's stationery, where one finds the motto Ut translatio natura—Latin for "nature as metaphor," an idea echoing religious and Romantic concepts of nature as a text to be translated, the scene of hidden meanings.

A diorama on the Cameroonian Stink Ant (officially known as Megaloponera foetens) may or may not embody this idea. Through the narration track, we learn that the occasional Stink Ant, while foraging for food along the rain forest floor, inhales a microscopic fungus spore, which, once seated in the ant's tiny brain, begins to grow at an accelerated rate. The afflicted ant soon appears troubled and confused, and for the first time in its life, leaves the forest floor and begins to climb a vine or plant. At a prescribed height, it impales itself onto the stalk. Within two weeks, a bright orange spike emerges from the ant's ravaged body, dropping new spores onto the forest floor for other unsuspecting ants to inhale.

Unless you're a tropical entomologist, it's hard to know whether this is the story of a real ant, or a parable of all-consuming obsession. It might well be both. The tale of the Stink Ant could also be an allegory for what happens to many of the MJT's visitors: exposed to the museum's exhibits, they initially become troubled and confused, but eventually persuade others to visit in order to be infected by this same experience. The idea of the exhibit-as-metaphor opens a veritable can of worms, partly because metaphor is malleable. Rather than conveying ready-to-digest information, the exhibits unsettle us with information about information. The artifacts we're supposed to be learning about start to dematerialize into a field of questions about display and the nature of knowledge.

One result is that the general parameters of what constitutes an exhibit grow fuzzy. On coming out into the lobby, it's easy to wonder whether the gift store is yet another exhibit, and perhaps even the brass plaque engraved with the names of the museum's supposed founders. Might not these displays also harbor veiled commentaries, something to do with the way contemporary museums increasingly exist for their merchandising operations and the aggrandizement of benefactors?

The suspicion that these exhibits are metaphorical induces minor paranoia. Of course a little paranoia goes a long way toward shaking up habitual perceptions. In certain cases, the uncertainty that the MJT instills in a viewer can produce what I call Stoned Thinking. When I refer to the Stoner, you may imagine someone poring over the cover of a rock album, decoding cryptic messages and its previously unconsidered cosmic implications. But the Stoner's rapture speaks of an experience of total involvement and immanent distraction, not unlike what we see in Vermeer's *Astronomer*. It's something close to a trance.

The effect of stoned thinking is to scramble our perception of boundaries, so that almost anything looms as a potential exhibit deserving an intimate once-over. To give an example, a friend once emerged from the exhibition halls and started examining an unusual object on the front desk — what he assumed was some kind of antiquated seismic instrument. Upon inquiring, he learned it was a tape dispenser temporarily out of tape.

The Stoner's fascinated gaze is also akin to the lover's regard for the beloved, which obliterates the rest of the world with its laser focus. A great part of love's maintenance is earned by paying close attention, and keeping this attentive vision alive. Inasmuch as it produces a similar gaze, I find the MJT to be a deeply romantic museum. Instead of asking us to suspend disbelief, it leads viewers beyond belief. It's not that it aims to discredit rational scholarship; rather it embraces its rhetoric as a peculiar and distinctive voice, but by no means a definitive one. The museum never discards categories such as history and fiction, or science and art; it simply implies they're not necessarily hygienic, that contagion and overlap between them is possible, if not actually quite common. It's a principle at work in the museum's own multiple identity. On leaving, visitors may wonder whether it's a real museum or a simulation, a science museum or an art installation? If it harkens back to the curiosity collections of the eighteenth and nineteenth centuries, can it also be a modern meta-museum — a museum about museology?

In accommodating contradictions and allowing for the existence of parallel systems of thought and parallel realities, the museum seems to be in agreement with the increasingly popular notion that historical perspective is relative. This staple of postmodern thinking has been turning up in all kinds of museums, but with an important difference. For the sake of comparison, I will consider a couple of examples.

First: Los Angeles's fifty-four-million-dollar Gene Autry Museum dedicated to exhibiting and interpreting the heritage of the West. At times, the Autry seems bent on charting the histories of all possible Wests — of the geographic area from Mississippi to California as well as the various Wests of popular imagination, spanning Frederic Remington and Buffalo Bill to Bonanza and the Marlboro Man.

In more than one exhibit, the museum stresses a relativist approach to history. In the Spirit of Discovery gallery, we learn of diverse cultural groups "who discovered the West in their own time period," including Vietnamese refugees who "discovered" California in the late 1970s. Elsewhere, a diagram of the OK Corral showdown drawn by Wyatt Earp is accompanied by a note that this shouldn't be mistaken for an impartial account since it only represents the victors' viewpoint. This relativist philosophy also informs the museum's equal treatment of historical fact and Hollywood fabrication. The Autry's curatorial premise, baldly stated, runs something like this: since much of what we know of the West derives from media imagery, these inventions are as much a part of the legacy as real events. Complicating matters, references to the historical West are irremediably tainted by myth and popular media. A knowing display-text accompanying a Billy the Kid mannequin concludes: "Myth overwhelmed fact, and today, no one knows the real Billy."

At the Autry, as at many more progressive museums, we're told that the history we encounter there isn't definitive, yet the museum's own authority remains unquestioned. Despite all this relativist posturing, the underlying politics of our viewing approach remain unchanged; we are looking for the truth. By contrast, the MJT places its very authenticity in doubt—not just the authenticity of what it exhibits. It does so not simply by mixing fact and fiction—an approach that isn't inherently subversive by any means. At the Museum of Jurassic Technology, duplicity is used as means of instruction, not as a way to bolster its authority. In a society where the line between news and entertainment is increasingly blurred, its labyrinth of confusion offers a canny reflection of what has actually become our daily experience of shuffling fact and fiction. If knowledge is power, then an awareness of the tenuousness of knowledge can only make us suspicious of how power is wielded.

Consider the Los Angeles County Sheriff's Museum, located in Whittier, California: this museum interweaves documentary and fantasy, but to a very different end. Outside its front entrance near the Sheriff's Training Academy, a restored patrol car—a modified 1976 Chevy Nova—is displayed along with a text describing it as a "mystical vehicle." Inside the museum, a giant vitrine of confiscated occult objects includes tarot cards, a Motley Crue banner, a press release from Anton S. LaVey's Church of Satan, and a variety of plastic dashboard saints. As a corollary to the occult section, several exhibits canonize the chief of the department, Sheriff Sherman Block. As if testifying to his supernatural election, one vitrine features a charred section of fuselage taken from an airplane hit by lightning while Sheriff Block was on board. Elsewhere,

Los Angeles County Sheriff's Museum, Whittier, California.

photographs depict the Sheriff's meetings with the Pope and Santa Claus. Now clearly no Chevy Nova, even one with a heavy-duty radiator, is a mystical vehicle; nor is the occult a major cause of crime in Los Angeles; nor is Sheriff Block anybody's candidate for sainthood. Here the mixture of fact and fiction is a consequence not of radical doubt but something more like radical certainty. It's used to create a mythical image of the department in which sheriffs appear as Christian crusaders battling Satan's legions; transcending civic issues, law enforcement is presented as part of an eternal battle of Good against Evil.

From another viewpoint, though, the Museum of Jurassic Technology reads as a metaphor for the fallible self, especially our capacity for unconsciously fusing real events with made-up ones—in memory as well as present time. But this museum isn't merely a model of something else—it's a technology for altering habitual ways of seeing and thinking. Abrogating its own authority is central to this process. In puncturing its institutional facade, it frees us from feeling beholden to the museum's traditional "objectivity," and opens the way to our recovering the authority of subjective experience.

In visiting the MJT, you go in ready to hold up your end of the bargain, only to find that thinking as usual doesn't work here. By subtly breaching our customary contract with museums, the MJT lures us into the process of forging a new one—and to experiencing point of view as a point of negotiation. Whereas the Gene Autry Museum tells us that history is made up of contending, but essentially stable, viewpoints, the Jurassic problematizes the very notion of point of view. One result is the radical reorientation that I call Stoned Thinking. The implication isn't that other museums are necessarily bogus, but that the meaning of any exhibit is open to negotiation because the museum isn't merely a place that preserves culture— it's involved in the process of inventing it in a deal worked out with each and every visitor.

The architect Louis Kalin once complained that most museums are so fatiguing that the first thing you want on entering is a cup of coffee. I think one wants that cup of coffee because so many museum exhibits attract our attention only to immobilize our curiosity. Their atmosphere of infallible authority is paralyzing. The deal they offer leaves little room for negotiation. The visitor, like the objects cluttering the museum's halls, is locked in an airless space.

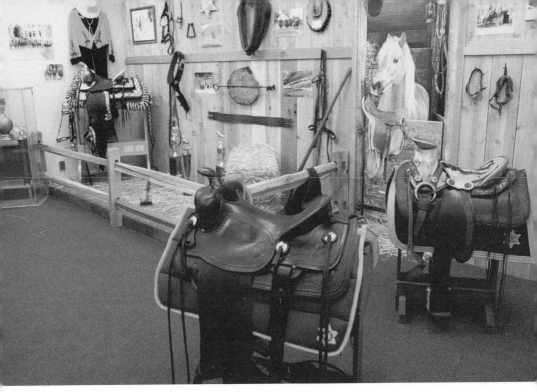

Los Angeles County Sheriff's Museum, Whittier, California.

Where there's no room for playful negotiation, there's no chance for seduction. As with any romance, once the negotiation process goes stale, the relationship is as good as dead. In working out a deal with its visitors, the MJT embodies a mischievous generosity. When it disorients and confuses us, it does so only to re-present this capacity as something infinitely valuable; it leaves us with the feeling that questions are worth holding onto as aesthetic acts, and that uncertainty is a key part of pleasure. In place of an encounter with profundity and depth, it offers an experience of an endless—because always changing—surface.

*   *   *

As I've noted, this museum mixes things—like religion and science, history and art—that are supposed to be kept apart. The very idea of law, on the other hand, is founded on the principle of separation. In ancient Greek, the original meaning of *nomos*, the law, is that which is divided up into parts.

From a psychoanalytic viewpoint, the museum might then conceivably represent what French analyst Janine Chasseguet-Smirgel calls "the perverse solution"—a forging of a hybridized vision through the dissolving of accepted boundaries. It's a vision that tempts us to replace a love of truth with a taste for sham.

The perversity of the MJT, though, is that it uses falsehoods as a way of conveying a type of experiential truth that escapes analytical approaches. In this light, it corresponds to what contemporary Italian philosopher Gianni Vattimo has called "weak thought"—a mode of reflection that stands in contrast to a metaphysics that is universalizing, domineering, and self-centered. Weak thought explores experiences of "diffused significance," approaching its subjects with a mix of nostalgia, supplication, tenuousness, and a respect for its own frailties.

Likewise, the MJT's curatorial policy is characterized by a tender regard for the frail, the pathetic, and the neglected. The word *curator* derives from the Latin to "care for," and here caretaking extends not simply to objects, but to our relationship with the past, particularly those portions that have been overlooked, dismissed, forgotten, or destroyed (as supposedly were parts of its own collection during the great wars). Here a home is provided for the marginal artifact, for things not usually prized or deemed worthy of serious display.

In the museum's Library for the Diffusion of Useful Information, an exhibit features letters sent to the Mount Wilson Observatory near the turn of the century by people wishing to explicate their own often highly personal cosmological theories to the observatory's astronomers. (It's worth noting that the experimental basis for the theory of relativity was developed at this same observatory). These letters, however farfetched, call to mind the proverbial "path not taken," and stand in for all endeavors that for whatever reason wander outside accepted paradigms. To the hubris of scientific certainty, they offer a hint of the way false data and experimental accidents often lead an individual off the beaten path and on to significant discoveries.

Which is why, speaking as someone who doesn't like to be pigeon-holed or labeled, I wouldn't mind being an exhibit in the Museum of Jurassic Technology. This may sound like an odd idea. Being put on a pedestal conventionally implies an uncomfortable alienation. To be made into an exhibit means suffering a metaphysical abduction, a not-so-latent violence.

This view was made poignantly clear to me at a panel I recently attended in Los Angeles on the legacy of the Black Panther Party. The organizer of the panel had dug up a collection of Panther graphics from the 1960s and early '70s, and had covered a wall with once-familiar posters of power salutes and heavily armed Panther leaders. One of the speakers, a former Panther, looked over at the wall and remarked that he felt like he was in a museum. It was a bittersweet statement: the price of seeing his own history enshrined as a museum piece was his present dislocation from ongoing political dialogue.

If a museum can disrupt our sense of distance from the objects it displays, it might not serve to isolate the past so much as to link it to our current experience. So as a living subject with a history still in the process of unfolding, I wouldn't be terribly worried—if I were to become an exhibit at the Jurassic—that visitors would walk away feeling sure they knew my entire story. I would be an exhibit whose truth one could only appeal to, but never possess. It is precisely the feeling of possession that is so fatal to romance. Deciding whether or not you'd care to be on exhibit in a given institution may not be such an unreasonable criteria for evaluating the deals museums offer us. Wherever you can display yourself without fear of being summarily judged, there's a chance for lasting romance.

Deprong Mori of the Tripiscum Plateau,
Museum of Jurassic Technology, Los Angeles, California.

My® **Weekly Reader** 4

Vol. 48 • Issue 4 • October 5, 1966

U.S. Gives Go Signal For Superjets

What will be as long as a football field, carry 300 people, fly 13 miles high, and travel at 1,800 miles an hour? America's SST or supersonic transport is the answer. The SST will be the giant airliner of tomorrow.

The race is on! Two airplane-building companies, Boeing Company and Lockheed Aircraft Corporation, are working hard on plans for an SST. Last month, each company sent its plans to the Government.

Lockheed's delta wing SST

Two SST Designs

The two planes are now being studied by a team of more than 200 airplane experts. Late this fall, one design will be chosen.

The SST's must cost no more to fly than today's passenger jets. The planes must be able to use today's airport runways and make no more noise than jetliners now in use.

The Boeing Company has planned an aircraft with movable wings. During takeoffs and landings, the plane's wings would move forward. At supersonic speeds the wings would swing back.

The Lockheed Company's plans call for a plane with huge delta wings. The wings would not move during flight. The wings are so large 100 cars could park on them.

Years of Testing

Once the Government chooses a design, two test planes will be built. The planes will undergo long and thorough testing. Years of planning, designing, building, and testing still lie ahead. The SST will not be ready for regular passenger service until 1974.

Boeing's swing wing SST

IN THIS ISSUE: Diagnostic Silent Reading Test Section

"U. S. Gives Go Signal for Superjets," My *Weekly Reader*, October 5, 1966.

VISUAL STORIES

A working country is hardly ever a landscape. The very idea of landscape implies
separation and observation. It is possible and useful to trace the internal
histories of landscape painting, landscape writing, landscape gardening and
landscape architecture, but in any final analysis we must relate these histories
to the common history of a land and its society.

—Raymond Williams, *The Country and the City*

A *My Weekly Reader* "Your Read and Study Guide" from 1966 posed these
questions to nine-year-old schoolchildren: "Study the designs of the superjets on this page and on the front page. How are the two planes alike? How
do the two designs differ?" One child penciled in this answer: "They are
pointed on the front. They have different wings and engens [sic]."[1] She drew
two of her conclusions from the visual evidence provided by the accompanying images, but her third answer required a conceptual leap since no significant differences between the engines of the two superjets are visible in either
set of images.[2] Evidently the student had been taught to attribute information
to images through conceptually related visual cues, in this case the different
shapes of the wings. This visible difference between the jets acted as a marker
of an invisible difference, and allowed looking to yield information, although
this information was not actually visible in the images.

Another *My Weekly Reader* article and study guide from the same year uses
images in a similar manner. The article, entitled "Packaged Power," contains
illustrations of familiar objects, such as clocks, cars, pencil sharpeners, and
television sets. Each one is depicted as a simplified, blue silhouette, while its
battery appears as a black-and-white photographic image inside. The study
guide asked students to name all the objects and then to extend their awareness of what was inside these objects to other objects used in their daily
lives: "What battery-driven toy have you enjoyed?" "What other 'cordless'
products have you used?" and "What electric products in your home may

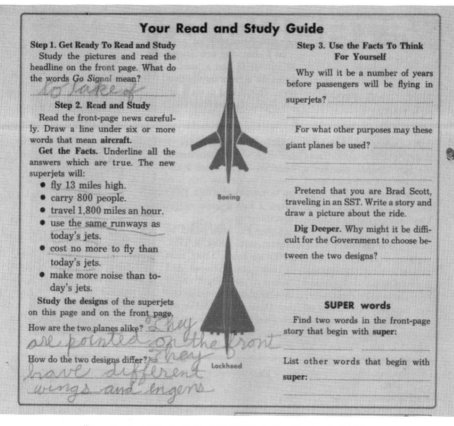

Your Read and Study Guide

Step 1. Get Ready To Read and Study

Study the pictures and read the headline on the front page. What do the words *Go Signal* mean? _to take off_

Step 2. Read and Study

Read the front-page news carefully. Draw a line under six or more words that mean **aircraft**.

Get the Facts. Underline all the answers which are true. The new superjets will:

- fly 13 miles high.
- carry 800 people.
- travel 1,800 miles an hour.
- use the same runways as today's jets.
- cost no more to fly than today's jets.
- make more noise than today's jets.

Study the designs of the superjets on this page and on the front page. How are the two planes alike? _They are pointed on the front_

How do the two designs differ? _They have different wings and engens_

Boeing

Lockheed

Step 3. Use the Facts To Think For Yourself

Why will it be a number of years before passengers will be flying in superjets? _____

For what other purposes may these giant planes be used? _____

Pretend that you are Brad Scott, traveling in an SST. Write a story and draw a picture about the ride.

Dig Deeper. Why might it be difficult for the Government to choose between the two designs? _____

SUPER words

Find two words in the front-page story that begin with **super**: _____

List other words that begin with **super**: _____

"Your Read and Study Guide," *My Weekly Reader*, October 5, 1966.

be 'cordless' in the future?"[3] The last two questions imply that a product's cordlessness is visual evidence of the presence of a battery inside, but this evidence or marker makes sense only after students have been provided with the illustrated look inside the silhouetted objects. Again, the designers of *My Weekly Reader* translated visible differences into markers of information that were literally invisible. And students were expected to make conceptual leaps in order to put what they had learned to good use.

The steps involved in making the conceptual or extra-visual leaps prompted by "marked" images need not be spelled out or even directly acknowledged in order for the lesson to be effective. In the case of the superjet example, the student made the connection between visible differences in wings and invisible differences in engines without needing any intermediary directions.

Such "successful" leaps, when demanded and performed week after week, begin to seem self-evident, especially when the lessons provide no forum for students to challenge the way the questions and their appropriate responses connect images and information.

The enhancement of visual images with additional layers of information does not result, however, in seeing more, only differently. Usually extra-visual leaps occur at the expense of aspects of these same images the lesson makers have determined to be irrelevant or detrimental to their educational aims. For example, a My Weekly Reader article on the Milwaukee Public Museum's soon-to-be completed diorama of a buffalo hunt provides an inventory of the items the diorama would contain, detailed descriptions of how each element and special effect is created, and general information on the importance of the buffalo in the life of the Plains Indians.[4] The magazine also contains two photographic views of the diorama, completed and under construction. The study guide's choices of possible responses to its question "If you could go to the new museum in Milwaukee, what might you see there?" are limited to those concerning how the diorama was created, such as "a diorama with a painted foreground," "eight live buffalo," and "two horses made in papier-mâché."[5] Another question, "What sound effects might you hear at the exhibit?'" continues this line of inquiry, while others separately address the historical relationship between the buffalo and the Indian with no reference to the diorama at all, as if the subject of the diorama and the diorama itself had no related educational function. My Weekly Reader's presentation of the diorama solely as a product of artifice unravels the diorama's illusionistic mysteries, but it ignores the museum curator's probable aim to teach the child about the subject of the diorama through the visual, audio, and textual elements of the diorama itself. As a result, the magazine's lesson on the buffalo seems more complete and direct than the museum curator's efforts because, in the former, visual fantasy appears to give way to hard "facts."

The articles and answers from the My Weekly Reader I have been using to describe the pedagogical process of extra-visual leaps come from my own copies of the magazine. I remember as a child I did not look forward to completing the "Read and Study Guides," even though I usually answered them correctly. Their questions still make me uncomfortable, but as an adult, I am better prepared to consider why this might be so.

My ® Weekly Reader 4

Vol. 48 • Issue 6 • October 19, 1966

PACKAGED POWER

Clocks, flashlights, radios, toothbrushes, food mixers, electric drills—and even some automobiles—are run by batteries. Car makers announced this fall that they are working on a new kind of battery-powered, all-electric car. The electric automobile may become the car of the future.

New Kinds of Batteries

Battery-powered electric cars are not new. Some of the first cars ever built were electric cars. However, batteries to power cars have usually been too heavy, too costly, and have had to be recharged too often.

Now, a new kind of "space-age" battery may make electric-powered cars practical. A battery that is light, low in cost, and doesn't need recharging often may be used.

New Uses for Batteries

One of the earliest uses of batteries was to power electric lights, called flashlights. That was nearly 70 years ago. Today, new and more powerful kinds of batteries work better and longer. The batteries power a long list of products. People can wear battery-driven wristwatches, listen to battery-powered tape recorders and radios, watch battery-powered TV, and even fish with a battery-driven spinning reel. The list of "cordless" products seems endless.

Battery power has made many products portable. "Cordless" shavers, TV's, and other products need no wall plug. They can be carried from room to room, used in cars, and even taken to the beach or on camping trips.

"Packaged Power," *My Weekly Reader*, October 19, 1966.

The creators of *My Weekly Reader* did not develop these questions and lessons for me alone. They reached a large number of elementary school students; many United States public school systems subscribed to the magazine in the 1960s. Once one understands the basic principles behind these lessons — and the creators of *My Weekly Reader* certainly did not invent them — one can also begin to recognize these same pedagogical principles at work in many other places, albeit sometimes in either more complicated or less obvious configurations.

An examination of the pedagogical philosophy of one man, Alfred Parr, and his groundbreaking proposals for the Felix Warburg Man and Nature Hall at the American Museum of Natural History in New York illustrates the ways in which educational institutions encourage extra-visual leaps. The history of the development and refinement of Parr's basic educational aims and the hall designers' accommodation of them through several types of visual display provide striking examples of how and why public educational institutions addressed the complex relationship between vision and education during and after World War II in the U. S. Through a historical analysis of such a well-documented case, the reasons why such lessons might have made at least some members of their audiences uncomfortable can also be addressed.

Alfred Parr came to the American Museum of Natural History (AMNH) during a period marked by profound financial and administrative crises. The Depression was responsible, in part, for AMNH's budgetary problems. Over half of the Museum's endowment was invested in railroad bonds, which were constantly defaulting throughout the 1930s. Because of the general collapse of the national economy, grants from wealthy supporters decreased dramatically. Moreover, New York's mayor, Fiorello La Guardia, was frequently forced to cut the city's financial contributions to the museum.[6]

During this same decade, AMNH's president, F. T. Davison, and directors, George Sherwood and then Roy Chapman Andrews, continuously mismanaged the little money the museum did have, and none of these individuals developed an overall administrative policy or guiding philosophy. Davison, Sherwood, and Andrews were not scientists either, so the profitable dialogue between staff scientists, trustees, and museum administrators, which previous leaders had facilitated, deteriorated rapidly. The balance between financial support for scientific research and public education became skewed increasingly in favor of the latter. This imbalance led not only to low morale among the scientific and curatorial staffs, but it also continued an uncritical and short-sighted support from the administration for the construction of spectacular and costly dioramas as the museum's primary form of educational display.

Diorama halls were first instituted in the 1920s by a previous president, Henry Osborn, in order to encourage large donations from private individuals. When fewer funds came from these sources in the 1930s, the construction of this expensive form of display required dipping into the museum's own internal funds. As John M. Kennedy, a historian of the AMNH, states, what began as glamorous projects "that were supposed to help carry the ordinary work of the museum, ended by devouring much of the Museum's income."[7] Kennedy also notes that the museum's remaining private patrons were increasingly skeptical of the scientific and educational value of the evolutionary and taxonomic studies embodied in such dioramas as the focus of current work in biology increasingly shifted to genetics.[8] Thus the dioramas and diorama halls were at the center of increasingly fractious debates concerning the museum's identity as a research and educational institution, and their cost was one of the primary causes of the museum's financial troubles by the end of the 1930s.

In response to these problems, the trustees and the scientific staff, through several independent initiatives, began a review of the museum's policies; together their studies led them to commission Dr. Alexander Ruthven, the president of the University of Michigan and the former director of its University Museum, to evaluate the AMNH's facilities and staff.[9] He concluded that the museum's director should assume the leadership role in solving both the administrative and financial problems plaguing the AMNH, and that the director should be a scientist. These recommendations led to the forced retirement of Roy Andrews in 1941. Alfred Parr became the museum's new director in March 1942 with a mandate to develop new types of exhibits to replace the dioramas.[10]

Parr was a scientist who came to the American Museum of Natural History with an already developed philosophy of museum education, and the intention to totally redesign the AMNH's exhibition halls according to the premises of that philosophy.[11] Parr believed that many of the AMNH's public exhibits taught nothing at all and were hopelessly out of date in terms of contemporary scientific knowledge. These installations showcased the museum's extensive and world-renowned specimen collections, which in turn reflected the museum's central and ongoing commitment to evolutionary studies and taxonomic zoology. Parr believed that both fields were moribund, while ecology, an area of research to which the museum had little or no previous commitment, was "scientifically promising," and therefore should be the AMNH's new research and educational focus. He felt that such a focus would also once again attract interest and so obtain financial support from wealthy New Yorkers.[12] In making these proposals, Parr effectively announced his intention to end the museum's life-long commitment to being a world-class resource and center for evolutionary studies.

As early as March 9, 1942, the Plan and Scope Committee initiated a general review of the AMNH and drew up a ten-year plan.[13] But already, one short statement of policy contained in the meeting's minutes cleared the way for Parr's changes: "No exhibit can accurately be termed permanent."[14] The committee's intended target was the traditional diorama.[15] The artists and taxidermists employed by the AMNH developed the diorama or what the staff called the "habitat group" in the early decades of the twentieth century; it rapidly became the basic unit of display in the design of new and renovated exhibition halls during the decades preceding World War II. Generally, these groups present life-scale, three-dimensional reproductions of particular places or events within enclosed showcases. The museum's artists achieved a high degree of illusionism in the groups through the use of sophisticated techniques for accurately transferring specific landscape views and individual specimens or casts of plants, rock formations, and indigenous wildlife from "the field" to the museum. Maps and written descriptions of the depicted area's topography, climate, and history, and often a narrative describing how particular specimens were collected hung on the walls beside the cases, suggesting that visitors consider two different, yet metonymically related places: one located outside the walls of the museum and the other, an exacting, although selective reproduction of it, located in the exhibition hall's display case.[16] The illusionistic beauty of the groups was meant to enhance the habitat hall's primary role as "the great silent teacher, a true exponent of visual education," which in turn would promote visits to the actual places and a deeper scientific understanding of the things represented in the halls.[17]

The Plan and Scope Committee's completed review contained a clear assessment of what the committee members thought of the efficacy of the museum's educational programs generally, and the habitat groups in particular, by 1942. The section on the habitat groups began by acknowledging their "keynote" status in a natural history museum, but wasted no time in pointing out their shortcomings:

> These groups have become large and expensive, and probably have reached their ultimate artistic perfection. What is now realized is that they have become ends in themselves. The beauty of the composition and not the natural history content is what the visitor sees. It has been suggested that such groups are 95% art and 5% science. It has been considered justifiable to use 95% art, if by that means only 5% of science could be "put over," but many are still skeptical.[18]

Aesthetic appreciation had overtaken educational purpose so that neither the learning of scientific facts nor an association between what one saw in the groups and in the world outside the museum was occurring; the groups were expensive, pretty, three-dimensional pictures.

In this same document, but in a different section entitled "The Museum's Visitor," the committee turned an old argument concerning the visitor's lack of intellectual abilities and powers of concentration—he is referred to as "a low-grade moron...who will not read labels, who will not look at an exhibit in logical sequence, who will not spend more than a minute before a $100,000 habitat group"—on its head by blaming the museum itself for the visitor's educational failings:

> He comes to the museum to see objects. He resents casts and models, even to the extent of boring holes into them with a pocket knife. Diagrams and charts he ignores. However he admires cleverness and skill, especially if the exhibition method is mysterious.[19]

In other words, the illusionism employed in exhibits such as the habitat groups provided a powerful lure, whereas the informational aspects of the displays did not. Illusionism, though, could not call too much attention to the elements that manufactured its mystery because they then would be revealed and their seductive power would be defeated. Between these two descriptions of the educational failings of the habitat groups and their entertainment value, one can appreciate the dilemma in which Parr and his fellow committee members found themselves: how to balance entertainment with education in individual exhibits so that the former encourages the latter but does not eclipse it.

Concerns for what would attract *and* educate museum visitors had already led Parr to call for a study of visitor behavior in his first months at the AMNH.[20] His list of directives for this study included a categorization of visitors by type and an account of how many visitors entered each individual hall, along with the comparative amounts of time they spent in each.[21] Parr requested that this latter group of statistics be measured in terms of how the visitors engaged with the displays, namely the average proportion of labels they read and where they used benches or "display[ed] a desire to remain stationary for an appreciable interval" because he believed that the AMNH's visitors were not considering the visual material in relation to the information supplied by the supplementary textual material, but were merely glancing at each image and then passing on to the next one.[22] In order for visitors to learn from these existing exhibits, Parr felt that their examination of the displays had to be focused by information external to the display images and for an extended length of time. The survey directives also required that all of the visitor observations be based on a specific comparison between "a representative hall, the primary purpose of which is educational and...a representative hall, the primary purpose of which is aesthetic appeal."[23] This requirement reflected Parr's belief that some halls failed to educate and that their original educational function had been replaced by aesthetic entertainment.

Various committees compiled these status reports on the museum as Parr began to promote his ideas for a new introductory hall, which he hoped would offer a totally new educational model for natural history museums. He stated in a 1942 letter to a museum colleague, Edwin Colbert, that this new hall, like the rest of the museum, should no longer depend on a strictly chronological format since such a model inevitably commences by taking the visitor "back to the thing that occupies the remotest possible position in time and space from the moment and the place in which he is living and from the phenomenon with which he is familiar and concerned in his own life."[24] According to Parr, the introductory hall:

> should be the hall in which we meet our public on the basis of its common experience, which is a point from which we have to start if we wish to guide our visitor from his own knowledge into ours and from his own everyday experience into the new experience which science may have to offer him.[25]

Basically, Parr planned to ease the visitor's transition from a "common" or shared set of everyday experiences to a new set of scientific experiences by explaining the latter in terms of the former. In this same letter to Colbert, he described everyday experience as present and immediate, and not something consciously understood as a result of or even a part of a historical continuum. He identified a corollary to this quality of "presentness" in what he called the "contemporary dynamics of nature," which he also claimed could not be adequately apprehended through historical schemes. He elaborated:

> If you want to express it in terms of the physicist you may say that the historical rate of change (geologically speaking) is so slow in relation to the rates of change of contemporary dynamic processes that in historical perspective we can regard all the processes as being in instantaneous equilibrium with their own cause. Then the historical picture can, with more than adequate accuracy, be described as a series of equilibrium states, which means that to interpret any one of the states we can disregard the historical factor.[26]

For Parr, the "contemporary dynamics of nature" were nature's own version of everyday experiences like those of museum visitors; these "dynamics" could be made to be immediately relevant without forcing visitors to deal with distant or abstract historical factors first.

Here and in other written presentations of his ideas, Parr used the term "contemporary dynamics of nature" as a synonym for "ecological subjects," and early on, he often openly referred to the new hall as an "Ecological Hall." The provisional title came as no surprise to his staff, given his well-known commitment to ecology, but many of the AMNH's scientists strongly resisted his plans to replace evolutionary theory and taxonomic classification with ecology as the guiding principle behind a hall's organization. One of these scientists, Dr. William Gregory, claimed that such a principle lacked intrinsic unity, since it necessarily required information from various scientific disciplines and a grouping together of specimens usually displayed in separate halls. Parr countered this particular criticism with an alternate definition of unity and a restatement of his general educational aims:

> I have always been considerably disturbed by the lack of unity in the particular kind of *a priori* displays you suggest. It has always seemed to me that the introduction and importance of alfalfa at one point, rabbits in Australia, Japanese beetles, force of gravitation, and so on at other points, merely give us tidbits of knowledge from all corners of the world and from all types of situations, which can never form an integrated totality in nature....By showing all the disciplines in separate treatment it fails to show how they depend upon each other and how they supplement each other in the explanation of the totality of nature, which is very far from being merely the sum of its parts.[27]

As plans for the introductory hall progressed, both Parr and others involved increasingly referred to the AMNH's explanation of the "totality of nature" as the "story" it should tell. The term "story" makes one of its earliest appearances in the concluding paragraph to a lengthy, internal memo concerning the museum's exhibitions in general:

> We have a great story to tell, yet the simple truth of the matter is that we tell it so incredibly badly that few of our visitors ever get the idea that there is a story here at all....In planning a hall the first question should be—not what objects do we want to place in the hall—but what STORY DO WE WANT THE HALL TO TELL. The objects should be used to drive home the salient points of the story and should (exceptions of course) no longer, except for study purposes, be regarded as sufficient unto themselves. The second question in planning a hall should be: what is the very best method we can devise for telling the particular story to the average visitor.[28]

This aim to tell a story, and to tell it so well that the visitor would recognize its unifying presence and message, goes hand in hand with Parr's desire to reveal the presence of science within and the relevance of science to everyday experience since for him storytelling embodied the repetitive rhythm of the familiar and the everyday and could easily describe nature's cycles and systems. Such scientific storytelling would not need to refer to the complete sets of specimens or stages that taxonomic or evolutionary narratives did. In the new halls, fewer and more familiar objects would play multiple roles in depicting both the cyclical and historical events that comprise the total story of nature, which Parr believed the museum was obligated to tell.[29] The same objects and images would appear in more than one display case and in a variety of combinations, and their repeated appearances would encourage visitors physically to double back as well as move forward among the individual exhibits rather than to "progress" sequentially through them. Through repeated viewing of these same objects from different perspectives and in various combinations, visitors would recognize that more was going on in these familiar images than met the eye. Gradually the pieces of the story of nature previously unknown or unacknowledged, such as evolutionary and geological changes, and other normally invisible processes, would come into view. And visitors would move beyond merely recognizing specific forms in a taxonomic chain to achieve an awareness of how the forms functioned within a total ecological system.

In keeping with his commitment to thread scientific understanding through the experiences of everyday life, Parr also determined early on that the new introductory hall should tell the story of the local landscape.[30] He solicited suggestions for sites containing a "considerable variety of environment to make an interesting total story," but he also required these sites to contain landscapes the AMNH's public "would feel represented home territory," even if the site itself was not actually located in the state of New York.[31] The idea, as Parr stated it in a memo, was to grasp the total story as it existed within a particular location but:

> not to tie [the hall] too specifically with the details of any particular location, but to design it so that it will give the visitor a feeling of familiarity with the landscape because it will represent any landscape he might be likely to see on a Sunday's drive.[32]

Parr insisted that a balance be maintained between the generally familiar and the specific natural features and history of the local landscape in the new hall's representation of the chosen landscape: "We do not propose to copy it slavishly so as to make it specifically recognizable, but we have to base the work on a real landscape, otherwise we are in danger of failing to create a true illusion."[33]

By distinguishing between specificity of representation and true illusionism, Parr acknowledged the traditional goals of habitat-group construction. The chosen site was to be painstakingly reproduced in its particulars—local specimens, samples, and views—but these elements were to be artfully recombined in order to create a perfected totality that both generally alluded to the original site and convinced the visitor of its visual truth on its own illusionistic terms. Illusionism got the habitat groups into their pedagogical trouble. But, in choosing such a local and familiar site, one that could be visited over and over again, unlike the sites depicted in the old habitat groups, which were frequently remote and outside most visitors' everyday experience, Parr ensured that the hall's display images could never be regarded as just pretty pictures. Visitors would be motivated to learn more from the hall's images because they already had some experience of them as familiar places; they could more readily connect what they saw and learned in the hall to the actual places and things to which the hall's images referred. For Parr, telling the story of the local landscape provided the key to maintaining both a constant connection between representation and referent and a unity that many of his scientist colleagues feared would be lacking in an ecological hall.

By 1946, Parr had settled on the Pine Plains Valley and Mount Stissing area of upstate New York as his particular model for the new hall's local landscape. But World War II and another period of financial crisis within the museum, due, in part, to rapid postwar inflation, slowed the pace of Parr's work.[34] Finally, in 1947 the museum trustees resolved to invest several million dollars of capital in Parr's modernization program in the hope that new halls would attract more income, and the Board of Estimate agreed to increase the city's appropriation to the museum by over three thousand dollars.[35] Construction of the introductory hall resumed, and the finished hall, called the Felix Warburg Memorial Hall of Man and Nature, opened on May 14, 1951.[36]

The Story of the
LANDSCAPE
by Henry K. Svenson
and Farida A. Wiley

Cover of the guidebook to
the Warburg Man and Nature Hall,
The Story of the Landscape, 1952.

All the press releases and most newspaper reviews of the hall identified ecology as the hall's guiding organizational principle, compared the hall's total cost of $150,000 to the $100,000 price tag of previous individual habitat groups, and noted the innovative aspects of the hall's displays.[37] Some of these displays were innovative for innovation's sake; after all, Parr wanted the new hall to provide a provocative first glimpse of the "museum of natural history of the future" that would generate renewed outside financial support. But most of these innovations functioned as means toward Parr's stated educational aim to "tell the total story of the local landscape."

The hall's entrance directs the visitor in on a diagonal. A curve of plywood and wood veneer paneling stretches out from the entrance door frame to promote this diagonal orientation, and the hall's initial habitat group counters this diagonal with an orientation parallel to the lines suggested by the outward curve of the doorway. All of these axially aligned curves and diagonals initiate a rather unorthodox pattern of meandering movement throughout the hall. As for the visual aims of the individual displays, the deliberately "off-kilter" framing of the entrance calls attention to the activity of framing itself and along with it, point of view.[38]

The first habitat group the visitor sees at the entrance is entitled "An October Afternoon Near Stissing Mountain." This group contains an image just as aesthetically pleasing and visually complex as many of the museum's earlier habitat groups, and its brilliant, autumnal colors and picturesque composition are calculated to lure the museum visitor farther into the darkened hall. Yet the designers of this group are not aiming for the same kind of mysterious verisimilitude that they achieved in earlier groups; the view depicted is obviously not equivalent to what the naked eye would perceive at the actual site, and the mechanics of the illusionistic process are also quite evident.

The animal, bird, insect, plant, and soil specimens occupy an unusually

Entrance to the Felix Warburg Man and Nature Hall,
American Museum of Natural History, New York, 1956.

narrow strip of foreground space trapped between the tall, painted background mural on the group's back wall and the glass front of the display case. And because the foreground area is so narrow, the mural is not much more than arm's length from the viewer—and even the artist's individual brushstrokes are visible.

The illusionistic space depicted in the mural is also rather shallow because it recedes from right to left at a slight angle across and back, rather than gradually backward through an established middle ground to the mountains depicted in the background. When examining the mural artist's black-and-white preparatory photographs taken at the site, one recognizes that he has mixed together several of the most picturesque views of the mountains in the background and almost completely eliminated the middle ground areas, so that the space appears to move up from the foreground and diagonally across the background along several different orthogonals. These strategies for compressing several sweeping landscape views to fit the limited area of a habitat showcase were commonly used in creating the background murals for the museum's earlier habitat groups; but here the artist seems to push the distorting process beyond the point of creating a mysteriously real effect. The results of these distortions heighten the dramatic picturesqueness of the scene when visitors view it from the entrance, but when they move into the space of the hall and approach the display, parts of the scene appear to be closer than they actually would be at the original site or even in an accomplished, highly illusionistic landscape painting. Even if the viewers cannot identify specifically what causes the spatial distortions in the habitat group's overall image, the visual effects are slightly disorienting, and they call attention to the fact that what the viewer is looking at is a *landscape*, a construction made manifest through various points of view.[39]

To eliminate the discomfort caused by the image's lack of visual coherence, visitors can either retreat to the entrance—not a very likely reaction—or move even closer to the display so that its overall image is no longer in view. Such close proximity invites inspection of the individual elements in the scene and their identifying labels, which run along the lower edge of the case and are printed on paper that is the same red hue as the sumac plants in the foreground. The visitors are now in a better position to learn from looking at the group. Thus the group's artists have used beauty as a device for drawing viewers in, made the slightly distanced space of purely aesthetic entertainment an uncomfortable one, and, as a result, encouraged a closer and longer inspection of both the image and its lessons. At least it is certain that the visitors were looking at the habitat group differently, which was an important first step.

To quote again one of Parr's remarks made during the hall's early planning stages: "the explanation of the totality of nature…is very far from being merely the sum of its parts."[40] He continued:

> It seemed to me that the unity of the hall would be very plain, in that it was
> provided by the very landscape itself taken as a whole, as the visitor would
> first see it when he enters and would have it more or less before his eyes all
> the time in the form of a central topographic scale model. In other words, the
> central theme would be our effort to analyze and explain this landscape and
> all it contains.[41]

Visitors came to this topographic model of the Pine Plains Valley and Mount Stissing area immediately after viewing the initial habitat group; they had to move in close and drop their gaze, as for the habitat group, in order to view the model, mounted on a low wooden base. This three-dimensional map was visible from many parts of the hall, and since the case it occupied was the only freestanding one in the hall, it anchored the other visual displays by its large physical presence and by offering the only complete view of the region.[42] The rest of the displays are fragmentary, and don't all add up in the way individual members of a particular species lined up in rows in taxonomic display cases do. The Warburg Hall's designers offered visitors new ways of looking at specimens. Through the foregrounding of the very devices of illusionism, they transformed the visitors' eyes into magnifying glasses, microscopes, or scalpels, which could reveal the invisible workings of a previously familiar but superficially understood natural world.[43] The familiar and aesthetically pleasing views of the initial habitat group, as it appeared from the entrance, were dismantled and then supplemented by new and unfamiliar images and perspectives. And the story of the local landscape unfolded through the visitor's deepening visual understanding of it.

In a section of the hall that deals with the relationship between plants,

MARL

MARL SEDGE — CAREX VIRIDULA

SHRUBBY CINQUEFOIL — POTENTILLA FRUTICOSA

Only a few marl ponds are known in New York State, and their borders are always occupied by unusual plants. Marl, composed chiefly of shells, was formerly used as a fertilizer, but it sometimes contains harmful substances. The shrubby cinquefoil, or hardhack, has its center of variation in southwestern China. In western Europe it is found in only a half a dozen localities, because its range has been disrupted by glaciation. The little marl sedge (Carex viridula) occurs along the seacoast and inland in calcareous regions from Newfoundland to southwestern Alaska.

The soil profile is composed mainly of shells.

"Relation of Plants to Geology and Soil," (one of a series of six display cases),
Warburg Man and Nature Hall, American Museum of Natural History, New York, 1951.

soil, and general geological features of the local landscape, six individual cases contain all the elements of earlier habitat groups: detailed two-dimensional background painting, a carefully rendered three-dimensional foreground, including exacting plastic or plaster casts of plants and rocks scattered with actual soil collected from the site, a map marking the origins of the material, textual information, and, in addition, a soil profile also taken from the site. But now each of these aspects of the display is present as a separate type of information. Text and pictorial images exist on equal ground and equivalent scale inside the display case, neutralizing the latter's tendency to distract the viewer with its illusionistic tricks.[44]

In a set of display cases entitled "Life in the Soil," located directly behind and around the corner from the hall's topographical map, vertical cutaways of the soil strata underneath the edges of a woodland area and of a farmer's lawn offer little of the familiar, three-dimensional space above ground for visitors to examine. But the display designers compensated for this loss by providing visual access to the normally invisible world below the surface of the ground during winter and spring. Earthworms, chipmunk and mole burrows and nests, a yellow jacket nest, an ant nest, a hibernating frog, and other forms of underground life and activity appear in the same square feet of soil. These glimpses into life in the soil restore missing bits of the cyclical story of the active and hibernating life of many species.

Other aspects of the soil's story are presented differently. For example, labeled, blown-up photographs of microscopic images of root systems detail the ways these systems absorb nutrients from the soil, and comparisons of actual soil profile specimens demonstrate the various effects of soil conservation. All of these soil displays contain enough formal similarities, such as the primarily vertical orientation of their images, the identical colors of their backgrounds, and similar kinds of specimens, to encourage visitors to make visual and then conceptual associations back and forth across the space of the hall. These associations add up to a fairly complete understanding of the soil of the local landscape and of soil in general.[45]

Another example—by far the most visually unsettling—of spatial manipulation used by the hall's artists depended on a new type of visual display called a mirrorscope. Each of the mirrorscope display cases contains a miniature habitat group mounted on the bottom of an individual case,

"Life in the Soil," Warburg Man and Nature Hall,
American Museum of Natural History, New York, 1951.

directly below and behind a rectangular opening positioned in the wall at eye level. The visitor peers into the opening and down a dark, horizontal tunnel to view a tilted mirror-reflection of the habitat group below. Viewers might not initially realize they are looking at a reflection. Eventually, they perceive how the mirrorscope works because of the unconventional diagonal orientation of the mirrored image. This contrived image calls attention to its reflective viewing process, and reminds visitors that the habitat groups are highly artificial images that indirectly reflect larger three-dimensional sites elsewhere.

From a distance these mirrorscopes appear to be small, rectangular black holes, which disrupt the larger images in the displays that contain them. The viewer must move in quite close to these displays to see what is inside the holes; the mirrorscope images encourage much more insistently the same type of movement the initial habitat does. The hall's designers also use this combination of two nested, but differently scaled, views to represent the relationship between local geological conditions and the lengthy trajectory of general geological history and evolution. In one display, the former is represented by a cross section of the Pine Plains Valley region, running the entire length of the display case, and the latter consists of a timeline of the earth's history located under this cross section, which also runs the length of the case. Small mirrorscope views of the local landscape during the Devonian, Pleistocene, and Triassic eras, located at the corresponding points on the timeline, physically link the general and the specific histories of the local landscape together. The contrasting visual experiences of the display indicate the local landscape's geological history, as well as geological history overall; both kinds of history are displayed with equal importance.

Another type of display could be called a "picture diagram" because it consists of one or more miniature habitat groups placed inside and set back behind a larger diagrammatic image painted on the outer display case wall. The diagrammatic components illustrate ubiquitous natural or agricultural processes, which are either visually imperceptible or occur over an extended period of time and thus could not be represented in one view. This type of display aims to identify the presence and effects of such processes in the local landscape. For example, the hall's "picture diagram" of the water cycle contains a miniature habitat group depicting the Pine Plains Valley region inside

"The Water Cycle," Warburg Man and Nature Hall,
American Museum of Natural History, New York, 1951.

a two-dimensional, diagrammatic picture of a similar, but more simplified landscape format. Both images share a similar arrangement of clouds, a source of light coming from the right, a valley or lake flanked by rises on either side, and a view of distant mountains in the background. In the outer diagram, the sun and its rays, clouds, precipitation, and evaporating water are schematically sketched in a limited range of colors on the blue background of the display case wall, and arrows indicate the counterclockwise movements of water through the various stages that make up the water cycle. Both the central habitat group and the surrounding diagrammatic picture are labeled at all of the same points with the same terms; these labels, plus the general resemblance between the two compositions, link them together formally and then conceptually. Thus the presence of a "contemporary dynamic of nature" in the local landscape emerges through these formal analogies drawn between the two- and three-dimensional versions of the same system.

All of the exhibition strategies developed by the Warburg Hall designers —thin, vertical soil profiles; cross sections of fields; blown-up, back-lit color photographs; microscopic views of root systems; and a general use of miniature-scale habitat groups—offered museum visitors visual access to the normally unseen workings of nature or to the distant historical and geological past of the region through what were then deliberately unusual display techniques. These strategies were meant to transform the daily activity of vision itself into a more self-conscious activity, extending it beyond its natural limits in time and space. Parr believed that the Warburg Hall's lessons would work because they began with and always referred back to a shared and already familiar site, the local landscape. But to benefit from these lessons, the museum visitors had to project what they had seen in the hall onto the local landscape itself, and these projections depended on conceptual associations, or extra-visual leaps. One cannot see, for example, the life underneath soil or the geological past of a particular site through looking alone; the soil and the landscape must be marked as carriers of this invisible information through related visual cues, such as the markings left on rocks from the movement of glaciers. The Warburg Hall displays, just like the lessons from My Weekly Reader, call attention to cues and offer views of the usually unseen aspects of familiar objects and sites; the visitor may then extrapolate from what was seen when confronting the local landscape itself.

Although Parr selected "common experience" as the starting point for his lessons, he did not assume that the AMNH's entire audience came to the museum with the same set of experiences. His early characterization of the visitor's "feeling of familiarity with the landscape because it will represent any landscape he might be likely to see on a Sunday's drive" indicates that he had one particular group of visitors in mind: city dwellers.[46] According to Parr, this group viewed the local landscape at a leisurely distance from their cars or picnic blankets, whereas the local inhabitants of the Pine Plains Valley and Mount Stissing area, whom Parr identified as mostly farmers, did not.[47] Thus his goal of creating a "true illusion" of the local landscape from a generalized copy of a real landscape was based upon an outsider's understanding of "truth." Parr had another reason for making the museum's landscape unrecognizable in specific terms: "We do not wish to have any libel suits from the unintelligent farmer we propose to include."[48] He knew that local farmers would be the only visitors able to recognize a slavish copy of property they owned; their particular familiarity with the local landscape was a liability if represented.

The city dweller's passive experience of the local landscape represented everything Parr believed to be wrong with the way museum visitors experienced the old habitat halls. So, by broadening and transforming their common experience into a more clearly self-conscious educational activity, he was able to address this old pedagogical problem of passivity. Parr's selection of the urban audience as his primary target group for the Warburg Hall was also strategic, since most of the wealthy former and potential donors to the museum belonged to this group. Yet, in privileging this group, Parr chose the same audience targeted by the old habitat halls and for the same financial reasons as his predecessors.[49]

Although Parr's choice of audience conformed to his general educational and financial goals, several crucial effects of his choice are troubling. His understanding of the urban visitor's a priori experience of rural, upstate New York became the visual starting point for every museum visitor. And since this initial point of view was never explicitly identified with any particular segment of the museum's audience anywhere in the Warburg Hall, it seemed to be a self-evident choice, universally shared.[50]

Because Parr was also committed to telling the "total story of the local landscape," he had to include man's participation in the appearance and productivity of the land. But he did not want to burden his targeted city audience with any but the most general aspects of these parts of the story because, although he wanted them to be better informed, he realized that they would primarily still remain consumers of what they saw. The completed hall contained only a few displays dealing with crop cultivation and animal husbandry—but every one privileged general principles over detailed explanations of the farmer's practical problems, and most emphasized products over production.[51] Even when production was the subject of a particular display, as in the presentation of the history of farming in New York State, all of the textual information was addressed to the layperson; for example, part of the caption explaining farming economy in the 1950s reads: "All this makes machinery a large part of the farmer's investment but it also permits him to reduce human labor and to increase his production per man hour."

One might ask, at this point, "What did the farmer learn when looking at these types of displays?" or "How was his or her 'common experience' as a producer or laborer being transformed?" Nowhere were these questions addressed in the hall.[52] So, not only was the Warburg Hall's visual story of the local landscape partial, but the community of mutual understanding and interdependence promoted through the hall was limited, as it was based on the interests of residents of a single geographic region and, primarily, the middle and upper classes, who occupied only one position in the region's agricultural economy.[53]

Parr developed plans for the Warburg Hall long before the end of World War II; by the war's end, his pedagogical ambitions had outgrown teaching museum visitors about the relevance of science to their local, everyday lives. In his 1947 essay "Towards New Horizons," published in the museum's annual report, he described the postwar moment in much the same terms as Karl Mannheim described the prewar period in his text *Ideology and Utopia*, although where Mannheim identified *ideology*'s work in building a national and global community, Parr used *education*:

> The greater the mental confusion of the times, the greater the challenge to education, and the greater the value of teaching properly conceived and

directed towards the elucidation of the problems which disturb the world....
In a world beset by hostility and want, the natural history museums have an
opportunity, never before equaled, to serve the development of peace and of
a better life for all by bringing their educational facilities and their scientific
knowledge to bear upon the task of creating a better understanding of our
own problems in relation to the country that surrounds us and supports
us, and of the problems of other nations in relation to their natural circumstances, to one another, and to us.[54]

After the war was over, Parr and museum president F. T. Davison increasingly described the ecological story of natural history as an antidote to totali-
tarianism.[55] Over and over again in his writings, Parr proposed a "total
conception of the whole of nature as a balanced system" as a model for social
cooperation and world peace. During this same period, Parr suggested that
the term "'expedition,' with its romantic associations with the idea of distant
and long voyages" should be replaced by such words as "'survey' or 'field
work' to describe the manner in which the task of exploration is carried forward today," since he felt that thorough scientific research could be conducted
in one's own backyard.[56] There are even a few subtle indications of this
larger purpose of global awareness in the Warburg Hall, though its displays
ostensibly address only the problems of the local landscape.[57] Displayed
world maps, for example, indicate where soil conditions in upstate New York
occur globally as well as nationally.

The wedding of rarefied science to everyday life in the design of the
Warburg Hall represents a significant ideological shift in the museum's educational agenda, not just a simple effort toward better education. What Parr
represented as an efficient or "economical" model for understanding the
total story of the local landscape and ultimately of man and nature was, in
fact, a model for naturalizing an economic structure of interdependence;
twenty years of financial instability had demonstrated how much the museum
depended on this economic structure for its own survival and growth.

Parr's desire to enlarge his public's visual understanding of the "familiar"
included social and political aims that could only be accomplished through
dazzling, truly extra-visual and clearly ideological leaps, which started and
ended with the experiences of only a segment of that public. Such disparities

could easily have caused visitors some discomfort, especially if they were not members of that chosen segment of the public.

Perhaps the *My Weekly Reader* "Read and Study Guides" made me uncomfortable because I wasn't among their ideal or targeted audience.[58] When faced with an institutionalized and pervasive pedagogical devices like extravisual leaps, individuals are prone to blame themselves for feelings of discomfort or to credit these feelings to those of inadequacy, especially since such devices do not value subjective responses as a way to differentiate ourselves and who we are from the institution's version of who we should be. Discomfort may be our only motivation to look harder at the agendas of pedagogical institutions and their devices, no matter how subtle. An assumption of universal appeal always masks a much more considered selectivity.

"88"

Sm-o-o-th!

"ROCKET" ENGINE AND OLDSMOBILE HYDRA-MATIC

Hydra-Matic Drive optional at extra cost on all Oldsmobile models.

This is the car . . . this is the power team that's completely different from anything else on the road today. The surging power of the high-compression "Rocket" Engine! The silken smoothness of Oldsmobile Hydra-Matic Drive*! Sm-o-o-th is the only word for it. Try the flashing "Rocket" Hydra-Matic "88" at your nearest Oldsmobile dealer's soon. Drive it today and discover the big difference in automobile performance yourself!

OLDSMOBILE

A General Motors Value

Susan Buck-Morss

ENVISIONING CAPITAL:
POLITICAL ECONOMY ON DISPLAY

1

You are looking, on a microlevel, at the social relations of a new industrial epoch (see the top of page 112). The image is a "sociogram," charting interactions among university professors and students as they cross-pollinate with industrialists at a university industrial research center. The spermlike penetration shows minimal administrative intervention into a budding embryo of research and development. It is upon such informal, nonhierarchical institutions that a brand new breed of capitalists pin their hopes. They have crossed the "second industrial divide," a restructuring of capitalism characterized by decentralized production and changed technologies of flexible specialization, technologies that impose a competitive strategy of permanent innovation— hence the need to nurture new ideas and to keep their profit-making potential gestating within the proprietary domain of private firms.[1] These idea-producing clusters are enmeshed in global webs that, according to United States Secretary of Labor Robert Reich, catch approximately one-fifth of the U. S. population up into the global economy with prospects for a prosperous future but threaten to leave much of the nation's work force out in the cold.[2]

To get a sense of how radical this restructuring is, compare its amorphous sociogram with the classic model of the corporate firm that dominated the economic landscape until two decades ago. This form dates back to the turn of the century (the "first industrial divide"), when continuous-process machinery initiated the mass production of standardized goods, leading to economies of scale that transformed the earlier system of family firms into "corporate" or "managerial" capitalism[3]—impersonally owned, giant corporations comprised of hundreds of operating units and thousands of workers, the internal operations of which were protected from competition. Each unit is managed by a hierarchy of salaried executives who, because surveillance and coordination are their primary tasks, have become vulnerable to replacement by computers, as disaggregating firms strive to trim their

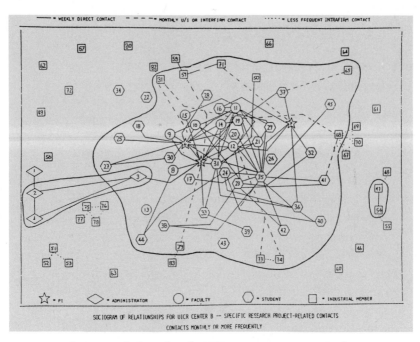

Sociogram of relationships for UICR center B. From J. D. Eveland,

Communication Networks in University/Industry Cooperative Research Centers, 1985.

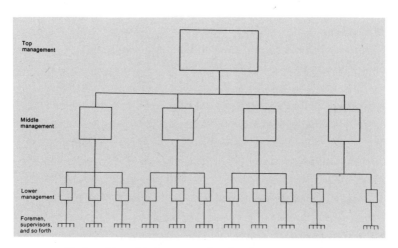

The basic hierarchical structure of modern business enterprise

(each box represents an office).

From Alfred Chandler, The Visible Hand: The Managerial Revolution in American Business, 1977.

hierarchies and turn the managerial "fat" into profits.

When giant corporations reigned supreme, their top executives, "corporate statesmen," were close to political power. In 1953, Charles Erwin "Engine Charlie" Wilson, the president of the world's largest manufacturing company, General Motors (its production equaled Italy's total gross national product), claimed no conflict of interest in becoming Eisenhower's secretary of defense: "I cannot conceive of one because for years I thought what was good for our country was good for General Motors, and vice versa."[4]

At the same time, everything hinged upon keeping these units distinct. This was the cold-war era, when life on the planet literally hung in the balance over the issue of how government and economy were related.[5] Of course, Lenin had adopted wholesale the disciplining structures of corporate capitalism— hierarchical forms, Taylorist "scientific management," assembly production—and the Soviets were early enthusiasts of Fordist principles. As for capitalism, as "convergence theorists" have pointed out, government regulation of industry, protection of labor, and welfare programs all became established principles of Western states, reflecting significant aspects of the socialist tradition. But it was not similarity in form but the flow of power— and goods—that counted. Because they owned the means of production, capitalists had no need to control the product. Whereas in capitalism power was a consequence of the distribution of goods, in Soviet socialism the distribution of goods was a consequence of power. Goods flowed out of the hierarchies of capitalist corporations to an anonymous market of consumers; they flowed into the hierarchy of the Communist party from producers whose personal relation to the party determined their power to consume.

It is the depersonalization of exchange within capitalist society that depoliticizes economic power, no matter how close capitalists and politicians may become. The point of market exchange is the null point of social community. Marx noted in the Grundrisse that in traditional societies exchange occurred at the boundary between communities; seen in this light, he argued, capitalist society is "unsocial."[6] Georg Simmel later countered in The Philosophy of Money that the lived experience of this loss of traditional community was liberating because money exchange sets limits to mutual obligation, thereby limiting society's claim on the individual.[7] Under capitalism, no matter how bureaucratic the organization, such points of market

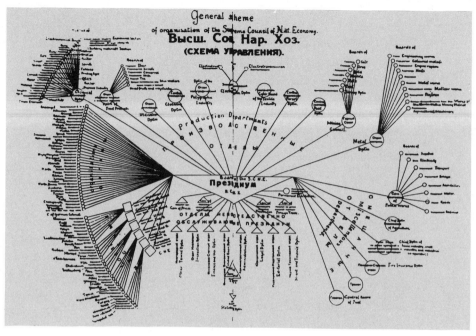

General scheme of organization of the Supreme Council of National Economy.
From *The Russian Economist*, January 1921.

indifference—and therefore of individual freedom—are productive of the very fabric of society. Under Soviet socialism, in contrast, a person's indebtedness was "infinite," even (indeed, especially) for party members; because symbolic social exchange—social obligation and sacrifice—was conceived to be without limits, it was transformed into "a monstrous technology of domination."[8]

Who can doubt that during the cold war capitalism proved itself superior in delivering the goods? The years 1945 to 1979 "witnessed the most dramatic and widely shared economic growth in the history of mankind."[9] Given the criterion of consumer plenty, Americans easily believed that the public interest was synonymous with the growth of national firms. U. S. corporations and their international subsidiaries dominated the "free" world. Yet because this new imperialism was not ostensibly political,[10] the organizing world-principle of nation-states allowed the soothingly comprehensible vision of polities as bound together by economic fate, all "in the same large boat, called the national economy" and competing with other national economies "in a worldwide regatta." This vision, claims Reich, is now simply "wrong." Due to the vast centrifugal force of the global economy, a shared economic fate that sets the terms for a "National Bargain" among business, government, and labor interests does not exist: "neither the profitability of a nation's corporations nor the success of its investors necessarily improve[s] the standard of living of most of the nation's citizens."[11]

The American polity, argues Reich, has become unstuck from the American economy (ironically, just when the postsocialist societies have been urged to adopt the model): "as borders become ever more meaningless in economic terms, those citizens best positioned to thrive in the world market are tempted to slip the bonds of national allegiance, and by so doing disengage themselves from their less favored fellows."[12] When members of the same society become aware that they "no longer inhabit the same economy,"[13] they are tempted to reconsider what they owe each other. This process raises the danger not only of a legitimation crisis of the welfare state (see early Jürgen Habermas, Claus Offe, and Michael J. L. O'Connor), but also of a deeper crisis in the social polity because it challenges the very definition of the collective—the idea of the "American people"—itself.

2

While it may be premature to say that this situation marks the end of an era, it at least makes us aware of the historical specificity of a particular vision of society, one that, as a part of Western modernity, has long been unthinkingly presumed. In fact, this vision has always been clouded by the blurred line between political and economic definitions; the problem is not as new as Reich implies. At a time when the ambivalent legacy of ethnic nationalism is resurfacing—often precisely among those groups left behind in the new global economy—it is worth emphasizing that it was not the political notion of nationalism but the economic notion of a collective based on the depersonalized exchange of goods upon which, historically, the liberal-democratic tradition rests. This basis has always been potentially unstable.

The proposition that the exchange of goods, rather than denoting the edge of community, is capable of functioning as the fundament of collective life necessitated the discovery that within the polity such a thing as an "economy" exists. This discovery can be traced to a particular historical site: Europe (specifically England and France) during the eighteenth-century Enlightenment. The economy, when it was discovered, was already capitalist, so the description of one entailed the description of the other.[14]

The discovery of the economy was also its invention. As Foucault told us (and neo-Kantians long before him), every new science creates its object.[15] The great marvel is that once a scientific object is discovered (invented), it takes on agency. The economy is now seen to act in the world; it causes events, creates effects. Because the economy is not found as an empirical object among other worldly things, in order for it to be "seen" by the human perceptual apparatus it has to undergo a process, crucial for science, of representational mapping. This is doubling, but with a difference; the map shifts the point of view so that viewers can see the whole as if from the outside, in a way that allows them, from a specific position inside, to find their bearings. Navigational maps were prototypical; mapping the economy was an outgrowth of this technique.[16]

The French Physiocrat François Quesnay provided the first such map in 1758.[17] His "economic picture" of society (tableau économique) traced the interdependence of three interacting sectors of the economy—farmers, landowners, and artisans—as they exchanged goods and labor across time. What was unique here was the organic representation of these sectors as an interlocking, self-reproducing whole. Quesnay wrote to his friend Mirabeau, "the zigzag, if properly understood, cuts out a whole number of details, and brings before your eyes certain closely interwoven ideas which the intellect alone would have a great deal of difficulty in grasping, unravelling and reconciling by the method of discourse."[18] The economic table had six variants, each showing the effects on circulation through the whole of a particular policy or social practice (for example, variant iii: spending on "excesses and luxury"; iv: "rapid effects" of taxes on advance; v: decay of husbandry; vi: "the destructive effects of the impost" when "overloaded by charges of administration").

It is significant that like many early political economists, Quesnay was trained as a physician.[19] The circulation of wealth was to him the lifeblood of society. There was a medieval precedent for this metaphor. Even before William Harvey's seventeenth-century physiological theories, the description

TABLEAU ECONOMIQUE.

Objets à considérer, 1.º Trois sortes de dépenses ; 2.º leur source ; 3.º leurs avances ; 4.º leur distribution ; 5.º leurs effets ; 6.º leur reproduction ; 7.º leurs rapports entr'elles ; 8.º leurs rapports avec la population ; 9.º avec l'Agriculture ; 10.º avec l'industrie ; 11.º avec le commerce ; 12.º avec la masse des richesses d'une Nation.

DEPENSES PRODUCTIVES relatives à l'Agriculture, &c.	DEPENSES DU REVENU, l'Impôt prélevé, se partage aux Dépenses productives et aux Dépenses stériles.	DEPENSES STERILES relatives à l'industrie, &c.
Avances annuelles pour produire un revenu de 600.ᵗᵗ sont 600.ᵗᵗ	Revenu annuel de	Avances annuelles pour les Ouvrages des Dépenses stériles, sont 300.ᵗᵗ
600. produisent net............	600.ᵗᵗ	
Productions		moitié partie ici Ouvrages, &c.
300.ᵗᵗ reproduisent net........	300.ᵗᵗ	300.ᵗᵗ
150. reproduisent net..........	150.	150.
75. reproduisent net..........	75.	75.
37.10.ˢ reproduisent net :	37.10.	37.10
18.15. reproduisent net........	18..15.	18..15
9..7..6.ˢ reproduisent net.....	9..7..6.ˢ	9..7...6.ᵈ
4..13... reproduisent net......	4..13...9.	4.13...9
2..6..10. reproduisent net.....	2..6..10.	2..6..10
1..3..5.ˢ reproduisent net.....	1..3..5.	1..3..5
0..11..8. reproduisent net.....	0..11..8.	0..11...8
0..5..10. reproduisent net.....	0..5..10.	0..5..10
0..2..11 reproduisent net......	0..2..11.	0..2..11
0..1..5 reproduisent net.......	0..1..5	0...1...5

&c.

_____

REPRODUIT TOTAL ....600.ᵗᵗ de revenu ; de plus, les frais annuels de 600.ᵗᵗ et les intérêts des avances primitives du Laboureur, de 300.ᵗᵗ que la terre restitue. Ainsi la réproduction est de 1500.ᵗᵗ compris le revenu de 600.ᵗᵗ qui est la base du calcul, abstraction faite de l'impôt prélevé, et des avances qu'exige sa reproduction annuelle, &c. Voyez l'Explication à la page suivante.

"Tableau Economique." From François Quesnay, *The Economical Table*, 1766.

was common of money "circulating" through the "body politic." Thomas Hobbes spoke of money as blood; in Thomas Mun's case money was the "fat" that had to be regulated so that this body became neither too thick nor too lean. But if the idea of a political economy was, indeed, a direct descendant of this feudal conception, this only makes the originality of physiocratic theory stand out more clearly.

The difference in Quesnay's scheme was that it accounted for the generation of wealth as well as its circulation. Landowners advanced capital to other sectors, but in this agrarian capitalist model only the farmers returned it (to the landowners) with a surplus. In contrast, the annual advance by landowners to artisans was returned without addition. Their expenses were unproductive—in Quesnay's term (and the metaphor is important), "sterile."[20] Quesnay drew on Sir William Petty's description of land as the mother of wealth, and the labor that cultivated it, the father. An admirer of the agrarian capitalism of England, where scientific husbandry had achieved visible results in an increase of general prosperity, he concurred with Petty's followers that if matter was fertile, the prudent labor of the cultivator brought it form. Together, matter and labor contributed with every new year a *visible* surplus or net product (*produit net*) in excess of what had existed before. Hence, the postulation of what I will call Quesnay's "fertility schema" is precisely what made the break from earlier theorists of wealth possible.[21]

Since the beginning of double-entry bookkeeping (in northern Italy during the quattrocento), commercial mathematics had assumed that exchange was a zero-sum game.[22] Because trade and barter involved the exchange of equivalents, mere circulation within a system could never augment the size of the pie. Mercantilist theory concluded that if one party grew richer from trade, it was at another's loss. Hence, according to Jean-Baptiste Colbert, mercantilism's influential seventeenth-century proponent, commerce, was a "perpetual and peaceable war of wit and energy among all nations."[23] The goal of this "peaceable war" was to gain wealth for real wars, and the wealth that counted was money. According to Colbert, "everyone agrees that the might and greatness of a State is measured entirely by the quantity of silver it possesses."[24] Quesnay's "Little Book of Household Accounts," as he called it, was an attempt to convince the French king that mercantilist reasoning was incorrect. In his essay "Grains" for the *Encyclopédie*, Quesnay argued against the theory of money as government wealth: "a kingdom can be prosperous and powerful only through the medium of products which are continuously renewing themselves or being generated from the wealth of a numerous and energetic people." In "Hommes" he wrote that in the economic life of an "agricultural kingdom," continuous exchange among the classes results in an increase of the wealth of the whole, and hence "the more wealth men produce over and above their consumption, the more profitable they are to the state." A century later, Marx would credit Quesnay with seeing that the "birthplace of surplus value is the sphere of production, not that of circulation."[25] At the same time, the "picture" Quesnay provided was one in which these two schemes, circulation (circular flow) and production (the fertility schema), folded into each other in the same social body. Of course, even the mercantilists had a "fertility schema." Colbert wrote to the French king:

> In view of the fact of having just one constant quantity of silver circulating in all Europe, augmented from time to time by that which comes from the West Indies, it is certain and demonstrable that if there are only 150 million pounds of silver in public circulation, one can only succeed in augmenting it by twenty, thirty, and fifty millions at the same time as one removes the same quantity from neighbouring States.[26]

Colbert was making a crucial distinction: trade within the European system could redistribute wealth by "augmenting" one nation's coffers at another's expense (with no net gain), but for its augmentation in an absolute sense colonies were necessary. Jean-François Lyotard, in a recent and otherwise disappointing study, makes the point that mercantilism imagined a "trading body" (the body of Europe) and a "victim body" (of barbaric foreigners). Colonialism entailed a trade of nonequivalents; it was looting a colony for precious metals, with trinkets given in return. Colonies were the necessary "exterior" of the system, "whose only role is to be emptied [cannibalistically], into an 'interior,'...the...body of Europe."[27] What I am describing as "fertility" was here the consequence of rape.

Among the Physiocrats, Quesnay's "economic picture" assumed a metaphysical, "near-mystical" importance. Influenced by Cartesianism, Quesnay frequently described the universe as a "gigantic machine," operating "according to natural laws of divine origin." Mirabeau described the "perpetual movement of this great machine" of nature, "animated and directed by its own springs" as in "no need of outside direction."[28] It was just a step to argue that the economic system had no need of government control. Quesnay did not take that step (as Adam Smith would do several decades later). His concern was advising the king, who, as "coproprietor"[29] of the land of the entire kingdom, could lay claim through taxes to its wealth: "agriculture is the inheritance of the sovereign: all its products are visible; one can properly subject them to taxation."[30] Such visibility, conducive to a compulsory patriotism, was lacking in mercantile, monetary fortunes: *"a clandestine form of wealth which knows neither king nor country."* The Physiocrats' political call was for *"legal despotism."*[31] Quesnay wrote, *"there should be a single sovereign authority standing above all the individuals in society and all the unjust undertakings of private interests."*[32] Only the king (with the aid of his Enlightenment advisors) was in a position to see the whole and govern according to the natural laws that guaranteed its rational functioning. Joseph Schumpeter writes in his monumental book *History of Economic Analysis* "Quesnay harbored no hostility either to the Catholic Church or to the monarchy. Here, then, was *la raison* with all its uncritical belief in progress, but without its irreligious and political fangs. Need I say that this delighted court and society?"[33]

3

Reading Adam Smith's *The Wealth of Nations* (1776), one is struck from the first that the audience he addresses is no longer limited, as with Quesnay, to the king and his authority.[34] We have crossed, within two decades, an intellectual and political divide. The "whole body of the people" that Smith is constantly considering forms the potential audience for his book. This social body that sees itself described is a new one.[35] It is no longer the traditional body politic of feudal theory that even Rousseau could still describe as "organized, living, and similar to that of a man," a moral being, possessing a "general will, which always tends toward the conservation and well-being of the whole and of each part," with the sovereign as head, the laws and customs as brains, and where "commerce, industry, and agriculture are the mouth and stomach which prepare the common subsistence; the public finances are the blood that is discharged by a wise *economy*, performing the functions of the heart, in order to distribute nourishment and life throughout the body."[36] With Smith the social vision clearly shifts. Not only is the body politic secularized,[37] it loses its ontological status and becomes pragmatic; it must be produced by doing. Now, even this has a precedent. Machiavelli described the prince as founder of the polis, capable of conceiving the body politic from out of himself. In the homely image of Francesco Guicciardini (his younger compatriot), the legislator is like a pasta maker. If he "does not succeed with his mixture the first time, he makes a new heap of all his materials and stirs them together again" in order to get the product right.[38] But Smith's "makers" are the laboring masses, although he did not use this term. They make society by making things. The economy is the place of creative action.[39] And politics recedes from center stage.

For Smith, the machine is no mere metaphor for the universe as it was for Quesnay (as well as for Rousseau). Machines are, literally, the means whereby labor, divided and specialized, becomes productive.[40] And although such division occurs to some extent in agriculture, only industry feels its full effect.[41] Smith's example is a pin factory—not a "great manufacture" but a "trifling" one—small enough so we can "see" the principle of the division of labor that governs the whole. This question of seeing is problematic. Smith will provide us with no perspective—that of God or King or Reason—from which the whole productive social body can be viewed. Nor will we ever see an object (such as land) that causes wealth to grow. We see only the material evidence of the fertile process of the division of labor: the astounding multiplication of objects produced for sale. Commodities pile up; in a pin factory "two or three distinct operations" are performed by ten men. Those ten persons, therefore, "when they exerted themselves...could make among them upwards of forty-eight thousand pins in a day." Each person who, working alone, "could not...have made twenty, perhaps not one pin in a day," now makes one-tenth of forty-eight thousand pins, or forty-eight hundred per day.[42]

Smith's fertility schema is the *multiplying effect* of a procedure, not something, nor even somebody. The machines (at that time rudimentary) are not themselves the source of value, but only the means of saving labor time and increasing worker dexterity.[43] Nor is the source the "capital stock" that puts labor "into motion."[44] And although labor is the source of *value*, it is not the source of fertility for growth. Workers are not promethean figures. The value they produce increases not as a result of their own strength but as "effects of the division of labour." This division causes the productivity of labor, machines, capital—not vice versa. As Schumpeter writes, "nobody, either before or after A. Smith, ever thought of putting such a burden upon division of labor. With A. Smith it is practically the only factor in economic progress."[45] The schema of industrial production—multiplication through division— is parthenogenic. Smith is obsessed with this character in systems to sub-divide from within with beneficial effects. It is fundamental to his theory of language. In his essay "Language," appended to the 1761 edition of *The Theory of Moral Sentiments*, he is fascinated by the fact that "mankind have learned by degrees to split and divide almost every event into a great number of meta-physical parts, expressed by the different parts of speech, variously combined in the different members of every phrase and sentence." Similarly, the advan-tage of money as a system is that it can, without any loss, be divided into any number of parts.[46] Philosophers, like machine inventors, make their trade in "combining together the powers of the most distant and dissimilar objects." At the same time their profession, too, benefits from an intellectual division of labor; the "subdivision of employment in philosophy, as well as in every other business, improves dexterity, and saves time. Each individual becomes more expert in his own peculiar branch, more work is done upon the whole, and the quantity of science is considerably increased by it." This astonishingly fertile division of labor has significant moral consequences, however, and they are negative. The same division that causes the social organism to grow in wealth also causes the individual worker to become impoverished. Smith's book does not dwell on this, but as he describes how "the whole of every man's attention comes naturally to be directed towards some one very simple object,"[47] the distressingly stultifying nature of divided labor becomes visible:

> The man whose whole life is spent in performing a few simple operations...
> generally becomes as stupid and ignorant as it is possible for a human crea-
> ture to become. The torpor of his mind renders him, not only incapable of
> relishing or bearing a part in any rational conversation, but [also] of conceiv-
> ing any generous, noble, or tender sentiment, and consequently of forming

any just judgement concerning many even of the ordinary duties of private life....But in every improved and civilized society this is the state into which the labouring poor, that is, the great body of people, must necessarily fall, unless government takes some pains to prevent it.[48]

Here is the paradox in Smith's view of *homo faber*: each real body is stunted in order for the social body to prosper. The latter becomes a production machine, and its individual, laboring members are reduced to what Stalin would later call, affirmatively, "little screws" within it. Now, Smith's philosophical heritage will not allow him to be satisfied with such a collectivist resolution. In order for the wealth of nations to be affirmed as the goal of social life, it must be a means to the end of the happiness of the individuals of which nations are composed. And so there is a sudden shift in focus. The impoverished producer shows up on the stage again, this time as the well-clad consumer. Smith lists the tangible benefits he or she receives on the domestic scene: "the woollen coat, for example, which covers the day-labourer, as coarse and rough as it may appear, is the produce of the joint labour of a great multitude of workmen." The same is true of "all the different parts of his dress and household furniture": shoes, bed, kitchen grate, coal, kitchen utensils, knives and forks, plates, bread, beer, and "that beautiful and happy invention," glass windows.[49]

With the wave of a hand, the victim of the division of labor becomes its beneficiary. Such shifts in focus are frequent in Smith's argument; in fact, the entire legitimation of the system depends on them. And yet these shifts involve a conjuring game. Gifted as Smith the philosopher is at splitting and dividing events into metaphysical parts and then reassembling them, combining the powers "of the most distant and dissimilar objects," he slides over an abyss (indeed several) in logic. (They will reemerge time and again in economic theory.) But it is as if he knows that he is proceeding through a philosophical sleight of hand. From the start, he gives the game away.

The "annual labor of every nation," Smith tells us at the very beginning of his treatise, is a composite "fund." Thus "thriving nations" can exist even if "a great number of people do not labour at all." The inequality of this situation might be justified if it reflected the natural order of things. But Smith candidly denies precisely this ontological premise. Natural talents are not very different at birth. Between a "philosopher and common street porter" there is less difference than assumed:

> When they came into the world, and for the first six or eight years of their existence, they were, perhaps, very much alike....About that age, or soon after, they came to be employed in very different occupations. The difference of talents comes then to be taken notice of, and widens by degrees, till at last the vanity of the philosopher is willing to acknowledge scarce any resemblance.[50]

It could not be clearer. The division of labor, upon which the wealth of nations depends, creates (against nature) a society of unequals. Class difference is the by-product of national wealth—and it is class difference that determines one's power in the marketplace, including the power to bargain effectively for the price of one's own labor. But by moving to the composite level Smith sustains the salutary picture; within the human species *as a whole*, differences in talents lead to "better accommodation and conveniency"[51]— which again begs the question of distribution because the *best* "accommodation and conveniency" goes to those who do not contribute to the labor "fund" at all.

What we are calling Smith's sleight of hand he himself called the "invisible hand." (There seems little doubt that Smith's use of this term derived from the tradition of natural theology, which saw effects of the hand of God everywhere in the natural world.[52]) And although this bedrock metaphor of capitalist economics appears much more rarely in Smith's work than the tradition of his reception would have us believe, the conception behind this term operates frequently, in fact, just at the points where he slides over the logical gaps.

So this hand is tricky, and it is easy to understand why many have dismissed it as a ruse, a legitimating gloss over (bourgeois) class interests. But being merely this would not explain its tenacity within the discourse of political economy. This unseen hand opens up a blind spot in the social field, yet holds the whole together. What is the social body to which it belongs? First and foremost, it is a body composed of things, a web of commodities circulating in an exchange that connects people who do not see or know each other. These things make it a "civilized" body. Having an abundance of

Left and Center: photographs from the French scientific expedition,
Tierra del Fuego (1882): "Men and women wore tiny aprons" and "Civilization advances."
Right: photo of Bridges's family, London, 1880:
"From left to right, Despard, Will, Mother, Bertha, Father, the Author, Mary."
From Esteban Lucas Bridges, *Uttermost Part of the Earth*, 1948.

"objects of comfort" is the litmus test that distinguishes "civilized and thriving nations" from "savage" ones, "so miserably poor" they are reduced to "mere want." It is trade that has caused certain parts of the world to progress, leaving others (inland Africa, northern Asia) in a "barbarous and uncivilized state." Commodities are the key to Smith's defense of the new social body; despite distinctions between rich and poor, *all* members of "civilization" can console themselves, because the *quantity of things they possess* marks them as superior to much of the world's population: "the accommodation of an European prince does not always so much exceed that of an industrious and frugal peasant, as the accommodation of the latter exceeds that of many an African king, the absolute master of the lives and liberties of ten thousand naked savages." The things-in-circulation that comprise the social body, like all matter—like planets in their orbits—obey nature's laws. What appears to individuals as their own voluntary activity is used, cunningly, by nature to harmonize the whole, so that each person is "led by an invisible hand to promote an end which was no part of his intention."[53] Foucault, in his late lectures, addressed The Wealth of Nations directly, speaking positively of the "benign opacity" of the economic system, the functioning of which is beyond the knowledge (and therefore the power) of the state.[54] There is a dark side, however, underneath the naturally harmonious whole, something monstrous in the system that, sublimely out of control, threatens to escape every kind of constraining boundary.

Expanding by parthenogenic division, invisible except in its commodity effects, insensate to human passions, impervious to human will, the thing-body of "civilized" society grows, theoretically, without limits.[55] It is vastly grander than the moral society that it encompasses and overruns. The social body of civilization is impersonal, indifferent to that fellow-feeling that within a face-to-face society causes its members to act with moral concern. The "pleasure of mutual sympathy," when I find my companion entering into my situation as I into his, causes me to moderate my passions so as not to exceed what is acceptable in the eyes of another who, as an "impartial" spectator, observes me from a sympathetic distance and provides the con-straining mirror through which I observe and monitor myself.[56] But the thing-society of civilization is blind to such constraints. Looking up from my work at this landscape of things, I cannot see the whole of its terrain. It extends beyond my ability to feel. And this blindness leaves me free to drop my sight to the short horizon of my own self-interest. Indeed, blindness is the state of proper action. Within that horizon, however, desire is free and knows no bounds. This desire expresses itself as a pursuit for things. The pleasure of mutual sympathy, when I find my companion entering into my situation as I into his, is replaced by the pleasure of empathy with the commodity, when I find myself adapting my behavior to its own—which is to say, I mimic its expansiveness. My desire multiplies to match the ceaseless multiplication of things, shooting so far past my needs that it appears as if my goal were anything but their satisfaction. The objects that I pursue with the fervor of a lover have little to do with needs for mere survival. I come to desire the plea-sure of desire itself. In fact it could not be otherwise. If desire were satiated, if it were not deflected onto a demand for commodities, the fashionable replacement of which knows no limits, then not only would the growth of wealth come to a halt but the whole social nexus of civilization would fall apart.[57]

This state of things is only weakly described by the utilitarian doctrine that individuals will strike a calculated balance between gaining the greatest satisfaction and expending the least amount of labor pain. Smith's schema is more radical and more extravagant. According to him, the invisible hand of the natural order counts precisely on the destabilizing surplus of a desire blind to the whole and ignorant of its effects. Again, it is at the collective level that this principle comes into play; the *deceptive* promise that happiness will be gained through the possession of objects is the decoy whereby nature ensnares the imagination and transforms it into a collective good. Smith is specific on this point:

> The pleasures of wealth and greatness...strike the imagination as something grand and beautiful and noble, of which the attainment is well worth all the toil and anxiety which we are so apt to bestow upon it. And it is well that nature imposes upon us in this manner. It is this deception which rouses and keeps in continual motion the industry of mankind.[58]

On the one hand, desire motivates the laborer to work, the promise of consumption growing proportionally to the difficulty of the labor. On the other hand and with equal importance, this desire creates what Simon Kuznets, writing in the twentieth century, called a "trickle-down effect" in the flow of goods. Smith describes the lack of subjective utility in the motivation of the landlord who lives off the labor of others:

> It is to no purpose, that the proud and unfeeling landlord views his extensive fields, and without a thought for the wants of his brethren, in imagination consumes himself the whole harvest that grows upon them....The capacity of his stomach bears no proportion to the immensity of his desires....The rest he is obliged to distribute among those, who prepare, in the nicest manner, that little which he himself makes use of....The rich ..., tho' they mean only their own conveniency, tho' the sole end which they propose from the labours of all the thousands whom they employ, be the gratification of their own vain and insatiable desires,...are led by an invisible hand to make nearly

the same distribution of the necessaries of life, which would have been made, had the earth been divided into equal portions among all its inhabitants, and thus without intending it, without knowing it, advance the interest of the society, and afford means to the multiplication of the species.[59]

Not demand, instrumentally and rationally calculated, but desire, deceived by commodities as decoys, is the motor force of Smith's "economy." We are caught in its orbit as self-interested monads who precisely in our unreason bring about reason's goal. Due to the deceptive nature of desire, it is impossible for the consumer to make a truly rational choice. This moment of irrationality has gotten lost in the tradition through which Smith's theory has been passed down. It makes the dynamics of the system enormously unstable. Consider the paradox that the efficiency of the division of labor, which alone causes wealth to grow, at the same time causes value to diminish because the value of something, its "real price," is the toil and trouble of acquiring it. Or consider the fact that the cosmopolitan promiscuity of commodities comes into conflict with the political limits of the nation, the wealth of which it is called upon to secure.[60] Self-discipline is required of the producer, and insatiable desire is required of the consumer; but since they are the same person the construction of the economic subject is nothing short of schizophrenic.

Colin Gordon, characterizing Foucault's position, writes that the invisibility of the economic system "means that the Physiocratic model of economic sovereignty is an impossibility; the knowledge intended to be compiled in [Quesnay's] Table is, even in principle, impossible for a sovereign reliably to obtain."[61] And yet Smith's economic theory would have had no conviction if one could not see the effects of the processes it described. Contemporaneous with Smith's work was a crucial innovation in the field of visual representation that made it possible to chart the effects of the invisible hand. This is an example of the work of William Playfair, whose *Commercial and Political Atlas* appeared in 1786. Note that rather than attempting to provide a God's-eye view of the whole, this form of data graphics correlates two measurements here: quantity (of British imports from and exports to America) over time (showing the effects of the American Revolution and the end of the protectionist Navigation Acts). Money is the measurement of eco-

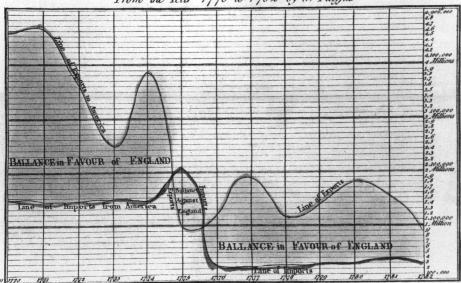

nomic activity, the universal representation of all commodities. The wealth of nations leaves a trace in money transactions that is charted. Brand new is the fact that, unlike earlier maps, the graphical design is "no longer dependent on direct analogy to the physical world.... This meant, quite simply but quite profoundly, that any variable quantity could be placed in relationship to any other variable quantity, measured for the same units of observation."[62]

"Relational graphic[s]" link "at least two variables, encouraging and even imploring the viewer to assess the possible causal relationship between the plotted variables."[63] In arguing to causes on the basis of effects, in showing correlations leading to decline or growth over time, data graphics show patterns of market behavior that emerge unintentionally from the aggregate of individual decisions, the seeming chaos of private persons and their self-interested desires. A later graphic by Playfair gives empirical evidence to support the Malthusian claim that the means of subsistence, because limited,

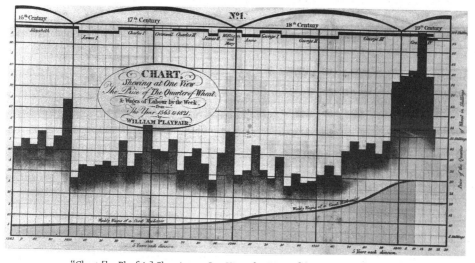

"Chart [by Playfair] Shewing at One View the Price of the Quarter of Wheat,
and Wages of Labour by the Week, 1565 to 1821."

From Edward R. Tufte, *The Visual Display of Quantitative Information*, 1983.

impose a limit on the increase of population (the inference is that an increase
in the cost of bread counters the tendency of workers to bear more children
in response to rising wages). Playfair's work lays the ground for the method
of producing knowledge within the new discipline of political economy —
not a picture of the social body as a whole, but statistical correlations that
show patterns as a sign of nature's plan.

4

It is difficult for us to appreciate what an extraordinary revision of the social
body the discovery of the "economy" entailed. The conception of the
progress of civilization as the unlimited increase of objects produced for sale
was a defining moment of modernity. Not just one of a series of social sciences, "classical" economics was philosophy in the grander sense. It sought
to place an anthropology, a political theory, a theory of social practice all
within the orbit of economic life, appropriating them from the realm of
political power and police control. As the state loses ground, the political
body splits off from the economic one. Thus we have two visions of the
social collective. While the tensions between them make their relationship
unstable, their separate existence allows for the critical exposure of the illu-

sionary elements of both visions. The ambivalent position of the individual —both an end in her- or himself and the means toward harmony of the social whole—was itself not new (one might mention the tradition of monopsychism connected with Neoplatonism in the premodern era). But the crucial role of fabricated things in social life, the significance of material objects or their money equivalents as the mediation of all social relations, deeply changed the conception of social existence.[64] The distinction between civilized and savage life was linked permanently to the abundance of commodities that became ciphers as they circulated promiscuously among invisible strangers. At the same time they were invested with social meanings and personal desires far in excess of their utilitarian value.

Smith called upon traditional notions of civic virtue to compensate for the moral inadequacies of the laws of political economy. This is a weakness in his thought because the civic society he desires is founded on principles inimicable to the economic society he describes. It was Hegel who drew out far more consequently the philosophical implications of political economy. In Hegel's writings, the antagonism first proposed by Smith becomes fruitful, indeed decisive. As a topological conception, "political economy" is centrally inscribed within the Hegelian metaphysical landscape, marking a break with earlier thinking that one commentator describes as nothing less than "epochmaking."[65] The more our archival knowledge of Hegel grows, the more indisputable this fact becomes.[66]

The crucial point is that the central Hegelian concept of civil society (bürgerliche Gesellschaft) is precisely the society created by what Smith called political economy. Here Hegel breaks from the traditional ancient and Enlightenment meanings of civil society (Smith's included), that were placed topologically on the plane of the political—the only meanings that Charles Taylor, for example, recognizes. (Taylor is a theorist in the Hegelian tradition who, despite his excellent early work on Hegel, totally ignores in his own work the topological displacement we are speaking about, and attempts to write political philosophy without any concern for economic theory.[67]) Not just Taylor's work but much of the contemporary discussion of the public sphere fails to do justice to Hegel's original insight that civil society, as "modern society," is produced by a historically specific form of economic interdependence, one that follows all of the principles of logic that Smith described.[68]

We have known only relatively recently that the young Hegel was profoundly influenced by *The Wealth of Nations*.[69] In a text from 1803–04, first published in 1932, Hegel referred specifically to Smith's pin factory, noting the tremendous productivity achieved by the division of labor.[70] Not only does Hegel fully acknowledge the emasculating effects (*Abstumpfung*) caused by the division of labor,[71] but he is also aware of the social inequality that the wealth of nations necessarily creates: "the antithesis emerges between great wealth and great poverty...to him who has, more is given." Factories and mines are based precisely on the misery (*Elend*) of a class, condemning "a multitude to rude existence." Strikingly, Hegel recognizes the sublime infinity of this "system of needs," the "insatiable" desire of consumers,[72] the "inexhaustible and illimitable" production of "what the English call 'comfort,'" and the deterritorializing "boundlessness" of the world market.[73] Civil society is a tremendous power, an abstract "territory of mediation where there is free play for every idiosyncracy...and where waves of every passion gush forth."[74] Although governed by natural laws, it creates a human interdependency that is "blind" and thus "accidental" (*zufällig*) — a strongly negative term in Hegelian discourse. In the early texts it is clear that this infinity of human needs, the limitless growth of both goods and human desires, frightened Hegel. He writes in the 1803–04 text, "Needs and labor...[create] a monstrous system of mutual dependency, an internally agitated life of the dead, which, in its motion, moves about blindly and elementarily, and like a wild animal, needs a steady and harsh taming and control."[75] The state, through law and the police, is the necessary oppositional power against the wildness of this system. It brings order, sets boundaries, tames the animal. Precisely in retreat from the monstrous nature of "civil" society, Hegel introduces the state as a *deus ex machina*,[76] for only through the rationality and centrality of the state is collective life accessible to individual consciousness and the central blind spot of civil society overcome.

In a real sense, it could be said that Hegel takes the vision of the social body of classical economic theory and, tilting it onto the perpendicular axis of time, reinscribes it onto the political realm, where, lifted out of the insipid, "accidental" events of the marketplace and relocated on the dramatic and bloody fields of battle, it is read as the history of freedom. In the same early period as his exposure to *The Wealth of Nations*, Hegel read Schrokh's

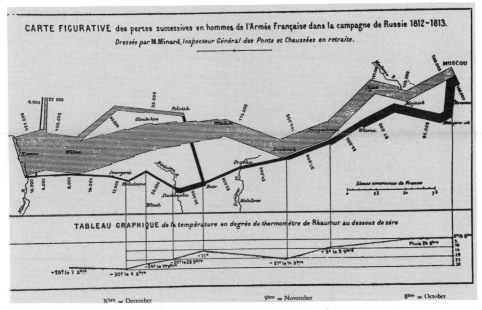

"Figurative map of successive losses in men in the French Army in Russia,
1812–1813." From Edward R. Tufte, *The Visual Display of Quantitative Information* (1983).
Charles Joseph Minard combines a data map and time series of Napoleon's
invasion into Russia. Beginning at the left, the thick band shows the
size of the French army, forty-two thousand men, when it invaded
in June 1812. The diminishing width of the band denotes casualties.
The dark band is the retreat, and it is linked to temperature scales, the bitter cold
Russian winter, through which the army struggled back into Poland.

Weltgeschichte (1785), which in effect conceives of world history as a pin factory because "no one has totally performed any action. Because the whole of
an action, of which only a fragment belongs to each actor, is split up into so
many parts," the rationality of history is only accessible through reflection:
"the work [of history] is not done as a deed but as a result which is thought."[77]

It is through the passions and desires of great men, political actors rather
than economic ones, that reason "cunningly" works its way out into history,
achieving, for collective action, a rationality denied to that of individuals. In
Hegel's 1819–20 lectures on the *Philosophy of Right* this analogy to civil society is explicit: "the secret of world history is…the reversal of particular goals
[so that they become the general goal of the realization of Reason]. This

reversal [*Umkehrung*] is the same as we have also seen in civil society [*bürger-liche Gesellschaft*]. Insofar as the individual carries out his particular goals he makes them objective."[78] Hegel even appropriates the root metaphor of political economy in order to describe the process of history. He writes in 1816 that despite Napoleon's defeat at Waterloo,

> the world has given the age marching orders.... This essential [power] proceeds irresistibly...with imperceptible movement, much as the sun through thick and thin. Innumerable light troops flank it on all sides, throwing themselves into the balance for or against its progress, though most of them are entirely ignorant of what is at stake and merely take head blows as from an invisible hand.[79]

Of course Hegel's is just as much a trick as Smith's original one, as Charles Joseph Minard's visual display (1861) of the French invasion of Russia graphically portrays.[80] Hegel's "cunning of reason" plays, on the politico-historical level, precisely the role that Smith's "invisible hand" plays on the socioeconomic level, including the ideological role of justifying the harm done to individuals in terms of "progress" for the social collective. What needs to be emphasized, however, is that both Smith and Hegel understood political economy as belonging to a more general philosophical discourse, one that entailed critical reflection—a normative dimension—as a necessary part.

5

The attempt to purge the "science" of economics from such concerns about normative values marks the deepest epistemological break between the classical economists of the late eighteenth century and the neoclassical econ-omists at the nineteenth century's close. If we were following here the canon of the history of economic theory we would trace precisely this develop-ment, describing it as the "professionalization" of the discipline. Economic theory is now concerned with the far narrower task of describing "laws" that account for regularities of market behavior as a self-interested rationality of means, while it remains totally indifferent to the normative questions about the reasonableness of individual motives or the substantive rationality of

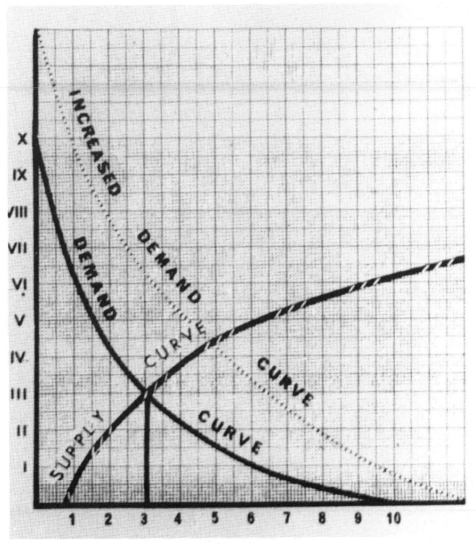

Supply-Demand Curve.

From Isaak Ilich Rubin, *Essays on Marx's Theory of Value*, 1972.

social ends. In the language of Alfred Marshall and his school, the anthropological premise of political economy is reduced to the formal "law" that "every man desires to maximize the difference between the sum total of his satisfactions and the sum total of his sacrifices, both discounted to the present moment."[81] And although in demand theory all value hinges on these subjective desires, their origin is shrouded in mystery. As the anthropologists Mary Douglas and Baron Isherwood have noted, "It is extraordinary to discover than no one [among the economists] knows why people want goods." Economists shun this question, "cleans[ing]" their discipline from "psychology" and taking "tastes" as given.[82]

Of course, the neoclassical economists of the 1870s marginal revolution drew (extremely varied) social and political consequences from their theories.[83] Yet crucial to their claim to be doing "science" was the deliberate reduction of their vision of the political economy to a point of normative indifference. Not qualitative judgement, but quantitative measurement was the criterion of scientific knowledge.[84]

The image prototypical of this vision is the supply-demand curve, described by Schumpeter as "demand *schedules* or curves of willingness to buy (under certain general conditions) specified quantities of a commodity at specified prices, and of supply *schedules* or curves of willingness to sell (under certain general conditions) specified quantities of a commodity at specified prices."[85] The "law" into which this translates is that there is a diminishing marginal productivity and a diminishing marginal demand, so that exchange takes place when the relative marginal significance of the commodity received exceeds that of the commodity given up for each party in the exchange. "This marginal significance is not a constant magnitude but changes with different persons and under different circumstances" — none of which are the concern of the economist: "all we know is the relative significance of an increment of one commodity to a decrement of another."[86] The whole problem of class polarization disappears in marginal utility theory because the "earnings" of labor and of capital are both determined numerically by the last profitable application of each (labor and capital) at the margin.[87] And so does the problem of a fertility schema. The marginal model presumes growth[88] and then focuses on individual economic behavior, wherein the same mechanism of scarcity and demand sets the price of labor's wages, interfirm purchases, and consumer buying. Consumer choice determines value, defined by the Austrian Carl Menger (1871) as "a judgement... about the importance of goods at their disposal."[89] The model is one of equilibrium in an essentially static frame. Not only is growth "given" as an exogenous variable but scarcity of resources, consumer motivation, population growth, and income distribution (class difference), are presumed as well. The economic problem is the pricing and resource allocation of fixed supplies.

Neoclassical economics is microeconomics. Minimalism is characteristic of its visual display. In the crossing of the supply-demand curve, none of the substantive problems of political economy are resolved, while the social whole simply disappears from sight. Once this happens, critical reflection on the exogenous conditions of a "given" market situation becomes impossible, and the philosophy of political economy becomes so theoretically impoverished that it can be said to come to an end.

6

There have been serious challenges to neoclassical demand theory in the last hundred years, but as this century comes to a close, market theory has seemed to weather the storms of political events most successfully. With its minimalist vision of economic transactions, it appears to make no metaphysical claims. No doubt many would say of philosophy's disappearance from economics, good riddance! Was it not, after all, precisely the problem of Soviet socialism that it believed it could plan economic production from a political center that claimed to see the whole and sought to command output, fix prices, and manage distribution in ways that violated every principle not only of market forces but of democratic political life as well? Has Janos Kornai not demonstrated conclusively that the true representation of Soviet economy is not a God's-eye view but rather the plumber's-eye view of a stopped-up flow, one that produces shortages structurally, due to soft budget constraints? Even Keynesianism—which at first had a hard time winning acceptance precisely because "planning," even in the limited sense of government policies for economic stimulus, smacked of socialism to some and fascism to others—never tried to deduce from the economy a vision of society as a whole. "The economy," according to Keynesians, might get "sick," "derailed," or need "repairs," but it was understood as a mechanism to be

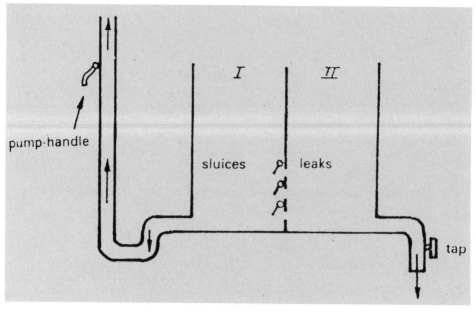

Leakage: the effects of soft budget constraints in socialist economies.
From Janos Kornai, *Contradictions and Dilemmas*, 1986.

tinkered with in order to effect social outcomes at the macroeconomic level, while leaving microeconomic actions free of government control.

Since the stagflation of the 1970s (inflation and negative growth that is unresponsive to Keynesian tinkering), game theory and rational choice have given a fashionable twist to neoclassical market theory, while neoinstitutionalism has corrected its most grievous oblivion to social context. At present, its hegemonic position appears ensured. In market theory, of course, the individual reigns supreme. Even when economic actors are states or firms, their profit-maximizing reasoning occurs without any vision of the whole. Indeed, its impossibility is the source of theories of the limited, hence "bounded rationality" of economic choice. As for the vast industry of econometric modeling, many of its practitioners pride themselves in *not* attempting to represent empirical social existence at all. Strangely out of step with history, the work of Nobel Prize winner Wassily Leontief has resurrected a vision as grand as Quesnay's original one. The matrix tables depict the entire economy, broken down into forty-two sectors, with the horizontal rows showing what each sector ships to other sectors, and the vertical rows showing what each consumes from other sectors. Again, as with Quesnay the point of these "input-output" tables is to demonstrate the seamless web of social interdependence produced by economic activity.

Leontief's tables satisfy a visionary need that the now hegemonic neo-classical economic theory proudly refuses to fulfill. When Foucault praises the invisibility of Smith's hand because it does not allow the sovereign sufficient knowledge to control the social field of individual desire, he forgets the other side, that the desiring individuals also lack this knowledge, and that such knowledge is vital for effective political response. Today, when the polities of nation-states are feeling deeply strained by the tug of a global economy, Foucault's affirmation of the incapacity to envision the economy can play into the hands of a reactionary nationalism that thrives precisely on the condition of blindness to the objective determinates of contemporary social life. In Moscow in 1993 the plan for economic transformation to capitalist markets was described by officials and the press in a representationally impoverished form as, simply, "the big bang" (English original). This mystical, invisible, sonar boom, imported by economists from Harvard, was supposed to provide for three hundred million Russian people some kind of cosmic rebirth out of the ashes of seventy years of Soviet rule. Heralded as the beginning of the new era, it seemed to the average citizen, on the contrary, to lead society ever deeper into a black hole. With no new vision of social life, with no way of refiguring their identity, Russians have responded by retreating into an equally mystical but culturally familiar collective identity of ethnic unity, one that finds a frightening voice in the political rhetoric of Vladimir Zhirinovsky. A philosophical, critical vision of the social body as it is produced by the global economy provides an alternative to the politics of renewed nationalism. Such an alternative vision has the healthy advantage of corresponding to the facts because economic interdependence, not ethnic purity, is what our world is really all about.

Why is it, today, that theory generally shirks the challenge of envisioning the social whole? Is it the taboo against "totalizing" discourses? If so, it might be noted that the global system will not go away simply because we theorists refuse to speak about it.[90] Or is it because the social contradictions that led both Smith and Hegel to beat a hasty retreat to theology

(God's invisible hand or *Geist's* cunning of reason) are bound to surface again, this time in a way that threatens the very institution of the nation, the wealth of which the discovery/invention of the economy was supposed to secure?

INDUSTRY PURCHASING

Table 1-1
Exchange of goods and services in the U.S. for 1947

INDUSTRY PRODUCING		1	2	3	4	5	6	7	8	9	10	11	12	13	14	15	16	17	18	19	20	21	22
agriculture and fisheries	1	10.86	15.70	2.76	0.02	0.19		0.01		1.21		0.05	*	0.01									
food and kindred products	2	2.38	5.75	0.06	0.01	*		0.03	*	0.79	*			*	*						0.01	0.02	*
textile mill products	3	0.08	*	1.30	3.88	*	0.39	0.04	0.03	0.01	*	0.44	0.09	0.03		0.01	0.02	0.05	0.15	0.01	0.05	0.08	0.07
apparel	4	0.04	0.20		1.96			0.01	0.02	0.03		*	*						0.10	0.01	*	*	
lumber and wood products	5	0.15	0.10	0.02	*	1.09	0.39	0.37	*	0.04	0.01		0.02	0.03	0.06	0.09	0.05	0.05	0.03	*	0.06	0.05	
furniture and fixtures	6			0.01			0.01	0.01							0.01	0.10	0.03	0.03	*				
paper and allied products	7	*	0.52	0.06	0.02	*	0.03	2.60	1.08	0.33	0.11	0.02	0.05	0.18	*	0.09	0.04	0.07	0.03	0.03	*		
printing and publishing	8		0.04	*					0.77	0.02						0.01	0.01	0.01					
chemicals	9	0.83	1.48	0.30	0.14	0.03	0.06	0.18	0.10	2.58	0.51	0.30	0.13	0.12	0.13	0.13	0.08	0.30	0.11	0.08	0.05	0.17	0.06
products of petroleum and coal	10	0.46	0.06	0.03	*	0.07	*	0.06	*	0.32	4.83	0.01	*	0.05	0.90	0.02	0.04	0.02	0.03	0.01	*	0.01	0.47
rubber products	11	0.12	0.01	0.01	0.02	0.01	0.01	0.01	*	*		0.04	0.05	0.01	*	0.01	0.13	0.03	0.30	0.01	*	0.04	*
leather and leather products	12			*	0.05	*	0.01	*					1.04				0.02	*	0.01	*	0.01	0.01	*
stone, clay, and glass products	13	0.08	0.25	*	*	0.01	0.03	0.03		0.26	0.05	0.01	0.01	0.43	0.21	0.07	0.07	0.12	0.19	0.01	0.03	0.06	0.02
primary metals	14	0.01	*		*	0.01	0.11		0.01	0.19	0.01	0.01	*	0.04	6.90	2.53	2.03	1.38	0.43	0.07	0.20	0.03	
fabricated metal products	15	0.08	0.61	*	0.01	0.04	0.14	0.02	*	0.13	0.08	0.01	0.02	*	0.05	0.43	0.82	0.54	0.37	0.10	0.07	0.04	*
machinery (except electric)	16	0.06	0.01	0.04	0.02	0.01	0.02	0.01	0.04	*	0.01			0.01	0.07	0.28	1.15	0.17	0.63	0.22	0.03	*	0.03
electrical machinery	17													0.01	0.05	0.24	0.58	0.86	0.62	0.12	0.03	0.02	0.02
motor vehicles	18	0.11	*		*					*				*	0.03	0.03	0.01	4.40	*				0.01
other transportation equipment	19	0.01								*	*				0.01	0.02			0.30				
professional and scientific equipment	20							0.01	0.03	0.01				0.04	0.04	0.01	0.07	0.09	0.18	0.02	*		
miscellaneous manufacturing industries	21	*	0.01	*	0.26	*	0.02	0.01		0.03		0.02	0.01	*	0.02	0.05	0.11	0.02	*	0.03	0.18		
coal, gas, and electric power	22	0.08	0.20	0.11	0.04	0.02	0.02	0.12	0.03	0.19	0.56	0.04	0.02	0.20	0.35	0.08	0.10	0.05	0.06	0.03	0.01	0.03	1.27
railroad transportation	23	0.44	0.57	0.09	0.06	0.14	0.05	0.22	0.07	0.29	0.27	0.04	0.04	0.15	0.52	0.13	0.16	0.07	0.23	0.04	0.01	0.03	0.15
ocean transportation	24	0.07	0.13	0.01	0.01	0.01	*	0.02	*	0.04	0.09	*		0.01	0.08	*	*		*			0.01	*
other transportation	25	0.55	0.35	0.08	0.03	0.14	0.04	0.12	0.03	0.10	0.47	0.01	0.02	0.07	0.16	0.03	0.04	0.03	0.07	0.01	0.01	0.03	
trade	26	1.36	0.46	0.53	0.37	0.06	0.06	0.18	0.03	0.17	0.02	0.05	0.06	0.05	0.38	0.20	0.26	0.14	0.06	0.07	0.04	0.05	0.05
communications	27	*	0.04	0.01	0.01	0.01	0.01	0.01	0.04	0.02	0.01	0.01	*	0.01	0.02	0.02	0.03	0.03	0.02	0.01	0.01	0.01	
finance and insurance	28	0.54	0.15	0.02	0.02	0.08	0.02	0.08	0.04	0.02	0.13	0.01	0.01	0.05	0.06	0.04	0.05	0.04	0.02	0.01	0.01	0.01	0.02
real estate and rentals	29	2.30	0.09	0.03	0.10	0.02	0.02	0.03	0.06	0.03		0.01	0.02	0.02	0.06	0.03	0.05	0.04	0.02	0.02	0.01	0.02	0.05
business services	30	0.01	0.63	0.07	0.10	0.02	0.08	0.08	0.03	0.42	0.04	0.02	0.05	0.01	0.03	0.05	0.04	0.03	0.02	0.01	0.03	0.03	0.05
personal and repair services	31	0.37	0.12	*	*	0.04	*	*	0.02	0.01	0.01	*	0.03	0.01	0.01	*	*	*	*	*			0.02
nonprofit organizations	32													0.03	0.01	0.01	*						
amusements	33																						
scrap and miscellaneous industries	34		0.02				0.25			0.01		0.01		0.01	1.11	0.02	0.05	*					
eating and drinking places	35																						
new construction and maintenance	36	0.30	0.12	0.04	0.02	0.01	0.01	0.04	0.21	0.04	0.03	0.01	0.02	0.03	0.10	0.03	0.05	0.02	0.04	0.02	0.01	0.02	0.27
undistributed	37		1.87	0.30	1.08	0.73	0.27	0.17	0.50	1.49	0.65	0.27	0.27	0.47	0.32	1.14	1.71	0.89	0.41	0.34	0.19	0.87	0.23
inventory change (depletions)	38	2.66	0.40	0.12	0.19	*	0.01	0.09	0.03	0.14	0.01	*	0.03	*	0.11	*	*	0.01	0.01	0.05	0.16	*	
foreign countries (imports from)	39	0.99	2.11	0.21	0.28	0.18	0.01	0.62	0.01	0.59	0.26	*		0.04	0.14	0.02	0.01	0.05	*	0.02	0.01	0.05	0.01
government	40	0.81	1.24	0.64	0.38	0.34	0.11	0.50	0.34	0.76	0.78	0.11	0.14	0.32	0.82	0.48	0.77	0.40	0.96	0.12	0.13	0.19	1.14
private capital formation (gross)	41	DEPRECIATION AND OTHER CAPITAL CONSUMPTION ALLOWANCES								ARE INCLUDED IN HOUSEHOLD ROW													
households	42	19.17	7.05	3.34	4.24	2.72	1.12	2.30	3.14	3.75	5.04	1.08	1.20	2.35	5.35	4.14	5.80	3.41	3.39	1.95	0.90	2.17	5.11
TOTAL GROSS OUTLAYS		44.26	40.30	9.84	13.38	6.00	2.89	7.90	8.45	14.05	13.07	3.82	3.81	4.84	18.89	10.40	15.22	8.38	14.27	4.00	2.12	4.76	9.21

"Exchange of goods and services in the U. S. for 1947."
From Wassily W. Leontief, *Input-Output Economics*, 1986.

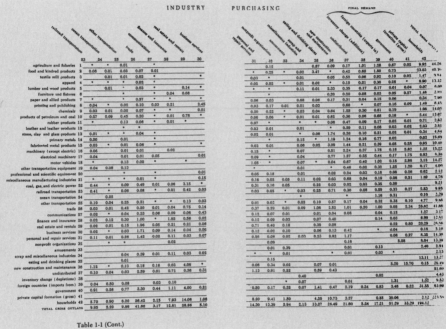

FINAL DEMAND

INDUSTRY PRODUCING

		23	24	25	26	27	28	29	30
agriculture and fisheries	1	*	*	0.01	*				
food and kindred products	2	0.08	0.01	0.03	0.07	0.01			
textile mill products	3		0.01	0.01	0.03	*			*
apparel	4	*	*	*	0.02	*			
lumber and wood products	5		0.01	*	0.03	*		0.14	*
furniture and fixtures	6			*		*	0.04	0.08	*
paper and allied products	7	*			0.57	*			*
printing and publishing	8	0.04	*	0.02	0.10	0.03	0.21		2.45
chemicals	9	0.03	0.01	0.02	0.07	*	*		0.01
products of petroleum and coal	10	0.57	0.09	0.45	0.20	*	0.01	0.78	*
rubber products	11	*		0.13	0.08	*	0.01	*	
leather and leather products	12			*	*	*			
stone, clay and glass products	13	0.01	*	*	0.04	*			
primary metals	14	0.20		0.01	*				
fabricated metal products	15	0.03	*	0.01	0.06	*			
machinery (except electric)	16	0.06		0.01	0.01	*	0.02		
electrical machinery	17	0.04		0.01	0.01	0.05	*		0.01
motor vehicles	18			0.15	0.02	*	*		
other transportation equipment	19	0.04	0.08	0.13					
professional and scientific equipment	20			*	*				0.01
miscellaneous manufacturing industries	21	*	*	*	0.01	*			0.15
coal, gas, and electric power	22	0.44	*	0.00	0.49	0.01	0.06	3.15	*
railroad transportation	23	0.41	*	0.06	0.08	*	0.01	0.42	0.03
ocean transportation	24		0.22						
other transportation	25	0.19	0.04	0.25	0.31	*	*	0.13	0.03
trade	26	0.03	0.01	0.42	0.20	0.01	0.04	0.75	0.14
communications	27	0.02	*	0.04	0.33	0.06	0.09	0.06	0.43
finance and insurance	28	0.02	0.12	0.30	1.00	*	1.85	0.56	0.02
real estate and rentals	29	0.02	0.01	0.15	1.96	0.05	0.21	0.21	0.06
business services	30	0.02	*	0.03	1.71	0.09	0.14	0.04	0.06
personal and repair services	31	0.11	0.01	0.26	1.42	0.02	0.11	0.03	0.07
nonprofit organizations	32			*	*		0.02		
amusements	33								
scrap and miscellaneous industries	34			0.04	0.39	0.01	0.11	0.03	0.02
eating and drinking places	35			0.01					
new construction and maintenance	36	1.12	*	0.13	0.18	0.18	0.03	4.08	*
undistributed	37	0.10	0.04	0.03	2.59	0.01	0.71	0.36	0.31
inventory change (depletions)	38								
foreign countries (imports from)	39	0.04	0.50	0.08		0.03	0.10		
government	40	0.91	0.28	0.77	3.30	0.44	1.11	4.00	0.21
private capital formation (gross)	41								
households	42	5.70	0.90	6.20	26.42	2.15	7.93	14.08	1.08
TOTAL GROSS OUTLAYS		9.95	2.29	9.86	41.66	3.17	12.81	26.86	5.10

		31	32	33	34	35	36	37	38	39	40	41	42	TOTAL gross output
agriculture and fisheries	1		0.12			0.87	0.09	0.17	1.01	1.28	0.57	0.02	9.92	44.26
food and kindred products	2	*	0.25		0.02	3.41	*	0.42	0.88	1.80	0.73		23.03	40.9x
textile mill products	3	0.03	*		0.01		0.05	0.52	0.06	0.92	0.10	0.02	1.47	9.84
apparel	4	0.02	0.02	*	0.01	0.02	*	0.15	0.21	0.30	0.28	*	9.90	13.32
lumber and wood products	5	*	*		0.11	0.01	2.33	0.35	0.17	0.17	0.01	0.04	0.07	6.00
furniture and fixtures	6						0.20	0.50	0.08	0.03	0.05	0.57	1.48	2.xx
paper and allied products	7	0.06	0.03		0.68	0.09	0.17	0.31	0.04	0.15	0.06		0.34	7.96
printing and publishing	8	0.03	0.17	0.01	0.01	0.03	0.68	*	0.07	0.16	0.09		1.49	6.4x
chemicals	9	0.20	0.22	*	0.03	0.04	0.04	1.25	0.30	0.81	0.19		1.96	14.05
products of petroleum and coal	10	0.06	0.06	*	0.01	0.01	0.82	0.36	0.06	0.68	0.18	*	2.44	13.67
rubber products	11	0.07	*	*	*	0.06	0.47	0.09	0.17	0.02	0.01		0.71	2.83
leather and leather products	12	0.03	0.01		0.01	*	0.39	0.11	0.08	0.03	0.03		2.03	3.81
stone, clay and glass products	13	0.02	0.01		*	0.08	1.74	0.38	0.10	0.21	0.02	0.01	0.34	4.84
primary metals	14		*		0.15	*	1.19	1.24	0.16	0.77	0.02		0.02	16.09
fabricated metal products	15	0.03	0.01		0.06	0.02	3.09	1.44	0.21	0.39	0.05	0.28	0.95	10.40
machinery (except electric)	16	0.15	*		0.07		0.51	2.24	0.37	1.78	0.18	5.82	1.22	15.22
electrical machinery	17	0.09	*		0.04		0.77	1.37	0.55	0.44	0.17	1.75	0.83	8.3x
motor vehicles	18	1.05	*		0.07	*	0.04	0.87	0.40	1.02	0.15	2.98	3.12	14.27
other transportation equipment	19	*			0.01		*	0.46	0.02	0.32	1.25	1.20	0.17	4.0x
professional and scientific equipment	20	0.05	0.18		0.01		0.03	0.34	0.03	0.18	0.08	0.26	0.82	2.12
miscellaneous manufacturing industries	21	0.16	0.05	0.08	0.11	0.02	0.03	0.88	0.04	0.19	0.08	0.31	1.89	4.76
coal, gas, and electric power	22	0.31	0.16	0.05		0.22	0.03	0.02	0.03	0.35	0.20			9.21
railroad transportation	23	0.03	0.05	*	0.03	0.25	0.71	0.30	0.08	0.59	0.33	0.27	2.53	9.95
ocean transportation	24				*			*		1.16	0.31		0.10	2.29
other transportation	25	0.01	0.02	*	0.02	0.10	0.57	0.17	0.04	0.32	0.35	0.10	4.77	9.55
trade	26	0.37	0.29	0.01	0.09	1.06	2.52	1.01	0.20	1.00	0.05	2.34	28.82	41.86
communications	27	0.12	0.07	0.01		0.01	0.04	0.08		0.04	0.15		1.27	3.17
finance and insurance	28	0.12	0.09	0.03		0.07	0.40			0.14	0.02		8.99	12.41
real estate and rentals	29	0.71	0.40	0.18		0.39	0.08			0.22	0.50		20.29	26.56
business services	30	0.12	0.02	0.10		0.06	0.13	0.42		*	0.04	0.18		5.10
personal and repair services	31	0.36	0.08	0.02	0.03	0.23	0.82	1.17			0.08	0.27	8.35	14.30
nonprofit organizations	32		0.09					0.16			5.08		4.04	13.39
amusements	33		0.01	0.39			0.01			0.13			2.40	2.94
scrap and miscellaneous industries	34	*	0.01			0.01		*		0.03	*			2.13
eating and drinking places	35		0.15										13.11	13.27
new construction and maintenance	36	0.06	0.34	0.02		0.07	0.01				5.20	15.70	0.15	28.4x
undistributed	37	1.13	0.91	0.22		0.59	0.43							21.60
inventory change (depletions)	38				0.40					0.02				4.43
foreign countries (imports from)	39			*	0.07			0.01			1.31		1.32	9.52
government	40	0.50	0.17	0.32	0.07	1.41	0.47	2.19	0.24	0.83	3.48	0.22	31.55	63.90
private capital formation (gross)	41													
households	42	8.20	9.41	1.50		4.20	10.73	2.27	*	0.85	30.06		2.12	223.5x
TOTAL GROSS OUTLAYS		14.30	13.39	2.94	2.13	13.27	28.49	21.80	5.28	17.21	51.29	33.29	194.12	

Table 1-1 (Cont.)

CONSTRUCTING ETHNICITY

Not long ago I met with a film director from the former Soviet Union, Nikita Mikhalkov. He stood six feet, four inches, wore a heavy walrus mustache, and spoke in a booming voice. His conversation was full of parables, belly laughs, and wry pessimism in the vein of Gogol. In short, Mikhalkov exemplified, and knew he exemplified—moreover, he tried to exemplify—what we think of as *Russianness*.

In conversation, Mikhalkov spoke at length of the Russian sensibility, the Russian way of life, Russian values and spirit. "Democracy can't work in the former Soviet Union," he said, "It's against the Russian character. The idea of democracy in Russia reminds me of when Gorbachev visited Sweden during the glasnost period. He saw the ample housing and social services, stores full of goods, comfort, and cleanliness. Back in Moscow, Gorbachev announced to the press, 'We should have more Swedish-style socialism in the Soviet Union.' To which I said at the time, '*There aren't enough Swedes in Russia!*'"

Mikhalkov has brought plenty of Russianness to the screen. *Oblomov* (1979) concerned an indolent aristocrat who was so apathetic he could not raise himself from the sofa to engage in the courtly rituals appropriate to his station. *Dark Eyes* (1987) won an Academy Award nomination for Marcello Mastroianni's performance as a charming bamboozler in late Czarist Russia. And *Close to Eden* (1991) told the story of a Russian truck driver stranded in the steppes of Mongolia.

After we had talked for a while, I asked the Russian filmmaker, "What is the Russian spirit? Can you encapsulate it for me?" Mikhalkov responded with a parable:

It's night. You're in the forest. Frost on the ground. A wooden cottage among trees. The sound of balalaika music in the air: "dinga-ling-a-ling-a-ling-a-ling." The music stops. The cottage door swings open. A barrel-chested man, shirt-less, barefoot, a balalaika in his hand, steps out. He bellows at the top of his lungs: "FuuuuckYoooooooou!" He slams the door and disappears. The balalaika resumes. That's the Russian character!

War Tourism

Mikhalkov's performance of "the Russian sensibility" presents an example of *constructed ethnicity*. A constructed ethnicity is a national, regional, sometimes racial identity produced in the presence of, and for, a spectator. This performative dimension within ethnicity is based on the presumption that culture is not written, as theorists of language might build their metaphor, but staged.

The tourist industry contains the clearest examples of ethnicity produced as an event. In fall 1992, I went to ex-Yugoslavia to write a newspaper story about the bombing of the Croatian city of Dubrovnik. A thousand-year-old

settlement on the Adriatic Sea, Dubrovnik was once the seat of a trading empire. In the twentieth century, the city became the main hub of the Yugoslavian tourist economy, which extended several hundred miles along the coast.

For an eight-month period in 1991–92, and again in early 1993, Dubrovnik was shelled with gunfire from the Serbian army. The old town was perforated by thousands of mortars, artillery from gunboats offshore, and Howitzers perched on nearby hills. When I visited, a United Nations truce had been agreed upon, and the Serbs had withdrawn from the perimeter of the city in the direction of Montenegro, twenty miles to the southeast. The worst damage was not in Dubrovnik itself, but in the tiny, picturesque villages in the path of the Serbian retreat. As they withdrew, the Serbs had burned everything.

Cilipe, a village with a population of 500, was once a showcase for the folklore of the Dalmatian coast. A former peasant village, Cilipe had been developed in the 1960s by the Tito government to attract tourists carrying so-called hard currency. The community was arranged in a circle around a central church. There were gift shops selling regional costumes, performances in the town square, and a little museum of peasant life. In short, Cilipe had an economy based entirely on constructed

ethnicity. Then the Serbian army arrived. After they had gone, 167 of the village's 184 houses had burned to the ground. When I visited, the village was empty of human life, save two or three people shoveling at the ruins.

Walking through the rubble, I met a woman called Marina Desin. She introduced herself as the director of the former museum of ethnography. We stood in the roofless hulk of her old offices and talked. She told me about the folk festivals that had been staged every Sunday in front of the church. People had dressed in the old local costume, played music, and organized dances. The museum had artifacts from around the region and was the center of village activity.

Looking around the ruins, I tried to imagine the former street life. A constant stream of tourists. Crowded cafés, people selling costumes and crafts, free-flowing wine, concerts in the town square. None of this was recognizable among the shards. Nothing was left except, standing in the museum's ruins, a giant stone wheel. The former director explained that the stone was once used to press olives, showing tourists how cooking oil had been extracted in the old days.

I asked Marina Desin whether she had any hope of rebuilding what had been lost, and she replied, "We aren't going to rebuild. We're going to restore." It was a cryptic remark. Only later did I realize what she meant. It was not "merely" that people might move back to Cilipe, take up their lives and put roofs back on their houses. The museum director meant that the whole apparatus of the tourist performance, seamlessly fused with everyday life—the consciousness of self and nation as an interlocking unit to be displayed—would somehow be put back together.

Returning to Dubrovnik, I found an architect who was assisting in the repair of buildings fractured by bombs. His name was Zvonimir Franic. He had a different idea of the effect of the war on the tourist economy. "No one will come here," he said pessimistically, "as long as the Serbian guns are nearby. Eventually tourists may come, but merely to see the damage. They will spend a day or two, look around, then leave. They will come to see what the war has done."

Franic's suggestion was alarming. The damage would not soon be put back to rights and the ethnic performance resumed. Instead, Croatia might see the formation of a new branch of "war tourism." Once the war was suspended, he implied, people might fly in to see the aftermath. And the locals, to carry the conjecture further, would obligingly show them around.

War tourism would differ from the traffic around historical monuments, a traditional destination in the travel economy. Many of us have been to old battlefields, climbed on towers, and looked out at the horizon, or stood at the war memorials in cities far from the old front lines. War tourism, by contrast, would take place at a site during the actual moments of shifting national identity. In place of displays of ethnic selfhood, there is substituted the destruction of cultural life. The destruction itself becomes the focus of interest.

Spectacle

In the shadow of such cultural developments, our ideas about display and visuality seem narrow. One of the most progressive notions of display seems still to derive from a text of the 1960s, *The Society of the Spectacle*. When Guy Debord and the Situationists, the avant-garde art cell, first began to circulate the notion of "the spectacle," it was as a principled attack on reification and commodification. Debord's *The Society of the Spectacle* (1967) observed the spreading out of the rule of exchange to the furthest precincts of daily life. For Debord, the spectacle meant the panoramic landscape of advertising, motion pictures, and television—an image world that transformed lived experience, depleted it, and finally substituted a homogenous performance of consumption in its place.

During the 1970s and 80s, picking up where Debord and the Situationists left off, Jean Baudrillard took the measure of the culture of *simulation*. In the realm of the simulacrum, representations have so far escaped lived experience that they do not even brush up against the flesh of events. Even war can appear to us, via the news media, as a visual and enthralling performance that does not link up with phenomenal reality. After the Persian Gulf War in 1991, Baudrillard wrote a pamphlet called *The Gulf War Did Not Take Place*. The essay argued that media coverage of the bombing of Iraq—being bloodless, and notoriously resembling a video game—displaced the war up to the realm of the signifier. There it remained, inaccessible, frozen as an experience.

I would like to embellish the notion of spectacle by linking it to three additional terms: Otherness, ethnicity, and performance. The spectacle is not restricted to economic phenomena (the intensification of capitalism), or to the culture of images (the growth of visual media). The spectacle is also an encounter with Otherness. It appears as a moment in the consciousness of the subject. For example, the individual witnessing representations of the Gulf War experiences—in addition to a narrative of bombing and military "success"—a consciousness of an object of wonder and ambiguity. The spectacle of the war appears as a shock, an unintelligible Otherness, which produces self-consciousness. This definition of Otherness corresponds to the Sartrean sense of "the Other" as a mysterious, existential alterity.

In recent years, there has been added to this existentialist meaning an additional connotation of Otherness, that of the ethnic/national/cultural

Other. Ethnic Otherness differs from philosophical Otherness in its being historical in content. Unlike philosophical Otherness, ethnic Otherness yields to the naming of difference (Chicano, Italian-American, Chinese, African American, white). Yet ethnic Otherness can be no less powerful a defining moment for individual identity—what "I am" versus what "they are."

I would like to import these twin senses—existential Otherness and ethnic Otherness—into an understanding of the notion of the spectacle. By doing so, we might have, finally, an idea of display that incorporates an experience of difference.

Carnival

In 1992, I was in New Orleans during Mardi Gras. The carnival season in New Orleans, the time of "masking," is a spectacular instance of crossover into ethnic and sexual difference. Tourists come to the city hoping to experience the "pure" difference of the public masquerade—women dressed as men (or vice versa), blacks dressed as whites, workers dressed as royalty, and so on.

One of the most popular aspects of the New Orleans carnival is the parading of the so-called Mardi Gras Indians. The Indians include seventeen clubs or "tribes" of mostly poor people, all black, who dress themselves in fantastical costumes of Native American derivation. The "Indian" tradition dates from 120 years ago, when black people, excluded from participating in white carnival balls and parades, formed Mardi Gras organizations of their own, with names like the White Eagles and the Wild Apaches. On Mardi Gras day, these "tribes" march through the streets chanting and drumming.

Why do black people imitate Native Americans? I put this question to the "chief" of an Indian group called Creole Wild West, Bertrand Butler. Butler explained that when black slaves ran away from their masters, Indians were the only people who took them in. He added, "Africans and Indians are almost identical people, anyway. They have a witch doctor, we have a voodoo man. They were warriors, we were warriors. We both lived in tents or huts. We both wore feathers. We're almost the same."

On Mardi Gras day, the marchers of Creole Wild West sometimes bump into other Indian groups in the street. When the tribes meet, each lets go a rant or chant in Afro-Caribbean patois. One of them sounds like this:

Hey-an dan dalu wild mamboula!
Handa wanda o mambo.
Said uptown rulers and downtown too!
Handa wanda o mama.

Indians coming from all over town.
Big chief singing gonna put them down.
Chock-a-mo feny hey de hey,
Indians the rulers on the holiday.

How do we talk about this subculture in the context of spectacle and display? The Mardi Gras Indians become "themselves" by encountering Otherness—specifically, the idea of the Native American. This encounter, in turn, is publicly performed in the street. I hope I do not exterminate the life of this beguiling show by applying to it the phrase from the beginning of this paper—constructed ethnicity. The case of Cilipe, the town in Croatia, presented an instance of constructed ethnicity in which the participants had created a modern tourist economy from the disused remnants of their peasant society. The Mardi Gras Indians, by contrast, construct an identity by assimilating the emblems of an Indian culture to African-American life. They recognize Otherness and absorb it, making the process of absorption into the act of self-creation.

Cultural Authenticity

Today, there is a compelling demand for more and more forms of Otherness. We clamor for the display of local cultures in their redolent authenticity. I'm reminded of the story of the indigenous Tasaday people of the Philippines. In the early 1970s, a group of anthropologists, working in a remote jungle far from Manila, discovered the Tasadays, a "primitive" tribe unruffled by the winds of modernity. A mere twenty Tasadays had managed to sequester themselves in the jungle. There they lived in thatched huts, used stone-age instruments, and foraged for food. The Tasadays had somehow escaped the grasp of colonialism, and more strangely, the even more powerful hand of industrialization. But following their discovery by an ambitious scientist, the Tasadays were sought out by ethnographers and subjected to numerous studies and interviews. Surprisingly, the "primitives" enthusiastically cooperated with their newfound fame, answering the questions of all visitors, and actually traveling to Manila to be interviewed on television.

A few years after this remarkable cultural emergence, a Dutch journalist traveling in the Philippines became a confidante of one of the Tasadays, and learned that the whole thing had been a hoax. Evidently the Minister of Interior in the Philippines government wanted publicity for his department, and to get it, he had arranged for a few native people in a remote village to perform a kind of "primitive" behavior for visiting scholars and news reporters. When the anthropologists and reporters were scheduled to arrive, these natives would take off the jeans and T-shirts that they normally wore, paint their bodies, and wait in a remote village of thatched huts built by the government. After the visitors left the Tasaday camp, the "tribe" put their jeans and T-shirts back on, and went back to their everyday life, driving pick-up trucks, listening to the radio, and carrying on like the hybrid cultural subjects that they actually were.

There is an insistent demand for the display of "genuine" ethnic identity, which is not often forthcoming. We ask for ethnicity to be performed, and we are disappointed when the result appears to be staged. By way of a conclusion, I would like to offer a final example of constructed ethnicity that appears to embody the ambiguities of cultural identity.

Japan is the capital of cultural hybridity. On the one hand, the Japanese historical culture—including traditions such as Shinto, tea ceremony, flower arranging, martial arts, cuisine, etc.—continues with great intensity, though at times some of these traditions appear to be performed by rote. On the other hand, the imported forms of especially American popular culture fill much of the daily life of the generations born after World War II.

In Tokyo, a vivid subculture grown from American popular music has become as Japanese as any tea ceremony or shogun's palace. Every Sunday, in the neighborhood known as Harajuku, in the parking lot that lies outside the Olympic Stadium, groups of high-school students perform dances. The teenagers are devoted fans of rockabilly. They have immersed themselves in 1950s American music, wavy hairstyles, and clothing (tight leather jackets for the boys, frilly dresses for the girls), and learned dances that date from the years after World War II. The teens dance in groups, the boys with each other, and the girls likewise.

The rockabilly dancers, in addition to affirming themselves as a group in an encounter with American Otherness, are an attraction for tourists, who go to the Olympic Stadium to watch the performance. In this way, the dancers have quite strangely come to represent (at least for the tourists) something

essentially Japanese. Throwing themselves against a popular music that was once a creation of mass marketing to Americans, these Japanese kids extract some identity for themselves, and at the same time, for the nation of Japan. The rockabilly subculture is personal, as well as being emblematic of Japan, a country whose social forms we have come to see as hybrid in the extreme. Here is the beguiling paradox of constructed ethnicity — the act is repeated until the performance itself becomes the authentic expression.

TALES OF TOTAL ART AND
DREAMS OF THE TOTAL MUSEUM

The first performances at the Cabaret Voltaire took place on a Saturday evening, February 5, 1916. The city was Zurich, which had become a cosmopolitan and artistic center during the war because of the influx of exiled and disaffected artists and political activists. The place was Hollandische Meiri café, which had already served as a venue for the Cabaret Pantagruel poetry readings. The instigator was the young German playwright and dramaturg Hugo Ball. Ball, who had arrived in Zurich from Munich at the end of May in 1915, approached the Meiri café's proprietor to book the space, then said to some of his friends, "Please give me a picture, a drawing, an etching. I would like to have an exhibition in connection with my cabaret."

Thus, from the beginning, the Cabaret was a makeshift gallery displaying both the performers and the artworks. Paintings by Wassily Kandinsky, Paul Klee, Fernand Léger, and Henri Matisse, etchings by Pablo Picasso, and an assortment of modern posters and work by fellow performers and friends were on the wall. Two years later, in March 1917, the defunct Cabaret was reinvented and transferred from the Meiri to a new space, the Dada Gallery on Bahnhofstrasse. This gallery also hosted simultaneous art exhibitions and cabaret performances, but the scale was now more ambitious, and included afternoon tea and a café called the Kandinsky Room. In April, Ball noted in his diary, "Yesterday I gave my lecture on Kandinsky. I have realized a favorite old plan of mine: Total art: pictures, music, dances, poems..."[1]

Thus, Zurich Dadaism was built around this project of "total theater," which would incorporate painting, poetry, music, and dance, and rejected, therefore, the separation of these forms into the streamlined institutions of the museum, the concert hall, and the theater. This post-Wagnerian project was also the inspiration for Sergei Eisenstein, who saw the cinema as its obvious location, and it also can be found influential in a different, but related form in the collaborative work of Serge Diaghilev and the Russian ballet, related experiments of Léger, and Oskar Schlemmer's Triadic Ballet, for example. Implicit in the practice of the heroic avant-gardes was the idea, not only of transforming and totalizing the arts, but also, as the necessary corollary, of transforming the site of visual display as no longer separated from auditory display and the display of bodies and representation.

According to this vision, dance began to seem all important because first, it was through the body that the senses could be naturally linked with art objects, and second, it was through dance that space and time were themselves combined into a unity, a four-dimensional continuum for the exhibition of movement. In dance, it seemed possible for the ontological division of the arts to be overcome. But, this conflict between the harmonious, measured, and rational Apollonian and the sensuous, frenzied, orgiastic Dionysian visions was to play itself out in strange and paradoxical forms.

Monte Verita and the Cabaret Voltaire

After their first meeting in Munich in 1912, Kandinsky had been Ball's greatest influence. Munich was the art capital of Germany at that time, widely considered the principal rival to Paris. Its Bohemian quarter, Schwabing, was the equivalent of Montmartre, or later Montparnasse. Kandinsky explained to Ball his theories about the unity of the arts, largely based upon the doctrine of synesthesia, the existence of an immanent correspondence between the senses. Kandinsky wanted to combine painting, music, and dance, and put them into movement to create total spectacle. He painted watercolors, which he then gave to the musician Thomas Von Hartmann, who would choose one and "play" it. Another friend, the dancer Alexander Sacharoff, would join them and, in turn, "dance" the music, concluding by pointing to the painting, which he felt best expressed his dance. Of course, the ideal outcome of this synesthetic experiment was when Sacharoff's choice coincided with Von Hartmann's. So, Ball, having begun with the philosophies of Friedrich Nietszche and Richard Wagner, was impressed by Kandinsky's experiments, and further moved on to seek a more radical strategy.

Hugo Ball met Alexander Sacharoff in Munich through their mutual friendship with Kandinsky, and shortly after Sacharoff moved to Switzerland where he joined the dance company of Rudolf von Laban, who became a key figure in this story. In 1913, Laban had been attracted to the Swiss mountain town of Ascona, overlooking Lago Maggiore. He began a yearly dance summer school for his students and admirers at a farm on the slopes of Monte Verita, where previously there had been a vegetarian colony with a number of wooden huts, sunbathing places, and meadows. Laban and his students expanded it, as he later described:

> Each morning from the veranda of my small house with its overhanging creepers I sounded a gong and everyone turned up for work. Tools were distributed and before breakfast groups went to the various gardens to weed, dig, plant and do other necessary jobs. Groups of women went into the sewing rooms, where they made dance costumes and sandals. We had a bakery and later even two weaver's looms which produced the fabrics we needed. Fruit was preserved and meals prepared and cooked in various shifts. However, our main concern was with the places for dancing.[2]

Rudolf von Laban, ca. 1914.

Stranded there, at the end of the summer when World War I began, Laban continued to maintain the school. In 1916 the school moved from Munich to Zurich. Laban was the son of a self-made officer in the Austro-Hungarian army who rose into nobility and became the military governor of Bosnia-Herzegovina, where Laban was brought up. For him, Bosnia was the source of all future inspiration, the "Land of Adventure" — as he invariably refers to it in later writings. Laban remembered two things in particular about his first home near Mostar, in a mountainous region inhabited mainly by Muslims: first, the power of the landscape, nature, and the earth. "In my childhood, the earth was my confidante. When as a child I roamed about in the mountains, woods, and meadows I always felt as if I received answers to questions which I could ask nobody but the earth."[3] It was the mountains that especially impressed and overwhelmed him; like giants in his imagination, the mountains, on whose flanks plants and crystals struggled for predominance, retained the potential to stretch, toss, and turn, crushing everything around before settling back to bask in the sun. He also remembered the dance of the dervishes, which he encountered in Herzegovina, where he'd been admitted under the protection of an imam to otherwise private rituals, presumably of the Bektashi. "The dancing dervishes are Muslim lay-brothers who perform their prayers not in words, but in body movements and especially in endless turnings…at first sight, [they are] completely incomprehensible, even almost repulsive in the wild whirling which goes on till the dancers froth at the mouth. It all seems quite mad to us, but it is probably in the madness that the sense lies."[4]

Laban saw the dervish dance as a kind of magic. He recalls seeing dancers drive needles and nails into their cheeks and stab themselves with knives. Comparing them with sword dancers he had seen in another mountain villages, he interpreted the dance as a magic ritual, conferring bodily invulnerability on the dancers. "Many of us may already have experienced how dancing can induce an enhanced, or at least a different kind of consciousness from our normal practical everyday awareness of the world. How far can this go, and whether one can attain extraordinary powers through dance, I could not judge at that time. Here it was simply a miracle that I saw with my own eyes, an unbelievable conquest of nature."[5] In his indispensable book *Mountain of Truth: The Counter-Culture Begins: Ascona, 1900–1920*, Martin Green suggests that in intellectual terms, it was the life-philosopher Ludwig Klages who most influenced Laban in the early formulation of his ideas.[6] Klages, best known as a graphologist, believed in the power of energy flowing outwards from the center as the key to both bodily and spiritual health, an energy flow impeded by the bodily regime of a spiritually impoverished modernity. He believed in youth, nature, community, and dance. It was a little later that Laban's life was changed by his encounter with Suzanne Perrottet, an ex-student of the Swiss music educator Émile Jaques-Dalcroze at his institute in the garden city of Hellerau, near Dresden. In the summer of 1912, Laban, then living in Munich, went to Hellerau to take a cure at the Weisser Hirsch Fresh Air Sanitarium, and embarked on an affair with Perrottet.

Dance of the Kadiri dervishes
(from the *Tableau Général de l'Empire Othoman*, 1790)

Mary Wigman and her dance group in *Wandering* from the work
Scenes from a Dance Drama, 1924.

Perrottet's mentor, Dalcroze, had developed eurythmics, a series of group
movement exercises in order to instill a sense of intrinsic rhythm in music
students, translating musical rhythms into whole-body rhythms, and then
returning to the piano with fingers attuned to a more total, less mechanical
sense of rhythm. Dalcroze also organized a festival at Hellerau, which featured collective dancing. Laban, through Perrottet, began to absorb Dalcroze's
eurythmics and choral dance into his own emerging vision of a new pagan
art. With Perrottet, he sought a place in the fresh air of the mountains in
Ascona—already a center of the emergent counterculture—where dance
could be regenerated as a new, healthy, and ecstatic culture, a culture of exalted
creators, rather than decadent inheritors. In fact, Laban actually practiced
in Ascona not only as a dance teacher, but also as a psychosomatic healer.
He believed that "the warped psyche of our time" could not be cured except
through dance education.

In many respects, Laban's theories derived from a rebellion within the
traditional world of German body culture. Germany had a strong gymnastic
movement since the Napoleonic wars, when the first gymnastic associations and fraternities had been founded by Friedrich Ludwig Jahn. These

Mary Wigman in the first version of *Witch Dance*, 1914.

associations were conceived as patriotic training organizations for German male youths, bonding them into fellowships of the fit, hard working, disciplined, and the so-called beautiful. The ideal of male beauty went back to the Greek revival, which was started by the eighteenth-century classical archaeologist and art historian Johann Winckelmann, and which dominated German nineteenth-century thought in a number of areas as Martin Bernal chronicles in his *Black Athena*.[7] At the beginning of the twentieth century, Dalcroze's eurythmics not only launched Laban and his pupil Mary Wigman on dance careers, but also Rudolph Bode, whose *Ausdrucksgymnastik* (expressive gymnastics) bridged some of the gap between gymnastics and dance.

In fact, Bode was a major influence for Eisenstein, who linked Bode's techniques with his borrowings from *commedia dell'arte*, his theory of the *salto mortale*, and his goal of achieving ecstasy through film. Later he also linked Bode to the "Montage of Attractions," which would allow the spectator to empathize with a series of bodily movements, and as late as 1929, he was invoking Bode in his support of his own theory of montage (known now as "dialectical") against director Vsevolod Pudovkin's "mechanical" theory of film editing. In an essay of 1929, Eisenstein described how the performance of music might bring an audience to leave their seats and dance: "What is this? Dionysian ecstasy? No. Dalcroze..." Like Laban and Wigman, Eisenstein was fascinated by group movement and collective ritual.

Laban's dance school, the "negative pole" to machine civilization, became a cultural center attracting a surprising number and variety of extraordinary people. Two of these people, aside from Sacharoff and Perrottet, were to play a part in the activities of the Cabaret Voltaire.

Sophie Taeuber was born in Switzerland at Davos. In 1910 she began to study textile design in Munich, where she played a prominent role in organizing carnival festivities and masquerade balls, as did Laban around the same time. Like a model for Paul Poiret, she is dressed in turban and harem trousers in a photograph from 1912. After graduation in 1914, she went to live in Zurich, staying first with her sister who worked as a librarian at Carl Gustav Jung's Psychological Club. Toward the end of that year, she met Hans Arp—better known now as Jean Arp—whom she later married. Arp was directly involved in the group who organized the Cabaret Voltaire, which also included Ball, Raoul (Richard) Huelsenbeck, Marcel Janco, and Tristan Tzara.

Taeuber by then had started attending Laban's summer school at Monte Verita, which became her regular summer haunt. In April 1916, she participated in the first of many performances at the Cabaret Voltaire and the Dada Gallery by members of the Laban dance school.

At Ascona, Taeuber met Mary Wigman. Another ex-student from the Dalcroze School, Wigman transferred to Laban's school on the advice of Emil Nolde, one of her greatest admirers. She became Laban's star pupil, spending seven summers with the man she later described as, "the magician, the priest of an unknown religion, [who] was lord and master in a dance-born and yet so real kingdom, a multiple man who could change like lightning from courtly lover to grinning faun."[8] There she created her *Hexentaz* (*Witch Dance*), which was the model for many dances to come that, along with those of Martha Graham, were to define modern dance as we know it. She described her experience as follows:

Summer 1913. A leap from the safe cultured academicism of Dalcroze into the full freedom of creative experimentation. Laban is in his first, strongest phase, which swings between the poles of a fanatical passion for theory and an uncontrolled lust to produce, the two in continual interchange mixing, driving, and struggling against each other. The center alone stands firm, dance as a primary art. This explosive power possessed Monte Verita like a whirlwind ... A strong existentiality pulses through the Laban circle, and the wonderful consciousness of venturing into an untrodden land."[9]

Soon, however, Taeuber, Wigman, Perrottet, Sacharoff, and others were to venture down from the mountaintop—where they danced naked and barefoot to the rising and setting sun and let the rhythm flow through their naked bodies in a mystic encounter with nature—to the confined, smoky space of the Meiri café and its bohemian attraction, the Cabaret Voltaire. In March and May of 1916, Taeuber invented "Sudanese" songs for the Cabaret. In April she, Wigman, Perrottet, and three other Laban dancers danced poems by Hugo Ball and a painting by Kandinsky. The next year, Taeuber danced at the Dada Gallery as Ball recited his notorious poem *Gadji Berri Bimba*. Oskar Kokoschka's *Sphinx and Strawman* was also performed. Taeuber danced her *Song of the Flying Fish and Seahorses*, the dance of a miserable demon who wanted to become a child or an angel but could not decide which. Wigman danced Nietzsche at the Café des Banques. These dances, often based on African or Dionysian rhythms and motifs, issued, in Hugo Ball's words, "an unrecognizable force and living power. From this moment on the dance of the future begins."[10]

Yet, perhaps because the dancers were almost all women, their role in shaping Dadaism has been undervalued and, indeed, remains under-chronicled. Also, their paths soon diverged, especially after the war ended. The men left for the art worlds of Paris and Berlin, where they moved into center stage. Sophie Taeuber left Zurich with Arp and gave up dancing (although she later designed the Dance Café for the Aubette in Strasbourg). Mary Wigman left for Dresden in 1919, and went on to great fame in the dance world. She remained in touch with the world of expressionism: her style was called *Ausdruckstanz* (expression dance) and her pupils Harald Kreutzberg and Kurt Jooss were widely seen as expressionist dancers. But, she pulled back from artists using other media, preferring to develop a "pure" dance—thrusting, leaping, leaping, whirling as though possessed, without stage settings or even music. Her mode of display continued that of Monte Verita rather than the Cabaret Voltaire.

There was a tension at the heart of Ball's project of "total theater" incorporating all senses and all arts, which surfaced perhaps most clearly in Laban's refusal to work with the Cabaret Voltaire despite the enthusiasm of the dancers. The underlying question, one stemming for many from the problem of how to interpret Nietzsche, was a matter of what was healthy and what was debilitating, what was magically powerful and what was scandalously perverse. He was not entirely enamored of the idea of his priestesses and maenads displaying themselves in strange masks and dancing to "negro" rhythms and nonsense verses, such as "ollaka, hollala/ anlogo bung/ blago bung/ blago bung/ bosso fataka/ u uu u..." For Ball, on the other hand, poems like "Karawane" were the equivalents of Kandinsky's "yellow sounds"—pure phonic emanations, with shock effect necessary to clear away the garbage of modern decadence. He planned to simulate madness in his poems to destroy "the dreary, lame, empty language of men in society." This implicit culture-theoretical battle between Laban and Ball, between Monte Verita and the Cabaret Voltaire, was to develop in terrifying ways that none could have possibly foretold.

Film still from *Olympia*, 1936, directed by Leni Riefenstahl.

Laban's watchwords were, first, *life-body-gesture-movement*, signifying *dance*, an outward, centrifugal progression, then *dance-sound-word*, encapsulating the progression of movement of the body, or *dance*, then *sound* made from bodily movement (internal or external), and finally, *word*, an even more distant articulation of primary movement and primary sound. Thus, his workshops at Monte Verita were on movement, sound, and word, but he also added one on form. He was seen as the *tanzformer*—the dance shaper, the theorist, and the organizer—which differentiated him from the other dancers, even from Wigman, who was seen as the mesmerizing performer letting go of all restraint.

The German gymnastics cult shifted in the early twentieth century, creating a new community of youth movement engaged not only with modern dance, but also with sunbathing, nudism, and countryside trekking. Expressionism, unleashing individual passions and impulses, is often seen as the opposite pole to the discipline of the youth movement. And, the modern dance movement founded by Laban and Wigman spanned the spectrum. At one end were Laban's movement choirs and pageants, dance ceremonies that celebrated the setting of the sun and continued until its rising, and later the huge pageants that involved thousands of participants, vast dance spectacles with knights, pages, nuns, and peasants set in the castle of the Teutonic knights. At the other end were the intimate, provocative Dada performances of Taeuber, Wigman, and the other Cabaret dancers. Consequently, not only did the body culture movement reach a point of crisis, but expressionism as a whole entered a troubled phase, as it mutated into Dada and beyond.

Degenerate Art and the Berlin Olympiad

The Berlin Olympiad of 1936 was designed as a massive festival in celebration of the human body, as idealized by the Nazi ideology: the body of the sportsman in harmony with nature, disciplined in the quest for unsurpassed achievement, hardened by struggle, recapturing the grace, beauty, and strength of the bodies of antiquity. Olympia of ancient Greece had a special place in collective German memory. It was Winckelmann himself who first proposed the Ottoman regime send an expedition to excavate there in 1776; the task was finally achieved in 1875 when the German archaeologist Ernst Curtius led a well-financed expedition to the site, uncovering myriad sculptures, temples, and sports grounds.

The 1936 Olympiad was the first in which the Olympic torch was lit in Olympia, and carried by an unbroken relay of runners to the Games, held in the brand-new, neoclassical stadium in Berlin. The stadium was placed, designed, and constructed under Adolf Hitler's personal supervision and, in fact, inaugurated his grander dream of reconstructing Berlin. From the start, the Games were planned to honor the cultural and supposedly racial ties that would bind together Greece and Germany, the glorious past and the glorious future.

The spectacle of the Games, presided over by Hitler himself, was doubled and surrounded by a series of other ancillary spectacles. Leni Riefenstahl's film *Olympia* was conceived in two parts, "Festival of the Peoples" (*Völker*) and "Festival of Beauty" (*Schönheit*), corresponding to the two weeks of the Olympic program, covering athletics and the sports, including, of course, gymnastics. Riefenstahl had abundantly proved her exceptional flair for capturing pageantry on film in *Triumph of the Will*, her previous work for Hitler, which memorialized another festival of massed bodily movement. Arnold Fanck, director of "mountain films" was the most recognized influence on Riefenstahl, as he launched her career as an actress and supplied her with many of her trusted assistants; he also provided the basic model for her first film, *The Blue Light*.

But, Riefenstahl's first mentor was her dance teacher, Mary Wigman, whom she studied with in Dresden in the early 1920s. Her roots, like Wigman's, were in eurythmics, which she used in the prologue to *Olympia*, set in Greece. Like Wigman, she was a charismatic figure, driven to climb the mountaintops to experience ecstasy at the peak. Like Wigman, she was fascinated by group dance, by rites at sunrise and sunset, by communal ritual and festival.

In fact, in making the prologue to *Olympia*, Riefenstahl sent her cinematographer Willy Otto Zielke to look for dancers in the Bode, Laban, and Wigman schools in Berlin. Zielke chose twelve, who were approved by Riefenstahl, and he took them to the Baltic to film the sequence in accordance with Riefenstahl's instructions. Zielke was an interesting choice for this assignment. Originally a *Neue Sachlichkeit* (New Objectivity) still photographer, he turned to film in the 1930s and made *Das Stahltier* (*The Beast of Steel*), a film for the German railways, which so infuriated Goebbels that the film was shelved and Zielke sent to an insane asylum. Riefenstahl, who wanted him for her film, was able to get him out of the asylum, brought to Berlin, and then sent to Greece. Seeing the sequences he shot, one can only admire her judgment and her tenacity. Zielke was able to film the naked bodies of the dancers, priestesses at the Olympia temple, with the swinging, ecstatic movements Riefenstahl had learned from the schools of Laban and Wigman. The dancers introduce body worship and the sense of sport as a sacred activity, which pervades the whole film. Riefenstahl preferred to film the bodily activity of the athletes from the beginning to the end of their physical effort. For example, in depicting the throwing events, she concentrated on the contact with the built up of energy, the peak of the effort, and the final outburst of ecstasy mingled with the relaxation after the throw, but she did not bother to show the outcome of it.

An Olympiad of the Arts was organized as one of the ancillary events surrounding the Games. The Dance Olympiad was placed under the direction of Laban, who had risen to an authoritative position in the Nazi regime, as head of the German *Tanzbühne* (Dance Stage), an official organization sponsored by Goebbels and the Nazi Ministry of Culture. A gigantic pageant was to be performed on the evening of the Games' opening, with thousands of performers and including, as a set-piece, a group dance by Mary Wigman and her company, *Totenklag*. Wigman's student Harald Kreuzberg and Werner Stammer performed a sword dance, apparently in favor of peaceful competition, befitting of the Olympics. However pacific the contributions of Wigman and her dancers, it was a strange path indeed that took her from Hugo Ball's Cabaret Voltaire to Adolf Hitler's Berlin Olympiad, where her work could be produced under the aegis of her ex-teacher Laban and filmed by her ex-student Riefenstahl.

Mary Wigman also played a role in the 1936 Olympiad, less exalted than Riefenstahl's, but still significant. By this time, Wigman was securely placed as the artistic leader of modern dance in Germany, which she no longer called "expression dance" or even "modern dance," but "German dance." In 1934 she wrote of how new German dance "searched for God and wrestled with the demon, because it gave form to the old Faustian desire for redemption as the ultimate unity of existence—because of all this, it is a German dance."[11]

Laban also spoke of "German dance" and divided dance into racial categories, arguing that black American jazz dance was simply borrowed from the English and "heightened into a virtuoso-grostesque style." He doubted:

> whether the negro is capable of inventing any dance at all. If one hopes to find any kind of negro dance culture here [America in 1926], one is in for a big disappointment. A gift for dance-invention as well as the higher development of the other arts and sciences seems to be the privilege of other races. The negro adopts our dance-inventions just as he adopts our stand-up collar and top hat, and uses them grotesquely, remodeled to fit his own feeling. Where music is concerned, he seems to possess an inborn talent, but only for rhythmic, melodic, unsophisticated expression. The fact that the white race has re-adopted distortions of its own dances only shows the lack of taste of the robot age and is not a sign of a complete dearth of original ideas. In America there are a great many pioneers of modern expressive dance, which is usually called "German dance" and indeed resembles our style of dance very closely.[12]

This passage from Laban's *A Life for Dance*, published in 1935, illustrates quite clearly how the counterculture of Ascona evolved into Nazism. In one breath, Laban denounced the black American for lack of originality, penchant for grotesquerie and distortion, while attacking the cosmopolitan white culture for degeneration of its own dance taste in the modern "robot age." At the same time, he found healthy elements in American dance (Martha Graham, etcetera), and claimed them as honorary Germans. He also praised Native Americans as remote, romantic, and unthreatening, whose sword dances reminded him of those that had impressed him in the Land of Adventure, Bosnia-Herzegovina. A splitting takes place in his thinking between healthy and unhealthy "primitivism." The Native Americans were portrayed as living in wild nature, suggesting "demonlike elemental powers," in a landscape of endless prairie and towering mountains. He wrote that their dances:

> never lead to frenzy…the postures often remind one of Greek or ancient Egyptian sculpture. The grotesqueness is not unsophisticated or evil in nature. Form and direction in space are especially cultivated, and the groups move along lines which make a decorative ground plan of great clarity and beauty[13]

—not unlike, it might be added, those of the dancers in his own movement choirs. Black dance, on the other hand, lacked "all symbolic form and therefore all clarity of line. Only the flow of energy is important to them"[14]— it could be reduced to "savage stamping" and frenzied "body shaking."

Thus, Native American dance, like Bosnian dervish dance, could provide a model because it sprung from contact with wild nature, with the sublime, and because it had more than energy and rhythm—it had "symbolic form," like the dance of Greece and antiquity. In Nietszchean terms, then, Native Americans could be honorary Greeks, combining the Dionysian with the Apollonian. It is hence no surprise to find him commissioned as a kind of new Richard Wagner to supervise the dance section of the 1936 Olympiad of the Arts. On June 20, 1936, after a week of community dancing, Laban premiered his *Vom Tauwind und der neuen Freude* (*Of the Warm Wind and the New Joy*), with text from Nietzsche's *Thus Spoke Zarathustra*, and four choric dances, also with themes drawn from Nietzsche.

Unfortunately for Laban, his precautionary splitting of good myth from bad, good "primitivism" from bad, good rhythm from bad, came to grief at the Olympiad. Like Nolde, he was shocked and disoriented to find himself under attack. Goebbels, who watched the dress rehearsal of Laban's Olympic display, thereupon decided to cancel its presentation during the Games. It seems the decision already may have been made, perhaps as a general shift of policy away from mass pageantry. The dancers were sent away, and after the foreign press had left, they were dismissed. Laban's work was denounced as "hostile to the State," he was abused as a Jew and homosexual and he too was sent away into a kind of internal exile, from which he managed to escape early the following year, crossing the border to France and making his way to Paris. He moved on again in 1938 to England, where he joined the former Wigman dancer Kurt Jooss at Dartington Hall, a boarding school and arts community founded on the basis of theosophical ideas, still today a center for modern dance.

Laban's next twist of fate was a particularly strange one, underlining once again, the paradoxes of his cultural stance, indeed of the whole Monte Verita project. In 1942, he was approached by a management consultant, F. C. Lawrence, and persuaded to construct a system of "Industrial Rhythm," which would combine Taylorist work-study with an approach to workers' movement drawn from expressionist dance. Laban approached this strange task by focusing on the question of "effort" and in 1948 published a book with that title, coauthored by Lawrence. As they write there, "the main thing, however, is to develop the man's capacity to control strength in the degree to which he is physically able to exert it."[15] It was to be done by achieving the "right proportionality of Weight, Space, Time, and the control of the Flow of movement."[16] Each movement has its own form and its own rhythm of exertion and relaxation. Each movement is systematically analyzed and graphically notated according to the system developed by Laban into categories such as strength versus lightness, directness versus flexibility, sustainment versus quickness, and free flow versus bound flow. This categorization enabled Laban to notate the difference, for instance, between a "shoving punch" with free flow, and a "throwing slash" with "free flow," when throwing the load on the shovel into the furnace.[17] Laban also advised dividing up the workers according to their personality types, separating those best able to deal with free flow, fine touch, flexibility, and sustainment from those best able to better deal with bound flow. He was then able to recommend who to use for different kinds of work, such as assembly work, lumbering, and hand forging. Evidently, Laban made his peace with the "robot age" and machine civilization, and contributed to the anti-Nazi war effort.

At base, his ideas on work effort probably derive from Ludwig Klages's analysis of handwriting, filtered through both Taylorism and its apparent opposite, Laban's movement theory. Laban's view of stoking a furnace or conducting a boardroom battle ("continuous pressing effort with a sudden explosion into a mighty thrust," countered successfully by "light flicking, short dabbing, some pressure soon relieved by floating") is conceived in terms like those in which Riefenstahl saw the battles on the athletics fields between long jumpers and discus throwers (except that her filmic version carries a romantic gloss missing from his analytically noted account). The emphasis was on the coordinates and sequences of movement, structured by the rhythm of effort and relaxation. Both knew, from their dance background, what to look for in the factory or in the arena—the path to health and effective movement—and turned away from the "unproductive," as Laban had described Dada, from their views of "debility and perversity."

The Degenerate Art exhibition opened in Munich in July 1937. The

Film still from *Olympia*, 1936, directed by Leni Riefenstahl.

south wall of Room 3 contained a special section devoted to Dada, including paintings by Georg Grosz, Kurt Schwitters, Wassily Kandinsky, Paul Klee, Emil Nolde, Conrad Felixmüller, Lyonel Feininger, and Heinrich Campendonk. Today, we only recognize Grosz and Schwitters as Dadaists; the rest are affiliated in one way or another with movements of the *Blaue Reiter* (Blue Rider), *Die Brucke* (The Bridge), *Der Sturm* (The Storm), or the Bauhaus.

Nolde, Mary Wigman's old admirer, the man who had first directed her to Laban, who painted her portrait and took a seat for himself and one for his easel at her concerts, who used her dance as a model for his painting *Candle Dancers* (1912), was a prime target of the "Degenerate Art" show. No fewer than twenty-seven of his paintings were exhibited there, and that was a tiny proportion of the 1,037 confiscated from German museums and sold, stored, or destroyed. Nolde was horrified and distressed at the way his work was pilloried. As a Nazi party member, he could not fathom how or why he was denounced in this public and summary way. He was a figure, one might

Two views of room 3 in the exhibition
"Degenerate Art," Munich, 1937.

say, like Martin Heidegger, who above all believed in peasant virtues. He held fast to his *Heimat*, his native Schleswig-Holstein, as Heidegger did to the Black Forest. He hated technology and the city and felt that Germany needed regeneration from the roots, and he felt that only the Nazis could achieve this task. Unlike Heidegger, who went no further afield than the Greeks, Nolde looked for inspiration from the people of Papua, New Guinea, then a German colony. Nolde felt that Germans could find there, as though by destiny, the primal life force needed to restore their vigor and lead them into a new era.

As for Zurich Dada, Arp and Janco were not represented in the show at all; the only artists with any real connection at all were the Munich artists Kandinsky (Ball's mentor) and Klee (whom Ball also knew and admired). Perhaps Zurich Dada was so performance oriented that no permanent work was ever acquired by German museums, and consequently was not available to be confiscated and displayed by the exhibition organizers. Making up for this deficiency, they attempted to suggest the atmosphere of a Dada cabaret as they imagined it. They hung the paintings askew on walls covered with their own hilarious pastiche of a scrawled-over Kandinsky and graffiti with George Grosz's slogan "Take Dada seriously! It's worth it!" They also added, for atmosphere, two pages from the Berlin journal *der Dada*, each prominently displaying the word *DADA* in heavy lettering, and an inscription drawn from Schwitters in which he praised nonsense and declared his love for it. Ironically, it is as if the organizers, driven to extremes by their overwhelming desire to destroy Dadaism, in fact tried to appropriate the same Dada agitational techniques that had been directed against all they stood for.

The "Degenerate Art" exhibition was not an exhibition in the conventional sense; indeed, it was much more like a political demonstration where all that the Nazis hated in the visual arts was held up to obloquy and disgust, pilloried and lampooned. So, in effect, it was more like the 1936 Olympiad than one might imagine. The Olympiad, too, in the minds of the organizers, was not so much a sporting event as a political demonstration honoring the values that the Degenerate artists were held to have desecrated. Hitler himself made this quite explicit in his opening speech at the House of German Art, which opened in Munich the day before the "Degenerate Art" show opened. It was intended as a contrast to show all that the Nazis held to be good in German art. It is clear from this speech, which was printed in the Degenerate show catalogue, that he intended to address not the mass audience of German sycophants gathered in the House of German Art, but the absent hordes of Degenerates whose work was displayed on the other side of the park. Simultaneously in Hitler's rhetoric, there are some uncanny echoes of the counterculture of Monte Verita. It was the Greece of Apollo that he evoked, though, instead of Dionysus—the Greece of trained athletes over the unruly maenads. He described the relationship between Degenerate art and the Olympic festival as follows:

Today the new age is shaping a new human type. In countless areas of life huge efforts are being made to exalt the *Volk*, to make our men, boys and youths, our girls and women, healthier and thus stronger and more beautiful. And from this strength and beauty there springs a new lease on life, new joy in life. Never has mankind been closer to antiquity, in appearance or in feeling, than it is today. Steeled by sport, by competition, and by mock combat, millions of young bodies now appear to us in a form and a condition that have not been seen and have scarcely been imagined for perhaps a thousand years. A glorious and beautiful type of human being is emerging: one who, after supreme achievement in work, honors that fine old saying, "Work hard and play hard." This human type, as we saw in last year's Olympic Games, stepping out before the whole world in all the radiant pride of his bodily strength and health—this human type, you gentlemen of the prehistoric, spluttering art brigade, is the type of the new age. And what do you create? Misshapen cripples and cretins, women who can arouse only revulsion, men closer to beasts than to human beings, children who if they lived in such a shape would be taken for the curse of God![18]

Mary Wigman's enigmatic maxim that men in her audience upon seeing her group of women dancers might say to themselves "I don't want to marry any of them!" might be recalled!

But, ultimately it was the responsibility of the critics and curators if the work of Degenerate artists was acquired and displayed—just as, in contrast, sports administrators were to take credit for the exploits of their athletes. In this sense, both exhibitions—the Olympiad and the "Degenerate Art" show— primarily reflected on an assessment of the strengths and weaknesses of the

Nazi state, its so-called healthy institutions and its so-called degenerate ones. It was the body of the State fundamentally at question. "The Degenerate Art" show can only be understood in terms of competing regimes of the body, which determined both representations exhibited in it and the ideology of the exhibition itself. The first relevant regime is that imagined by the exhibition's organizers. This body, as Hitler himself indicated, is the Greek body, as elaborated by Winckelmann. It is the body of the Olympic athlete—a disciplined, sporting body, given a modern edge by Riefenstahl. This healthy Greek body was contrasted to the medical-aesthetic body of nineteenth-century positivism and racism.

The second body at issue was the expressionist body—Nolde's reading of the dancing body of Mary Wigman, for example—intense, primal, possessed. This body displaced the body of nineteenth-century nationalist gymnastics into a new form, drawing on self-expression to seek revolutionary sources of energy in order to combat the supposed reduction of the modern body to mechanized robot and urban decadent. In extreme form, this body also represented that of the Cabaret Voltaire, outrageous and scandalous, turning the healthy, Hellenistic body inside out and upside down, appealing directly to Ball's carnivalesque Other. These competing bodies, in all their paradoxical complexity, must be placed alongside their representations in order to understand expressionism, its history, and its enemies. And, so far, the museum as the site of visual display has proven inadequate, as it effaces the role of the body and performance by privileging the durable artwork as object and severing other related forms of representative display culture, such as dance.

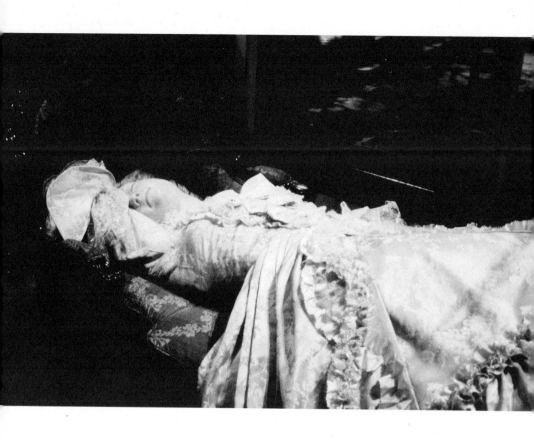

Sleeping Beauty, ca. 1765, is the oldest figure on display
at Madame Tussaud's museum in London.

Marina Warner

WAXWORKS AND WONDERLANDS

The eyes are wide. They cannot address
a helplessness, which has lingered in
the airless peace of each glass case:
To have survived. To have been stronger than
a moment. To be the hostages ignorance
takes from time and ornament from destiny. Both.
To be the present of the past. To infer the difference.
With a terrible stare. But not feel it. And not know it.
—Eavan Boland, "The Doll's Museum"

The oldest surviving waxwork in Madame Tussaud's museum in London is the Sleeping Beauty. She is a life-size sculpture of a small woman reclining in a pose often referred to as abandoned, for it suggests either that the subject sleeps alone, or that she is entirely trusting of any chance beholder. Her face is hard to see, unless one goes around her to look at her upside down — and then the upturned angle offers her throat and breast (in French, *gorge* means both) to the spectator's attention before anything else. This is indeed the most spectacular aspect of her: her breast rises and falls with her breathing.

She had a clockwork mechanism until the turn of the century, when she was electrified. She is lying on a couch, fully dressed in day clothes, and has kept her shoes on; her hair is now ringletted, a style for presenting oneself in public, but in a previous version it was loosened, as if at bedtime. The caption states that she was modeled by Philippe Curtius, Madame Tussaud's uncle, in 1765, and that she's a portrait of Comtesse du Barry, the mistress of Louis XV.[1]

Ten years ago, Sleeping Beauty was the centerpiece of a much more elaborate pageant, devised by the stage designer Julia Trevelyan Oman: she lay under a canopy in a four-poster bed, with several attendant observers, all in wax, emphasizing her 200-year role in the museum spectacle. A Victorian gentleman and lady were portrayed gazing at her, while at the foot of the bed, her page, an eighteenth-century "blackamoor," kept vigil. She has always been strategically placed in the arrangement of the museum: formerly the centerpiece of the entire room of celebrities, today, significantly, in a gazebo of her own at the junction of the new "Garden Party," a display featuring current stars of screen and stadium strolling together— a kind of curtain raiser before the tour takes visitors into the past.

In her book *Sexual Visions*, Ludmilla Jordanova analyzed the gendered politics of knowledge evinced by such supine, passive, sadistically exposed, and scrutinized forms as wax models of female bodies.[2] The waxwork image of the sleeping woman will be developed further here, as a figure in contemporary popular entertainment, as a dreamer and vehicle for communal dreams, aroused and shared in public, and, finally, as a site of and stimulus for wonder.

Philippe Curtius, who modeled Tussaud's Sleeping Beauty, was a Swiss physician and he first took up wax sculpture as a pastime. But he was so successful at it that he abandoned medicine and became a professional artist instead. He was patronized by a varied clientele, whose portraits he made. His original French patron, the Prince de Conti, invited him to Paris in 1766; later his subjects included freethinkers and radicals like Jacques-Louis David, Marat, and Robespierre, who gathered at his table. When Curtius went to Paris, he took his sister with him, and her six-year-old daughter Marie Gresholtz, whom he had cared for since her father had died before she was born. He soon apprenticed Marie, the future Madame Tussaud, in his studio, where he began teaching her his art of waxworks, then called with a flourish of science and learning, ceroplastics.

Curtius was also one of the earliest entrepreneurs in the business of commercial, popular visual display. In 1770, he opened the first of two *Wunderkammer* to the public, Le Cabinet de Cire, which exhibited contemporary celebrities in the Palais Royal. It included a life-size death effigy of Voltaire in the guise of the dying Socrates—an example of the strategy discussed by Jordanova of acquiring value by imitating the past. This cabinet was soon followed by another on the Boulevard du Temple, which included a large tableau of the Royal Family dining in public at Versailles after Sunday Mass, as was their custom. An engraving of the period shows how the waxwork busts were arranged on shelves around the scene, a library style of presentation that the Madame Tussaud museum curators continue to favor today. If you couldn't take the coach to Versailles to see them in person, you could enjoy that same sight in effigy. Curtius also immortalized more exclusive special occasions: for example, an Orientalist tableau showed Indian envoys received with full pomp at court. And in 1783 he added the Caverne des Grands Voleurs, a prototype of the Chamber of Horrors, with recreations of the scene of the crime, and portraits of famous criminals.

Marie Gresholtz was first commanded to Versailles as an attendant for the King's sister, Madame Elisabeth; there she made wax flowers and medallion profiles from life—ladylike pursuits at court. But when the Revolution started, she returned to the metropolis. Her uncle and guardian Curtius had connections with the Jacobins, which developed into enthusiasm: he took part in the storming of the Bastille, it seems, for he later signed documents adding after his name, *Vainqueur de la Bastille*.

The family skills in wax were much in demand from the revolutionaries. Two days before the fall of the Bastille, when Philippe d'Orléans and Necker fell from power, there was an immediate protest in the streets of Paris at the removal of these popular champions, and one of the focuses of the riot was Curtius's wax cabinet: the busts of the two heroes were seized, veiled in mourning crêpe, and paraded through the streets by the angry crowd. The demonstration met a detachment of soldiers who set upon the wax effigies and their defenders. There were one or two casualties—the very first of the revolution—including Necker's portrait.

The outburst seems to have been spontaneous: the waxen portrait busts of the heroes were treated by the crowd in exactly the same way as reliquary busts or cult statues of thaumaturgic saints are carried in effigy on their feast days to stations through the local town and countryside. It is the hope of the faithful that by contact or sight the energy of the statues' sanctity and their holy power will be renewed and flow through the place that claims their protection. Later Jacobin pageantry and ceremonial—such as the spectacular public *Fêtes de la Liberté, de la Raison*, and so forth—consciously adapted the Catholic church's brilliant strategy of crowd control to mobilize a new faith—the revolution. Curtius's waxworks were a novel medium for the relation between politics and imagery, that is, between money, the people, and representation.

The French Royal Family, modeled by Madame Tussaud, includes *Madame Royale*,
the Duchesse d'Angoulême, daughter of Louis XVI;
The Dauphin, titular King of France from 1793 and second son of Louis XVI;
Louis XVI, guillotined in 1793; and *Marie Antoinette*, daughter of
the Holy Roman Emperor Francis I and wife of Louis XVI, executed in 1793.

The connection between political movement and image was soon tight-
ened by design. The Jacobins' feeling for crowd entertainment inspired
the National Assembly to commission Madame Tussaud; at the request of the
artist David, she took a death mask from Marat's corpse immediately after
Charlotte Corday had murdered him. "I was ordered to come at once," she
is reported to have said, "and to take with me what appliances I needed to
make an impression of his features. The cadaverous aspect of the fiend made
me feel desperately ill, but they stood over me and forced me to perform
the task...." This passage appears, it should be noted, in the biography by
Madame Tussaud's respectable *English* grandson, well established in anti-
revolutionary England.[3] For, however cadaverous Marat might have been

moments after death, however desperately ill Madame Tussaud felt, she continued her unusual task throughout the Terror of making death masks of its victims.[4] Many waxen aristocrats and former revolutionary favorites, as well as Charlotte Corday, have been lost over the years of museum tours and accidents—such as a bad fire in 1925. However, Tussaud's original portraits of the King and Queen, made when they were still alive, are still on view in the museum.

The descendants of Madame Tussaud in England took pains to disinfect her of any revolutionary sympathies. Indeed, the waxworks were presented as exemplary and horrifying testimonials to the atrocities of the French. They toured the country from 1802 until she established her permanent

Jean Paul Marat, 1743–93, modeled by Madame Tussaud from a death mask.

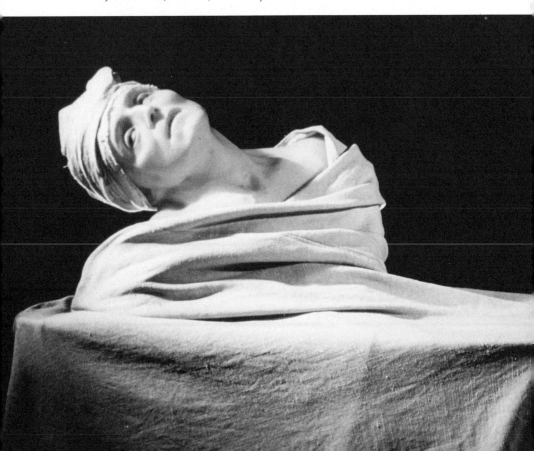

show in 1833 in the Bazaar, Portman Square, near the museum's present site on Baker Street in London. Tussaud herself covered her tracks well, and nothing at all is known of her attitudes or political views before the end of her life, when her pious and sentimental memoirs were ghosted.

Curtius and his niece incorporated the death mask of Marat in a valedictory tableau, showing Marat in his bath. It was opened to the public soon after the murder to scenes of great commotion, pity, and lamentations, with Robespierre adding his own personal accents of grief to the general clamor. It is still on view, in a third- or fourth-generation cast from the original, with a fresh sheet and newly painted wound. David, at the same time, was composing his key work of revolutionary piety, Marat as the dead Christ. The two portraits, his and the Curtius-Tussaud, interestingly echo each other, and underline the vital link between political imagery and religious iconography.[5] David's famous icon annexes Catholic ritual for the purposes of revolutionary, not religious, metaphysics; and the waxwork to this day recalls Passion Week effigies of the dead Christ on his bier, exposing his wounds.

Madame Tussaud's last self-portrait in wax, 1842.

Real beheaded villains were displayed on pikes as a warning during the Terror; the representation of severed heads or piteous corpses could work to exalt as well as to blame, to admonish the survivors through the likenesses of virtue (Marat) as well as vice (the King and Queen). Marie Tussaud received heads straight from the guillotine and modeled their portraits in wax. In some cases (Jean Baptiste Carrier, for example, who died in 1794), she depicted — in relief and of course in color — the blood splashing up their cheeks from their severed necks. As the revolution continued, she modeled more and more portraits of its victims — many of them Jacobins, like Robespierre, who had sat for her at the height of influence, as well as many noblemen and women whom she had known at court before the Revolution.

Though Madame Tussaud was summoned before the Committee for Public Safety on one occasion, she survived and left for England as soon as she safely could, arriving in London with a collection of waxworks and memorabilia in 1802. Curtius had died in 1794; she had married soon after, but the union did not last. She then took up her uncle's legacy on her own with a flair for timing and a grasp of the public appetite for the gruesome.

Her inheritance included three Sleeping Beauties, all of them victims of the guillotine from the gilded court society: the Princesse de Lamballe, Madame du Barry, and Madame de Saint Amaranthe.[6] These reclining figures were secular tomb effigies. Their relaxed, even languorous sleep — representing a wishful fiction about death — would lead to the familiar Victorian aesthetic confusion of erotic femininity and narcotic catalepsy. Madame du Barry is the only "Beauty" who had sat in life for her portrait. At the age of 22, she was modeled by Curtius, thirty years before her death. As for the other two reclining figures, Curtius or his niece had modeled their likenesses from their severed heads. A contemporary, who claimed to be an eyewitness, described how deftly Curtius rearranged Madame de Saint Amaranthe's rictus with finger and thumb in the Cemetery of La Madeleine. She was one of the few victims who protested violently at her death. "He made up the face with a posthumous smile, rendered her beautiful and charming."[7] He then poured a layer of wax straight onto the turf at the side of the grave, and rolled the severed head in it to take an impression of her features.

By the time the earliest catalogues of Madame Tussaud's were drawn up, only one of the three reclining figures survived; she is our present focus. In order to keep the gory toll of the Terror before the eyes of the public, this Sleeping Beauty was provided with a different, spine-chilling idealized story. She was reidentified with unabashed, and highly inventive, royalist loyalty:

Taken from life, a few months before her execution. Madame Saint Amaranthe was the widow of a Lieutenant-colonel of the body-guard of Louis XVI, who was killed in the attack of the Tuileries on August 10, 1792. She was one of the most lovely women in France, and Robespierre endeavoured to persuade her to become his mistress; but being as virtuous as she was beautiful, she rejected his solicitations with indignation. Robespierre, who never wanted a pretext for destroying anyone who had given him offence, brought Mme. St. Amaranthe before the Revolutionary Tribunal, and at the age of twenty-two, this victim to virtue was hurried into eternity.[8]

In Madame Tussaud's own self-portrait, Madame Saint Amaranthe, victim to virtue, lay on a couch while Tussaud stood at the head of it in poke bonnet and specs, resembling a little old loving governess, either watching over one of Freud's hysterical patients, or perhaps praying for the intercession of a powerful saint. In this tableau, the thread connecting waxworks and death, religious wonder and the modern idea of the hysterical woman, begins to unravel.

*   *   *

Waxworks exude the spirit of death and life equally. In the embalmer's art of the dead and the verisimilitude of Tussaud's popular art, both morbidity and the promise of immortality coexist. These different but related approaches to wax find their origins, as will be seen, in the same place: the reliquaries of Christianity.

Wax belongs in the embalmer's pharmacopoeia; working with wax is a forensic skill. Waxen artifacts, even when removed from the clinical ground of their origin and their medical uses are no longer apparent, retain their challenge to the stuff of life, their antithetical connection with bodies and embodiment. Wax has been used, for instance, for ex-voto plaques showing limbs and organs from Neolithic times to the present day; a shrine to a goddess in Cyprus yielded figurines with accompanying miniatures of breasts and bones to encourage her to help or to give thanks for help received.[9] In Sicily and Bavaria, two Catholic strongholds, it is still possible to buy wax pendants of breasts, lungs, or eyes, to offer at the shrines of saints—

say, Lucy, the patron saint of eyesight. (Oddly enough, the present museum of Madame Tussaud has not forgotten the antecedents of the trade, and the limbs and heads of former heroes in the pantheon are displayed in the workshop section of the tour, like so many ex-votos and relics.)

Wax preserves by sealing matter from air, so the very substance can be understood to bring about imperishability, to stall the passage of time, and prevent its marks. Denis Diderot, in one of his earliest disquisitions on art, *L' Histoire et le secret de la peinture en cire*, singled out the wax medium of encaustic for praise because it partook of eternity; describing how classical sculptors covered their sculptures in a layer of painted wax, he was moved to a telling use of somatic imagery: "The ancients thus made for their statues an epidermis of wax with which they countered the damage of air. Every year we regularly tear the skin from our statues with sponges laden with a hard gritty liquid. On the days of that cruel operation I flee the Tuileries Gardens, just as one leaves a public place on the day of an execution."[10] Ten years before Curtius made his Sleeping Beauty, Diderot was binding living flesh and statues together through the metaphor of a waxen epidermis, and, significantly, introducing a simile that invokes summary death.

Wax is also a material like alabaster, which holds the light within itself, rather than deflecting it, and it has in consequence a natural, glistening surface as well as an inner glow, as if alive. (One of the peculiarities of the stuff is that it cannot be photographed to resemble its appearance to the naked eye with a flash because the light doesn't bounce off the waxy surface but soaks into it.) Thus its preserving properties and inner luminosity symbolically challenge the corruption of the flesh and seem to overcome death. The affinities of its surface appearance with skin, wax's especially fair, glistening, slightly moist condition, lent it to the simulation of flesh—sometimes even in erotica. Indeed, Curtius furnished private clients with curiosities of this kind.

Wax has been used literally as a stamp of authenticity since the beginning of written documents, as the medium used for sealing, since when it sets, it sets hard and can only be broken, thus revealing tampering. Wax creates a relationship to truth for the viewer, and can be mobilized to fortify conviction as well as faith.

The bodies of saints, miraculously preserved with wax, exemplify this faith. Incorrupt after death in honor of their spiritual wholeness, "immaculate," meaning unmarked literally and metaphorically, they can be seen in many Catholic churches, in their *urna* or casket. Santa Fina, who died in San Gimignano in 1253 at the age of fifteen, is brought out twice a year in procession. Santa Vittoria, a virgin martyr, preserved in wax in her glass coffin, is in full view in Santa Maria della Vittoria, Rome, in the same church as Bernini's *Ecstasy of Saint Teresa*. Bernadette Soubirous, the visionary of Lourdes, reputed to be incorrupt, can be seen embalmed in her nun's habit in the convent at Nevers, where she died in 1879. The incorruptibility of the flesh betokens the unbesmirched soul of these saints.

But waxworks are not identical with reliquaries. Unlike the urn of Catholic devotion, reliquaries do not reassemble corporeal remnants, only attributes (clothes and possessions); they are imitations of bodies, simulacra, and to do this most effectively, they borrowed methods from scientific practice: in the waxwork of the Age of Enlightenment, reason meets the marvelous to produce a convincing representation of the human body and individual personality.

It is difficult to find good photographs of predecessors of Snow White in their glass coffins because they are truly sacred relics, still venerated, beyond blasphemous handling and investigation. According to the beliefs that invest them with this numen, they are furthermore natural wonders, bodies not arrested, but suspended in time with wax. Hence, they are defined not as *objets d'art* but as historical individuals. These effigies are missing from art history books, and even from the most scholarly accounts of the history of wax.

Madame Tussaud, however, fully understood the effect of relics; in this, too, she was something of a pioneer, pursuing the humblest objects of her heroic cast of dummies with a modern fan's enthusiasm. She bought the blade of the original guillotine, or so it's averred, from the executioner himself, who was glad of a penny or two now that trade had slowed. She acquired Napoleon's coach from Waterloo and his cloak from Marengo, and, with various other articles, these were arranged in "The Shrine," or "Golden Chamber," of the "Relics of the Emperor Napoleon," admission sixpence.

The embalmer's art drives toward simulating life; the remains should be a living likeness so that the onlooker exclaims in wonder at the skill. The Liverpool *Kaleidoscope* was very struck by wax modeling's powers when the exhibition toured there around 1820, and invoked the scene in *The Winter's Tale* when Hermione is unveiled by Paulina as if she were a statue: "Would you not deem it breath'd? And that those veins Did verily bear blood?" To which the reply comes, from one onlooker: "Masterly done: The very life seems warm upon her lip."[11]

The illusion produces wonder, and wonder, as Stephen Greenblatt has argued in the context of medieval and Renaissance travelers, acts to define self. Wonder implies inquiry into the realms of the unknown—a going forward—and it also implies awe—a falling back. Both in the propulsive energy of inquiry and the state of arrest of the latter, the "I" of the humanist self finds a means of knowing itself; this self establishes ownership and distinctiveness by recognizing both the similarities and the boundary of difference between itself and the object of wonder. Wonder is composed of mixed feelings: "When we wonder," writes Greenblatt, "we do not yet know if we love or hate the object at which we are marvelling; we do not know if we should embrace it or flee from it." He quotes Descartes's view that "Wonder has no opposite and is the first of the passions."[12]

Waxworks reproduce horrors and marvels, villains and heroes, and induce the dual shiver of wonder; they familiarize the spectator with their subjects, and they mark a difference between the two. The beholder possesses life in all its mysterious fullness. As living likenesses, who, unlike Hermione, cannot cross the river between the quick and the dead, waxworks function as memento moris, teaching the meaning of life, the difference between life and death. The simulacrum quests for authenticity.

The first portrait waxworks in the seventeenth and eighteenth century reproduced hair and clothing and eyes in painted wax, constituting a variation on the finest medalist's art. The simulacrum makes a virtue of its honesty. But it does so by duplicitous, sorcerer's methods. For, in order to create the illusion of being what it is, a waxwork has to resort to material equivalents, to the actual matter from which the original itself was composed. Thus, although glass eyes, taken over from optical science, were introduced at the beginning of the nineteenth century in Vienna,[13] by the time of Curtius and Tussaud, organic substances were preferred on the whole, to anything counterfeit or illusory.

Waxwork makers began to incorporate the subject's own hair, as in a saint's effigy, as well as articles of dress that had belonged to their subjects. Madame Tussaud's grandson even attributes the idea to no less a personage than Robespierre, who volunteered, he writes, to give his portraitist a suitable outfit from his own wardrobe to clothe his waxwork. Whether or not Robespierre is behind the present-day brouhaha about which dress Princess Diana should donate to the museum or that of Michael Jackson's jeans, using authentic clothing is a practice which has remained central to the impact of overall authenticity. Again, religious cult was the earlier context where artists strove for this fullness of naturalism, with actual hair, clothes, lace, ribbons, and jewels.[14]

An important line to draw between fine art and religious imagery — Tussaud's art is somewhere in between — distinguishes spectators from participants; a painting or fresco is used as an object of contemplation, a stimulus to prayer, a door to mysteries, but it does not invite handling, stroking, combing, adorning, robing, disrobing, touching, and kissing, as relics do. An icon that is the object of a cult, or any thaumaturgic image becomes part of a process, is treated like a doll, as the principal of a cast of *dramatis personae* in an unfolding game of make-believe.

Figures of the Christ child, for instance, made in wax, were and still are introduced into their decorated cribs on Christmas Day traditionally in Germany and Italy; this form of pious play-acting, inspired by Saint Francis's own practice in the thirteenth century, continues to be performed in many Catholic family homes on Christmas Eve as a domestic coda to midnight mass. In a highly uncommon cult of a baby girl, the Augustinian monks at Monte Oliveto Maggiore in Italy have reversed the sexes of this sacred game of pretend in their worshipping cult of La Santissima Bambina. It is not the Christ child, but Mary as an infant. On the feast day of her nativity, her waxen image is taken from a glass case on the altar, and processed by the all male, celibate community through the grounds of the monastery before she is returned to her shrine with perhaps a little more paint and a few more jewels.

The authenticity of the paraphernalia, its nonmetaphorical state, lends authority and truth to an image, bringing it back to the plane of the actual and the living. Devotion to the holy child inspired different costumes for different aspects of his power. He appears, for example, as the Good Shepherd in an eighteenth-century wax figure from Bavaria. The Christ child of the Santa Maria in Ara Caeli, Rome, worshipped since the fifteenth century, is entirely swaddled in gold and gems. In Seville, la Macarena, belonging to one of the most ardent cults of the Madonna in the world, is carried aloft by a rapturous crowd every year on her feast day. She has real eyelashes implanted and glass teardrops—as well as a finely modeled expression of grief. The importance of the icon's dress, not only as a precious offering to the divinity, but as a stamp of her actual and immediate presence, is revealed in the holy pictures that are on sale. They are themselves textured and encrusted, to give palpable, tactile substance to the two dimensional semblance, expressing the virtuality of the Madonna's power in real glitter glued to the surface and real thread stitched to clothes, crown, and halo.

The use of color in statuary, like the addition of proper matter functioning as itself, degraded the artifact to the lower echelons of art, according to the philosophy current in nineteenth-century England and Scotland. Henry Weekes, a Royal Academician, developed a theory of color and its moral worth in his *Lectures on Art* in 1880, inspired by John Gibson's *Tinted Venus*, a neoclassical nude with slightly enhanced complexion. Gibson's attempt at realism had caused a scandal. Weekes admitted that the Greeks had painted their sculpture in the brightest colors, as Diderot had pointed out, and he gave the reason for it: "Their colossal colored statues stood or sat in the midst of the temples....There was a crowd of ignorant devotees to be impressed with wonder, to be made to conceive a real presence, and to feel awe at its power..."[15] Weekes would just about countenance colored surfaces in the Greek past, but he came out strongly for colorlessness in the present:

> That a too literal rendering of Nature renders a work of Sculpture common-
> place, if not still more offensive, I need not urge to you....The absence of
> Colour in a statue is, in short, one of the peculiarities that remove it so
> entirely from common Nature that the most vulgarly constituted mind may
> contemplate it without its causing any feeling of a sensuous kind.[16]

He thus banished from the canon of high art the whole Catholic effort to awaken exactly those sensuous feelings. Wax, unabashedly colored, remained deeply associated, however, in Victorian times, with an important aspect of morality: the acceptance of death. In spite of its powers to seal and preserve, wax is a deliquescent substance, and while it does not decay, it can melt. It thus offered a metaphor for the deliquescence of flesh. Wax implies change, and in the form of a candle, has symbolized the transitoriness of life since the invention of candlelight in images of *vanitas*;[17] or in the related iconography of penitence, as adapted in Georges de la Tour's *Wrightsman Magdalen* with its contemplation of the vanity of earthly life.[18]

A late seventeenth-century wax diorama, the Sicilian Giulio Gaetano Zumbo's *La Corruzione dei corpi*, which Ludmilla Jordanova reproduced and discussed in *Sexual Visions*, meditates with swooning morbidity on the triumph of death; the very medium of wax implied mortality. Zumbo is typical of early wax sculptors, not only because he indulged a taste for queasy Catholic symbolism, but because—recalling Sleeping Beauty and Madame Tussaud— he worked in Italy and France as an anatomical model maker.

In Bologna and Florence, medical museums still display the remarkable medical wax figurines made in the seventeenth and eighteenth centuries for the study of the body and its organs. A close link exists between anatomical mannequins made of wax and theme-park figures like the Sleeping Beauty. Curtius, remember, had started life as a physician, and originally modeled in wax for his students.[19] Waxwork makers in the medium's secular history, making commemorative portraiture or edifying monuments, were following in the immediate footsteps of forensic science, even while obeying broad principles of sacred representation. Paradoxically, the more scientific the approach, the deeper the marvelous character of the work.

As Jordanova has observed, the outer bodies of female subjects in medical displays were presented in the language of erotic art. These wax women were laid on velvet cushions, bedecked with jewels, and recognized, from their langorous poses, as "Venuses." Their secondary sexual characteristics were stressed; their abdomens were revealed and interiors opened up to show the archaeology of innards in removable parts. Jordanova makes the acute point that anatomical models of male bodies are presented standing up, their genitals not usually emphasized or dissected. The men serve to illustrate bodily functions such as the circulation of blood or the apparatus of muscles, which correspond to the supposedly manly qualities of strength and reason; whereas the women, those recumbent, sleeping

Venuses, document the nervous systems—affect and eros.

The Tussaud Sleeping Beauty bears an uneasy affinity with certain so-called Venuses of scientific art.[20] The "Little Venus" in Bologna was made by the eighteenth-century ceroplast Clemente Susini, who modeled her with a five-month-old fetus in her womb, adding hair and pearls to her outer form. Indeed, one wonders whether the alleged Madame du Barry did not begin life as a medical model, and her body cavity, where the clockwork was placed, did not once hold replica organs.

*   *   *

Madame Tussaud's museum is one of the most popular attractions in Britain, with over two million visitors a year. The Sleeping Beauty is one of the rare figures of fantasy in the current pantheon at Madame Tussaud's; Just William, from Richmal Crompton's books, Batman, and Edna Everage as impersonated by the drag queen Barry Humphries are likewise fictions of the imagination. But they are few and far between. In the past, many more tableaux were inspired by nursery rhymes, folklore, children's books, and fairy tales. As the museum's public has grown older and more international, these fantastical waxwork dioramas have been given new homes in children's hospitals.

Today's museum characters evoke a powerful, complex wonder in visitors, closer to Christian relics and ritual than to folklore. The sense of involvement with a simulacrum, a wax figure, overrides its actual fakery. Today almost all museum characters are real, historical individuals of world-wide fame—athletes, politicians, monarchs, artists—and fantasy flowers in the relation of the public to them, not in their very identities. The fantasy is stimulated by the public's proximity to the stars, by the possibility of touching or being photographed with them. The first displays of the waxworks placed them all on daises; now the royal family stands on a dais, cordoned off, and a few stars, like Madonna in her conical bra, or Joan Collins coming down a monumental showbiz staircase, are held at a distance. Otherwise the figures stand at ground level, as if mingling with the crowd. Photography is encouraged: the illusion of bringing the commoners up to the level of the mighty and the mythical.

In his essay, "Some Reflections on Dolls," Rainer Maria Rilke describes the

Joan Collins with her wax portrait at Madame Tussaud's, London.

way imagination stirs to fill a void, to stop the love for a doll from expiring on the blank slate of its response. He writes,

> I know, I know it was necessary for us to have things of this kind, which acquiesced in everything. The simplest love relationships were quite beyond our comprehension, we could not possibly have lived and had dealings with a person who was something; at most, we could only have entered into such a person and have lost ourselves there. With the doll we were forced to assert ourselves, for, had we surrendered ourselves to it, there would then have been no one there at all...it was so abysmally devoid of phantasy, that our imagination became inexaustible in dealing with it....[21]

In waxworks, something similar occurs. The subjects are drained of semantic and narrative particularity while simultaneously crammed and

Dalai Lama with his wax portrait at Madame Tussaud's London.

A group of American presidents at Madame Tussaud's, London.

heaped with visual and tactile specificities. Story cedes to spectacle in this kind of show, on purpose, encouraging the mythic imagination of the visitor to make up for the semantic emptiness. Madame Tussaud's effaces differences of time and place. Everyone is present simultaneously; history plays like a tape on a loop, and geography no longer conjures a mental sphere but something more like a record, with adjacent grooves from which one can skip as easily as a needle: Teng Tsiao Ping sits next to Juan Carlos of Spain, and various American presidents are taking a group bow. The displays offer false narratives, not fictions; the dominant structure to which they belong is the photo call. Valhalla has become an eternal photo opportunity.

The power of these fabrications is literally lethal, in the etymological sense that they lead to forgetfulness (and Lethe was, appropriately enough, one of the rivers of the classical underworld). The case of Sleeping Beauty illustrates forgetfulness well: her role as the fairytale character has taken precedence over her possible historical connection with a king's mistress under the ancien régime. The slippage of Madame du Barry from history (however putative) into fairytale purifies her story: a notorious courtesan

Benjamin Franklin, Madame Tussaud's, London.

becomes the virtuous nubile nymph of the French fairytale, first written down for children by Perrault in 1697. She lies in timeless defiance; it is interesting that visitors hang back from her with more anxiety than other standing waxworks— she is not only uncanny, but also intimate, and the pressure on desire she exercises invites a closed door and a moment or two alone.

The sculpture's only impact is erotic, and specifically erotic with a necrophiliac edge, but this does not encompass all the feelings it now provokes whatever its origins in the murky convergence of eighteenth-century science and libertinism. The museum, by taking her out of bed and laying her down on a couch, has interestingly shifted emphasis away from the fairytale and the awaited prince. Placed where it is today, the waxwork illustrates a growing theme in contemporary iconography, which invests the image of a dreaming woman with hope—not of possessing her, but of identifying with her, of becoming her. She is available for psychic entry. The spectator looks at the Sleeping Beauty, and while the expectation of a prince's kiss interrupting the eternity of sleep dominates the familiar plot, the museum spectacle draws the spectator into wonder about her inner life. She solicits imitation, not assault.

For the illusion of her permanent sleep denies the reality of death; with her rising and falling breast, the Sleeping Beauty functions as an anti-memento mori, positioned in the antechamber of the Great Hall where the images of great men (and a few women) appear also to have conquered death through glory and fame. Sleep is a refuge from death, a deception that can cheat death itself. The Sleeping Beauty's false flesh offers a lens to the visitors through which to look at the waxworks to come. While these serve as eerie reminders that all flesh is grass (unless it be wax) and that even the most accurate and lifelike simulacra can never possess vitality itself, the Sleeping Beauty promises immortality as the suspension of time.

The Sleeping Beauty waxwork is a vehicle of fantasy into which visitors step in order to travel to wonderland. Hypnos, the god of Sleep, was depicted winged; he offered imaginative flight; his presence evoked a journey to an elsewhere beyond the actual moment and place. The Tussaud sculpture was made during the rise of interest in states of unconsciousness, in suspended animation, that is neither sleep nor waking nor indeed coma; this was hypnosis. The theorist, magician, and healer Anton Mesmer enjoyed a huge social esteem at the time, and when a commission was set up to investigate his theory and practice of Mesmerism, no less a figure than Benjamin Franklin chaired it. The commission reported in 1784 that there was no foundation to Mesmer's theory of animal magnetism, but it allowed that therapeutic benefits could be achieved through the powers of the imagination. Franklin was one of the many people who sat for Curtius, and though a small crossing of the ways must not be argued as a greater philosophical convergence, it would be interesting to explore the evolving ideas about sleep and dream states in the period when waxworks became popular, and perhaps Franklin and Curtius might have influenced each other.

The hypnotists who came after Mesmer in the late nineteenth century took over the Greek word for sleep because they perceived a similarity between sleep and the form of suspended consciousness that their patients experienced. The mind lowered its guard, became both suggestible and guileless; sensitivity to pain decreased or even disappeared.[22] Saint Bernadette, who later becomes in death a waxen effigy of a sleeping beauty, was scientifically tested during her visions in 1854; she was pricked with pins and burned with candles and felt no hurt—to the wonder of the attendant crowd. Lewis Carroll, in his preface to Sylvie and Bruno Concluded, defines three states of the psyche: in the first, ordinary state, there is no awareness of wonders like fairies at all; in the second, "eerie" state, the subject is conscious but simultaneously aware of an enchanted dimension. But, in the third state, a form of trace, the sleeping subject can travel out of the body to experience fairyland in full. The wonderland Carroll invented for Alice wasn't a mere fancy to him.[23]

One of the most popular novels of the 1890's, George du Maurier's Trilby, dramatized the suggestible dream state of the heroine when hypnotized by Svengali, and her access, in that state, to higher powers of expression through her song. Somnambulism figures vividly in the stories of Edgar Allan Poe and in films inspired by them; The Cabinet of Dr. Caligari (1919) focuses on murders committed by a sleepwalker, only to reveal that a hysterical female subject who lives in a dreamlike state has produced the whole drama out of her own hypnotic fantasy.

These cognate states of the entranced subject share something with a visitor's receptivity to the fantasy of theme parks, with wonders both pleasant

Animal Magnetism: The Operator Putting his Patient into a Crisis,
anonymous etching, 1794.

and unpleasant. The Surrealists used the work of men like Dr. Charcot, famous for his photographs of his hysterical patients, to explore the hypnotized state as a passage to the marvelous. The theme of hypnotic trance persists in contemporary culture where surrealism's influence flourishes so strongly: Eric Rohmer's film *The Marquise of O* translated Kleist's romance about honor and forgiveness to the screen, drawing on Sleeping Beauty's enchanted trance to represent the crisis at the heart of the story, which was the rape of the insensible Marquise by the protagonist. The state of suspension literally depicts the held breath of wonder and horror and dread, the state of knowing ultimate things—sexuality, death.

In all the various categories of effigy introduced here, the figures are usually of females or children and sometimes both combined. It would be absurd to suggest, however, that all cult statues, all of Mesmer's clients, all hysterical mediums and patients were or are female. But as Franklin's commission on Mesmer noted, women were in the majority among his following, as they were among Freud's and Josef Breuer's pioneering patients and analysands. Josephine Hilgard, in a study of hypnosis, has linked susceptibility to hypnotism with the imaginative capacity to lose oneself in a book, film, or soap opera, and has drawn attention to the mingling of fantasy and reality in the subject of hypnosis, the readiness to play pretend and make-believe games, to be malleable, impressionable, and ductile, like wax. Hilgard connects the hypnotic condition to the state of childhood, which raises the point of how intertwined the perceptions and definitions are of women and children.[24] The virgin martyrs—from Santa Fina to Bernadette—are historically youthful, and their posthumous cults preserve them on the childlike threshold where death does not mark them.

In the image of Tussaud's Beauty, ancient religious wonder and modern science have been transformed into an amalgam of hypnotic magic and culturally defined womanhood; and all the elements of the Beauty coalesce in the idea of a girl's enviable, trancelike death. Through her femaleness and her youthful smallness, the Sleeping Beauty at Madame Tussaud's conveys with special aptness the liminal state of the virgin martyrs, which is, in a sense, the desired condition of the visitor to the theme park, regardless of his or her identity: a return to the imagined perceptions of childhood, an entranced floating out of range of all coordinates (as the French call names and addresses), a liminal openness to impression, like a proverbial woman buried in a romantic novel, like wax before the mold of the waxwork maker shapes it.

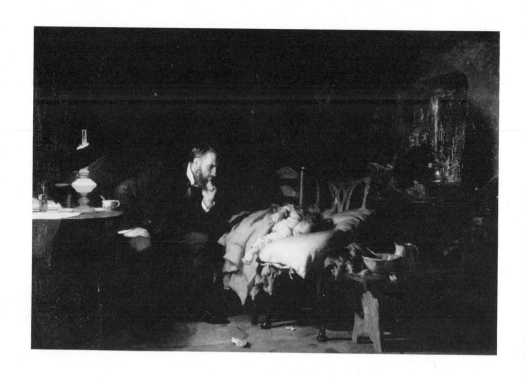

Sir Luke Fildes, *The Doctor*, 1891.

Ludmilla Jordanova

MEDICINE AND GENRES OF DISPLAY

The theme of display bears an important and complex relationship to medicine, but it does not always do so in expected ways. A probing of this relationship naturally leads to the issue of dissection, where the body is put on display often in a somewhat ritualized manner, ostensibly for the purpose of learning. Explanations that appeal to practicality are particularly common in studies of science and medicine, where claims about disseminating knowledge, communicating with students, and doing things in the easiest, cheapest, and most direct manner marginalize broadly defined aesthetic questions.

By the eighteenth century, many sumptuous books were available that recorded the results of dissections, and these became vehicles of display in their own right. Even if at this time dissections themselves increasingly were carried out behind closed doors, the audience for these books could not be controlled or vetted. The accuracy of such productions was certainly vaunted, as were their beauty and high technical quality — paper, drawing, engraving, and printing. *What* was displayed was rather elaborate; yes, it was the human body, its insides, and a detailed, specialist knowledge of body parts. The skill and connoisseurship of medical authors in selecting and working with artists, engravers, and printers were on display. Thus, patronage networks were on display — a point reinforced by the dedication pages in medical books of the period. At another level, a special kind of good faith was displayed, in that the validity of what was shown was propped up by mere assertion, since no other form of support was available. Hence, the authority of medical images was inevitably derived from claims that were fundamentally on moral ground, in that they rested on the honesty of the medical practioners, artists, engravers, and printers. In effect, a pledge was offered by the person who carried out the dissection. The author's name and reputation was at issue: "this is really what we saw, please accept it as true." It was for this reason that the other partners in the enterprise — the artists, the engravers, and printers — were so important; it was a tacit guarantee that they had altered nothing.

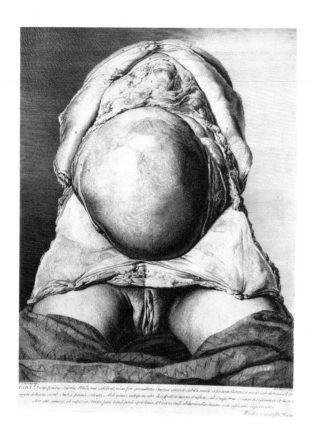

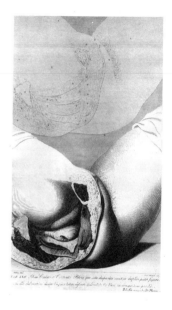

William Hunter, *Anatomia uteri humani gravidi* (*The Anatomy of the Human Gravid Uterus Exhibited in Figures*).
Published by J. Baskerville, Birmingham, 1774.

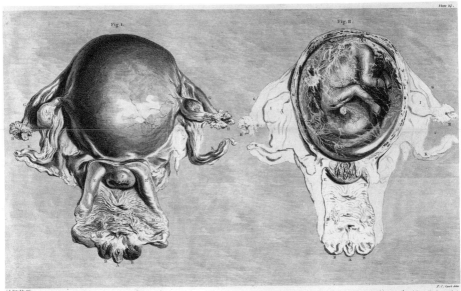

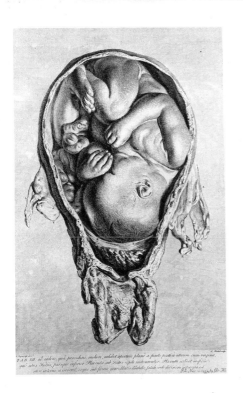

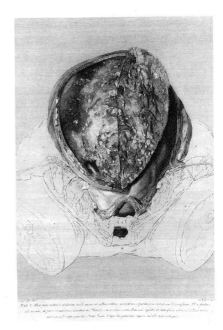

Thus, these conspicuously beautiful, illustrated medical books displayed both the trustworthiness of the authors and the epistemological quality of medicine. Medical practitioners were intensely concerned about the quality of their knowledge—what marks late nineteenth- and twentieth-century medicine is not so much a lessening of such concerns as the existence of a much wider range of techniques for defending the authority of medicine. The very nature of clinical practice, that is, of individuals looking and making fine visual discriminations, raises acute problems for the more public representation of medical knowledge, and, as a result, display of that knowledge presented particular challenges. But, much more than "knowledge" was necessarily on display. In the face of relentless critical scrutiny and merciless satire, eighteenth- and early nineteenth-century practitioners had to display their nonconformity to negative characteristics and stereotypes. This may sound tortuous, but it conveys an important theme in medicine: the drive to display the absence of those qualities associated with the quack, the charlatan, the empiric, and with the insecure, unreliable knowledge they deployed. The critical scrutiny of medicine and, above all, its clinical practice became more pressing as public expectations were altered about the prevention of illness and death. These expectations were widespread among the general public for the first time; of course, practitioners themselves did much to cultivate such expectations, but all too easily fell victim to them when they failed to prevent and cure serious illness. The constant criticism of medicine in the period can be read as a product of puzzlement, grief, and anger at medicine's failure to deliver the goods.

Doctors were well aware of their dilemma, and, in response to satire and threats from quacks, they sought ways to display their safeness in, for example, their gentlemanly attributes and appeals to science. They certainly deployed the expected routes for this display, and five key areas are relevant here. First, practitioners displayed their educational qualifications and their links with learned patrons or teachers. Second, they displayed their institutional affiliations with colleges and learned societies; some of these institutions exercised genuine power over the profession, and all attempted to exercise cultural control through the display of portraits and commemorative medals of their most famous men. Third, practitioners displayed their scientific knowledge, clinical expertise, and professional probity in periodical publications, which hardly existed before the eighteenth century and grew markedly in number during the mid-eighteenth century. Fourth, they displayed humanity and public spirit by participating in philanthropic activities, by making visible their concern for the health of less fortunate members of society. Finally, they displayed their social acceptability by participating in activities such as writing and collecting art—activities already a part of polite culture—and by participating in networks of people who already enjoyed societal status, for example by attending members of the court and aristocracy.

Other routes for displaying safeness and acquiring cultural power were also available. Physicians could invoke their classical heritage and display their classical learning. Medical men could celebrate the lives of practitioners as eminent men on the world historical stage through portraiture, eloges, obituary, editions of works, biographical dictionaries, and medical histories. Their publications, especially those that were collections or compilations, were used as vehicles of display. The deployment of the encyclopaedic mentality took many different forms—books, charts, maps, and statistical tables, as well as museums.

In the second half of the eighteenth century, the diverse activities of the brothers William and John Hunter beautifully illustrate the trends generally discussed here.

The first volume of the *London Medical Repository* (1814) contained a medical topography of London. Medical topography, which examined the relationships between a specific physical location and the experience of morbidity and mortality within it, was a popular genre during the late eighteenth and early nineteenth centuries. The impulses for this activity can be understood in three ways. First, they were a result of the encompassing environmentalist approach to health and disease—perhaps the dominant paradigm of the time. Second, these impulses were an expression of the passion for collecting medical data. This passion was not confined to practitioners but was part of a larger interest in what we now call demography—the study of the facts of life, birth, marriage, illness, and death, and the study of their relationship to the facts of nature and of society—in fact, the totality of factors that make up the environment, including the man-made. Third, they embodied the desire to have an all-encompassing, perhaps panoramic, vision-commanding assent. In producing a new kind of map, one that presented

London in terms of its medical features, the *Medical Repository* gave visual expression to a particular kind of display that represented a claim to power.

The collection of data was the basis for another major genre of medical display: bills of mortality (especially clear when publicly displayed). In the mid-eighteenth century, the reformer Jonas Hanway successfully argued that London parishes should be obliged to make public their rates of infant mortality. In effect, this was to shame them into taking better care of poor children—he assumed that simply displaying such information could be an instrument of change. Hanway himself was not a medical practitioner but a well-known, middle-class merchant philanthropist with an interest in patterns of health and well-being, especially among children. Perhaps he had an unusually well-developed sense of the power of displaying such data but medical practitioners shared his broader concerns.

Another significant example of medical display in the search for cultural power and social acceptability was portraiture. In the eighteenth century, a number of devices were used to convey the gravity of medicine, its respectability, and its aspiration to be a part of polite culture. The portraits of William and John Hunter by Allan Ramsay and Joshua Reynolds, although different in style, pose, and accoutrements, may be judged highly successful in their capacity to display illustrious medical figures in socially acceptable forms. By the early nineteenth century, the display of a small number of medical heroes was well-developed, with the result that a single master image such as Reynolds's portrait of John Hunter, spawned many derivatives, including a wide variety of print versions and a statue.

Surely a discussion of display implies, if only in the fantasies of displayers, an audience or a group of onlookers. It may be tempting to approach this in terms of public/private distinctions—"medical displays made public what once had been private"—these formulations simply do not work; they can all too easily assume an undifferentiated public constituting the main audience for scientific and medical displays. For example, medical advice books were a category of display that was of growing importance from the eighteenth century onward. These popular works might be seen as addressing a general public by broadcasting insights previously held in the "private" domain. Although they often contained information, usually about medicines, to which everyone would not necessarily have had access, their more important purposes were, first, to impose a medical framework on health and illness in everyday life, and second, to address the differences between social groups through their distinctive medical profiles. Eighteenth-century medical advice books were rather vitriolic, usually about specific class fractions—which ones depended on the author in question. They deliberately set groups against each other by using emotive vignettes of irresponsible behavior associated with specific groups, and then pointing to the larger social costs of such behavior. In these cases, although the interests of a larger collectivity was invoked, the display of medical knowledge and its moral-cum-political entailments was pointedly directed and worked precisely around the images people had of themselves and of each other. In this case, the display of medical authority implied *specific* audiences, even as the format, the advice book, suggested a wider readership.

It is likely that when practitioners wrote advice books, they were addressing their peers, whose approval they sought despite the fact that they were also competitors. In general, at least in the period discussed here and perhaps to a degree since then, the principal audience of medical display has been other practitioners. Certainly patients and potential patients can play the role of audience, but nonmedical audiences are often the cultural elite. The invocation of an audience of peers was even more prominent in the eighteenth and nineteenth centuries than it is today; to explain this we can refer to the idea of witnessing. Simon Schaffer and Steven Shapin, in their highly influential work *Leviathan and the Air Pump: Hobbes, Boyle, and the Experimental Life*, understand the origins of experimental science as an authoritative ideology in terms of a new stress on the importance of collective looking, of witnesses who vouch for occurrences, especially in a time when the self-consciously new experimental philosophy was establishing itself.[1] Because of the fragile status of natural knowledge in the seventeenth century, witnesses had to be carefully chosen. They could not be of low social status; they had to be educated. That is, they were to be the experimenter's peers.

Shapin and Schaffer are principally concerned with the second half of the seventeenth century. With Isaac Newton, the prestige of natural philosophy was assured by the early eighteenth century. Medical men certainly wanted to draw upon that prestige for their own purposes, but their practice possessed distinctive features that resisted the easy translation of witnessing from natural philosophy to medicine. The main techniques for assuring and displaying the quality of knowledge were difficult to arrange when overall medicine was not fully institutionalized and most practicing doctors worked alone. Indeed, it is revealing how often eighteenth-century medical periodicals appealed to these isolated men to send in their own first-hand observations as a way of advancing the field. Thus this form of publication became a surrogate for collective clinical and experimental activity. Without the witnessing of experimental natural philosophy, medical men were made more epistemologically vulnerable, unless they could appeal to what Shapin and Schaffer have called virtual witnessing, or the production of words and images that convey what happened so precisely that the reader or viewer was almost there.

The magnificent obstetric atlas produced by William Hunter in 1774 might be understood as an act of virtual witnessing, but it was unusual for the period. More typical perhaps were the medical periodicals, which were meant to counteract this medical vulnerability, first by displaying knowledge or detailed information to peers, not to the public at large, and second, by insisting on individual probity and professional correctness. It is hard to judge how successful medical periodicals were in their quest for medical authority, but the cultural energy they deployed is historically significant. Supposedly, reputations were being made, prowess was being displayed and judged, and, improvements and progress achieved. At stake here was the identity of medicine and its practitioners. Medical forms of display were ways of imagining medicine, of testing possibilities, of making claims and assertions. It follows that the audience was not, nor could it have been, the mass public, but instead it was made up of those who could read and interpret the displays, appreciate their significance, and, above all, act on the messages issued by them. This accounts for the marked growth of interest in medical biography over the eighteenth and nineteenth centuries. Representations of lives offered the chance for direct identification, satisfaction, comfort, and shaping of one's own life in response. Taken together, such representations provided a sense of security about what was, and to some extent still is, a fragile, unstable, and dangerous enterprise.

Display concerns what is hidden as much as what is revealed, for these are two sides of the same coin. What then did these types of medical displays conceal? First, faction and internal conflict were to be concealed. Medical unity was a desirable goal (or rather the appearance of it was), yet the *material* culture of medicine did virtually nothing to support such unity. At one level, then, display was a defense against splitting. Second, display concealed danger. Medicine was fraught with transgressive potential. In sexual terms, medicine is necessarily explicit, in a manner that cannot always be easily distinguished from pornography—and this was already true and recognized as such in the eighteenth century. More generally, medicine was associated and identified with disease

Anonymous, *Dr. William Hunter at a Confinement*, n.d.

and death. Doctors not only dealt with the dead and dying, but those who were cynical about medicine's claims could represent them as the agents of death. Third, display masked the processes of which medicine was composed, exhibiting instead its static products. It has no place for the uncertain, since uncertainty resists reification. In other words, display requires that the abstract and processual be translated into a visible and frozen form, easily seen and apprehended.

Understanding display as a way of making medicine simpler, more manageable, perhaps accounts for the appeal of bills of mortality, smallpox inoculation and vaccination, and studies of epidemics. Patterns of illness and medical responses to them took on more tangible, even quantifiable forms, which could indeed be put on display. *Cordons sanitaires* and quarantine arrangements, for example, could be appropriated for the purposes of medical display. Medical practitioners did not invent, at least not single-handedly, these systems for dealing with the spread of disease. But they did summon them as part of the rational man-management. Epidemics, the most dramatic threat to a population, hence offering the most dramatic opportunities for medical men were of central importance in the medical imaginary of the time. It is surely no coincidence that the most visually represented practitioner of the time was the inventor of the smallpox vaccination, Edward Jenner,

J. Thomas, *Portrait of William Hunter*
for Pettigrew's Medical Portrait Gallery, 1838–40.

whose achievements were so visually conspicuous. Jenner was represented not only as a hero in the fight against smallpox, but also as someone who helped people avoid the disfigurement associated with it.

It is obviously important to see how specific historical conditions inform genres of medical display. The sense of chaos in medicine was high during the late eighteenth and early nineteenth centuries; the conviction that medicine was in the process of becoming a (respectable) science was still fragile. It was difficult to display the fruits of medical knowledge directly (except in anatomical illustrations or, more dubiously, models), medical efficacy was the subject of relentless satire (the endless parading by practitioners of the very small number of instances where medicine did seem effective) — so, what remained? The answer was the men themselves; they were the vehicles through which medicine was embodied and displayed, hence the significance of portraiture, of the face as a sign of professional competence, and, as a further sign of the man, their signature, often reproduced under printed portraits.

The key to turning negative qualities (nonquack, for instance) into positive ones was the cultivation of conspicuous benevolence as a central part of the medical image. Benevolence entails giving rather than taking, controlling personal desire, and invoking the notion of universal humanity. By the early nineteenth century, the process of demonstrating medical benevolence was well underway, as practitioners were praised for their philanthropy. One striking example is the description by the historian of Royal College of Physicians in London of John Coakley Lettsom:

of his real merits as a practitioner, we know but little, but of his character as a philanthropist, it is impossible to speak too highly. The name of Lettsom was to be found associated with every project for the public good; he was on terms of friendship with most of the distinguished characters of the day, and from all parts of the kingdom, from the colonies, and America, he received most flattering proofs of the estimation he had excited.[2]

Lettsom (1744–1815) was well known as a Quaker philanthropist and prolific writer on medical good-works and medicine in general. As the author of *History of the Origin of Medicine* (1778), he conspicuously displayed his learning and wrote up medicine—his interest was in eminent persons, who had been, in his phrase, benefactors to the community; they redeemed the "victims of disease, pain, and misery," and they exercised a dignified and sacred function. Lettsom was showing off about the benevolence of medicine, writing against the grain of the evidence, to hold up medicine before other practitioners; his history originated in an oration to the Medical Society of London. His kind of display offered an idealized, desirable picture to his peers, while pretending he was only showing them a mirror. In praising him in the quotation above, the historian tells us not directly of his philanthropic deeds, but of the admiration he excited in others.

The important thing was to be *seen* doing good. We are reminded of the episode in *Les Liaisons dangereuses* when the rake Valmont acts philanthropically only to curry favor with the object of his desire, and is astonished to find it quite pleasurable.[3] Initially his motivation was display in a form readily understood at the time. The philanthropic claims of medical practitioners were, in somewhat fragile in that they made a living from private patients out of necessity. The cultural effort required to make the occupation hold the moral high ground was, and still is, considerable—as has become evident in medical defenses of new reproductive technologies. How the moral high ground is reached and then occupied has clearly changed markedly over the nineteenth and twentieth centuries. In the absence of national, state-endowed structures, practitioners in Britain and the United States were particularly vulnerable in the earlier period, hence the need for moral superiority, and the desire for cultural products that could act as permanent testimonies to the goodness of medicine and of its exponents became useful stabilizing

Still from *The White Angel*, 1936. Starring Kay Francis as Florence Nightingale.

factors. The big historical change is perhaps the use of the mass media to cultivate a sense of medical benevolence, with the result that professionals themselves no longer have to work so hard at it.

These shifts have taken place over long periods of time. They have had to counteract skepticism about the wonders of medicine—taking the form of satire and ridicule or political-cum-intellectual critiques. And stories of real-life medical heroism show no signs of abating in the twentieth century. In particular, types of display that tapped audience sentimentality were and still are especially effective. Child patients have a special role to play here, as they have since the eighteenth century, when they became accepted figures through which the collective vulnerability could be represented. One aspect of this role—benevolent medical attendant with vulnerable sick child—was consolidated by the late nineteenth century. A compelling example is Luke Fildes's canvas, *The Doctor*, which depicts the inside of a Cornish cottage. Images of sick children were hardly new, but previously they had not been used as vehicles of medical display. Here, in a condensed form, is the benevolent practitioner, and the fact that the scene it represents is implausible, serves to highlight the significance of the image: a well-dressed doctor sitting by the side of a sick child from a humble family. The poor found it hard to pay for medicines for their children, let alone home visits. Fildes could address a more general public because by the end of the nineteenth century, practitioners felt more secure in their constructed professional roles. They had convinced themselves of the lofty philanthropic calling they practiced, and were beginning to establish this as a general sentiment among the general public, whose idea of goodness they readily invoked. These are the historical preconditions of Fildes's canvas, which displays medical benevolence by disavowing any showiness.

Not only doctors, but nurses too learned techniques of display. Indeed, they were in more urgent need of it, given the absence of organized training, at least in Britain, until the mid-nineteenth century, and in the presence of vicious negative stereotypes and poor working conditions. In France, by contrast, where nursing had long been undertaken by nuns, there was a ready fund of religious imagery through which their occupation and its values could be displayed to the public, to doctors with whom they were in a sense in direct competition, and to their wartime employer, the government.

Moreover, nurses in general were impelled to display a benevolent image of a job that was becoming a profession in the nineteenth century, in order to encourage aspirant nurses of the right social background to identify with it. The Florence Nightingale Museum in St. Thomas's Hospital, London, is the direct product of these processes. The 1936 bio-picture about Nightingale developed sentimentalism into a high art, and includes scenes reminiscent of the Virgin Mary attending to the dying Christ. Nurses could identify with the image and feel themselves as the *mater dolorosa*. Patients, by the same token, could imagine themselves the recipients of such devoted tenderness.

These examples from popular culture are testimony to the success, not just over decades but over centuries, of sustained attempts to cultivate certain medical qualities, such as benevolence, to externalize them, so that they could assume an apparently independent life of their own, and then, once separate, be used to reinforce the original feeling. Here medical display gives shape to fantasies of power and authority, and actually helps mediate their acquisition. There is, of course, an elaborate history to this dynamic— a complex interplay between the labor processes of medicine, the identities of those who practice it, the views of medicine expressed in popular culture, and the media through which all these are represented.

The notion of display has a huge potential for understanding medicine over long periods of time. My old Penguin edition of Roget's *Thesaurus*— and Roget, after all, was a medical man—suggests three principal ranges of meaning for the word *display*: the first is how things look or appear; the second is exhibition, demonstration; and the third is ostentation, showing off. We can see all of these at work in the history of medicine, as well as the *strategic* blurring between them. The second two meanings suggest the artfulness of display, but the first indicates mere description by domains that have special claims to know how things look or appear. Medicine used many genres of display. In all cases, we need to ask how the resulting objects and texts participated in the processes of forming individual and collective identities, and in generating thereby a medical culture, which primarily served the needs of practitioners. It is characteristic of late nineteenth- and early twentieth-century cultural practices to refuse the separateness of earlier medical cultures and insist on the re- or decontextualization of forms of medical display. But these appropriations, as found for example in the Surrealist's interest in

"Marcus Welby, M.D." (ABC Television).

medicine have only been possible because medicine and medical practitioners no longer require the devices, especially the visual ones, mentioned here to assure them of power and authority, which are propped up by other means, not in the domain of visual culture. Indeed, now a popular culture of medical benevolence exists that usually is in stark contrast to the experience of the majority of patients. Patients who have been the recipients of spectacular medical successes, ironically, now have become the objects of display in their own right, as have the relatives, especially of heroic child patients. There have been vast shifts in modes of medical display—shifts with wide-ranging implications for contemporary visual culture.

Lynne Cohen, *Laboratory*, n.d.

Lisa Cartwright

GENDER ARTIFACTS: TECHNOLOGIES OF BODILY DISPLAY IN MEDICAL CULTURE

In recent years, artists, scholars, and cultural critics have focused increasingly on the display of the human body and its transformations in the high-tech medical culture of late Western capitalism. In 1993 there were few art venues in New York that did not mount at least one exhibition that dealt with this theme; few academic conferences were without panels devoted to bio-medical culture. Methodologically, this work has run the gamut from cautionary technophobia to euphoric technophilia. Why this frenzy around technological culture and its display of the body? An examination of the representation of the female body in the new medical imaging technologies might identify contradictory strategies of bodily reconfiguration both within medicine and in medical countercultures; these strategies attempt to mediate between, on the one hand, the distrust of high technology expressed by some cultural critics analyzing institutionalized fields such as medicine, and on the other hand the utopian embrace of new technologies as unproblematic tools of social transformation.

The latter position of embrace is exemplified in a 1992 *Computer Graphics World* article in which high-tech medical imaging displays are described as part of a revolutionary new field where "patients in advanced stages of disease are often the recipients of diagnostic and therapeutic technologies that are light years beyond the available procedures of ten, or even five, years ago."[1] Using superlatives like "revolutionary" and "explosive," this article celebrates the new imaging technologies as perhaps the most important breakthrough of this century. While it would certainly be a mistake to dismiss the importance of these technologies, it is also important to keep in mind that during the same period of their ascendancy there have been increasing disparities in access to them: predominantly white upper- and middle-class patients have access to private, technologically up-to-date, medical practices, while many communities rely on the underfunded, technologically retrograde public health-care system.

This situation suggests the need for intensified focus on the class, race, and gender politics of bodily regulation and surveillance demonstrated by these techniques. Rather than condemning new technologies, activist media producers, artists, and health-care advocates visibly and intensively engaged with the politics of medical treatment, health-care technology, and media culture during the same period of medical imaging's ascendancy. Through the work of groups, including AIDS Coalition to Unleash Power (ACT UP) and Women's Health Action Mobilization (WHAM!), there has been a vital revisioning of medical culture; this work has consistently foregrounded the centrality of visual media in medicine's cultural politics in the public sphere. The emergence of health-care media activism is a direct consequence of the fact that we are seeing the emergence of new imaging modalities at precisely the same time that we are experiencing major health crises locally and globally (including the resurgence of the tuberculosis epidemic, the deterioration of public hospital services and technology, and the dramatic polarization of private and public health care). These crises are generating some crucial transformations in medical cultures, as well as some interesting medical countercultures. Medical imaging technologies are, then, an emergent sphere of media politics whose images, techniques, and instruments are concurrently being critiqued and reconfigured by heterogeneous groups of "nonspecialist" imaging agents and activists. Medicine is a cultural field whose meanings are created not only by the elite managers of technoscientific laboratories and research centers, but also through the intervening forces of popular media forms and by media activist countercultures.

The simultaneous emergence of multiple optical techniques in the medical context has created an apparently monolithic new field in which only those with extensive training have access to medicine's specialized visual knowledge. In other words, the meaning of the highly technical and abstract images of our bodies produced in Computed Tomography (CT) and Positron Emission Tomography (PET) scans, sonograms, and magnetic resonance images (MRIs) appear to be totally inaccessible to those of us who are lay users, precisely because they function within cultural codes far removed from everyday forms like the photographic, the televisual, or the cinematic. These images can easily be decoded as compositions that metaphorically represent in familiar conventions the ostensible future of genetic technologies.

How do we begin to negotiate the relationship among more conventional biomedical representational forms and more abstract kinds of systems?

Through its complicated range and mix of techniques, medical imaging forces the lay viewer to be an outsider to medical interpretation. The idea that the new field of medical imaging is off limits to patients and the lay community is suggested in the introduction to a recently published medical textbook on magnetic resonance imaging. In the introduction, the authors stake out the boundaries between the field of popular cultural imagery and their elite fraternity of imaging specialists. "I don't know about you," the authors write, "but when I turn on my TV to watch the football game, electromagnetic waves, transistors, and picture tubes are the furthest things from my mind. I have no trouble applauding a touchdown pass without understanding the operation of the television set." Having thus implied that the TV set and the MRI apparatus have something in common technologically, the authors then go on to separate the lay viewer from the elite initiate of medical visual culture. "Unlike in the case of the 'boob tube,'" the authors warn, "some understanding of the rudiments of magnetic resonance imaging is absolutely necessary in order to even vaguely understand the image. Without this knowledge, one runs a serious risk of ineffective, or even erroneous, interpretation."[2] This anecdote establishes magnetic resonance imaging as a mode of male spectatorship that, unlike the "low" culture of televised football, is limited to an elite group of initiates, reinforcing the idea that medical-visual knowledge is off-limits to patients and lay viewers — that is, to those of us whose bodies and health are at stake in imaging practices; and it encourages the idea that the patient or lay person should surrender agency and control over the body to those specialists trained to "read" the complex body images provided by the new technologies.

In their introduction to the anthology *Technoculture*, Constance Penley and Andrew Ross note that, within leftist critical discourse, the high-tech instruments and apparatuses of Western industrial capitalism have routinely been regarded as monolithic — moreover, as dangerous forces enlisted in a program of social control.[3] Strategically, there is little to gain in representing modes of high technology as totalizing systems with little potential for local intervention. There is a need, instead, to focus on the moments of rupture and resistance within the culture of high-tech imaging. Perhaps the medical textbook authors are in fact belittling the media knowledge derived from television viewing that is in fact crucial to the understanding of specialized media forms. Can the physician really leave at the clinic door the knowledge of visual conventions that he or she has gained through the consumption of what are arguably closely related media forms? Indeed, the author of the *Computer Graphics World* essay notes that it is not, finally, the physician, but rather the computer graphics artist who really knows how to build, operate, and interpret the mix of technologies that constitute the medical imaging center. She claims that the computer artist is the real authority behind medical imaging systems, blatantly challenging the idea that the physician is the locus of medical knowledge, and suggesting the potential for "nonspecialist" agency and authority in this apparently monolithic field.

This is not to say that medical expertise is tainted by the forces of popular media culture, but that medical discourse is constructed through popular modes of reading visual culture. It is this intersection of medicine and the popular that constitutes a potential point of rupture and intervention. Some instances of medical image interpretation are clearly influenced by popular views about gender, sexuality, and cultural identity, rather than solely or primarily by ostensible medical needs and clinical knowledge. For example, the professional spectatorship and interpretation of ultrasound images in obstetrics are driven, to a great extent, by visual pleasures and desires that go beyond the apparent exigencies of medical knowledge.

The Place of the Popular in Elite Medical Imaging Analysis

In a well-known essay on ultrasound in obstetrics written almost a decade ago, Rosalind Petchesky analyzed the use of sonograms by anti-abortion groups to support claims of fetal identity and subjectivity; she also considered the by-now common phenomenon of the sonogram as a take-home fetal "portrait" and the implications of this practice for the politics of reproduction, and the possible uses of the sonogram as a means of reinforcing women's agency in obstetrics.[4] More recently, writing in feminist cultural studies on obstetrical ultrasound has raised questions about the technique's actual medical advantages, safety, and possible overuse. Rayna Rapp, for example, has recently noted that although an estimated ninety percent of the pregnant women in New York City have been placed under sonographic surveillance,

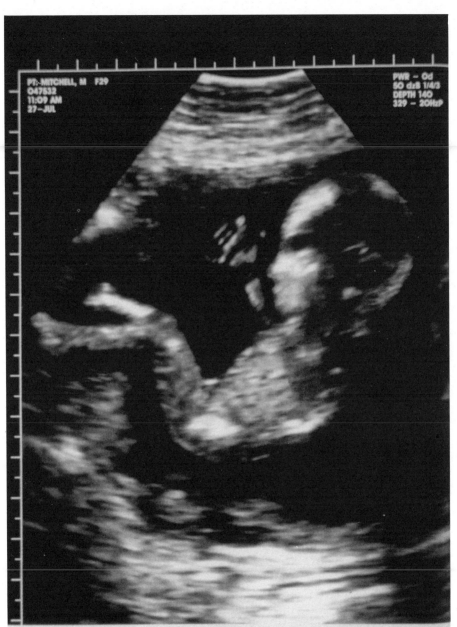

IS SOMETHING INSIDE TELLING YOU TO BUY A VOLVO?

and the jury is still out on the technique's risks and benefits.

Other writers have focused on the increasing prevalence of the fetal sonogram in the psychical life of the pregnant woman, and in the public sphere—a place where the image has come to function, as Janelle Sue Taylor and Carole Stabile have argued, as an icon of conservative family values.[5]

The fetal sonogram also circulates in the form of colorized, gender-encoded displays on book jackets, in popular journals, and in advertisements. The sonogram functions here as an artifact of the natural, anatomically complete body, a relic used in the management of cultural anxieties about shifting and disintegrating familial, sexual, and corporeal models. The artist Howard Sochurek's decorative fetal portraits, for instance, have been distributed in a popular coffee-table book, called *Medicine's New Vision*.

Very recently, a six-year medical study showed that routine use of prenatal ultrasound does not improve the outcome of designated low-risk pregnancies, thus tacitly confirming what many feminist scholars have been arguing—the only real benefits that ultrasound may have in the routine course of most pregnancies are cultural and psychical. Ultrasound continues to have proven uses in other areas of obstetrics—primarily in prenatal testing for genetic abnormalities, and in prenatal sex determination. The identification of the sex of the fetus through the sighting of the genitalia on the ultrasound display continues to be routine and expected in most obstetrical evaluations in the United States.

Ultrasound, it would seem, is wreaking havoc with conventional developmental theories by imputing gender and sexual identity to the fetus almost before the actual formation

Fig 1. Scrotum with bilateral hydroceles (arrow) in a male fetus at 38 weeks of gestation.

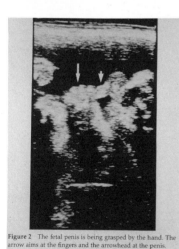

Figure 2 The fetal penis is being grasped by the hand. The arrow aims at the fingers and the arrowhead at the penis.

Pages from a 1987 issue of the *Journal of Ultrasound in Medicine*.

of sexual anatomy. Sex determinations through ultrasound are often
constructed as fantastic dramatic
narratives in which the fetus is
granted subjectivity and identity
through the pictorial act of endow-
ing it with sexual anatomy.

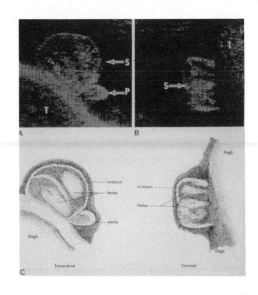

The construction of "fetal sub-
jecthood" has close ties to the medical deployment of the sonogram
as an analogue of the photograph.
Take-home fetal portraits emerged
at about the same time that research
in obstetrics began to focus on the use of ultrasound to identify, in the words
of one obstetrician, "structural defects" in the fetus.[6] But as another physician
notes, "While the major concern [in obstetrical ultrasound] is fetal anom-
alies, one cannot ignore the fetal sex organs" that appear in the image. As
in more conventional body photography, the image of sexual anatomy is a
source of visual pleasure and anxiety, an aspect of the image that must be
managed by the viewer through narrative and pictorial investments. The
real-time ultrasound display functions in the context of the clinic in part as
a means of establishing a developmental narrative that inscribes the fetus
as a properly social human being—that is, one invested with a normative
sexual identity.

A study documenting a scene of supposed fetal sexual deviancy, dramatized in the pages of a 1987 issue of the *Journal of Ultrasound in Medicine*, begins
by noting that ultrasound determination of fetal sex has become an accepted
part of obstetrical practice, potentially replacing amniocentesis as a means of
assessing the state of the fetus. The author, a physician, refers the reader to
two sonograms. According to his analysis, "the fetus at 28 weeks' gestation
was observed grasping his penis in a fashion resembling masturbation movements."[7] The narrative of male sexual behavior relies heavily on the two
sonograms, frame grabs from the real-time video in which the doctor spot-
ted this ostensible sexual act in progress. Interestingly, this narrative reads
something like a primal scene in reverse. Freud describes the primal scene as

a fantasy, activated by the sounds of parental copulation, a scene that is retroactively constructed by the child in the form of an image. Here the physician, like Freud's child, creates a narrativized scene on the basis of the evidence of sexual conduct suggested to him in the visual display. Just as Freud's mythical child hears the sounds of parental sexual conduct too early to comprehend them, the technician catches a covert glimpse of what he imagines to be the fetus's first sexual act.[8] Likewise, this doctor "sees" signs of sexual behavior perhaps too early for him to comprehend them.

Alessandra Piontelli, a psychiatrist who has analyzed the professional territory of sonographic fetal behavioral analysis, has noted that individual initiative and choice of movement is usually identified in the eighth week of gestation—a developmental point that is also associated with the appearance of more clearly identifiable male or female genitals in the sonogram. It is rather perplexing then that, in this account of "fetal masturbation," the physician is anxious to "see" genital sexual conduct not only before socialization has begun, but also when the first traces of distinctive sexual anatomy might be visible.[9] Even Freud, who seemed to advocate the intra-uterine investigation of fetal conduct before the advent of ultrasound, had the sense to state that there is absolutely no justification for attributing psychical content to stimulation of the genital zone in *utero.*

The physician retroactively constructed a narrative of sexual pleasure and desire in the barely legible, barely formed fetal body. As someone trained in the analysis of film and video, it is impossible to read this account without considering the erotic investments and the mechanisms of voyeurism and identification that structured this physician's experience as a spectator in his own private video "theater." This is not to say that the doctor has perverted objective medical knowledge of the facts of development by constructing a fantasy on the basis of the real-time video image, but to suggest just how strongly the conventions of popular reading can assert themselves in the professional space of the clinic.

Fetal Gender Masquerade

Another case of sonographic fetal sex determination suggests the instability of the cultural codes used to inscribe the fetus into a narrative of gendered and sexual identity. The *American Journal of Radiology* published a study in 1992, written by a group of ultrasound technologists, which studied sonograms of 112 pregnant women to determine the sex of their fetuses. The group found that they were accurate in only a little more than half of these cases. Sonograms were reproduced in the journal article; however, rather than simply interpreting these images for signs of sexual identity and behavior (as the authors of the previous account did), these technicians rendered interpretive charcoal drawings of the images that appeared on the monitor. The ambiguity of the image of genitalia as it appeared or did not appear in the sonogram was "cleaned up," and sexual identity more firmly established in visual form.

This case illustrates a certain shrewdness about imaging on the part of technologists. Unable to find biological proof of gender in the sonogram alone, they manipulated the image with a more traditional technique—the charcoal drawing—to prove the fetus' sexual anatomy. The manipulation of the image was not a terribly successful means of securing evidence of sexual anatomy in the image. For example, in twenty of the forty cases where no clear evidence of fetal genitalia existed (and thus the fetus was assumed to be female), the sex turned out to be male. Rather than chalk up these "false determinations" to their own interpretive errors, the technicians attributed blame to the maternal body. In some cases, they explained, the "wrong" part of the maternal body imposed itself in the image, casting a shadow over the area of the fetal genitals, as in cases where "maternal obesity" obstructed the view of the fetus, or in cases where the pregnant woman's bowels shadowed the fundus of the uterus and the fetal genitalia. Indeed, in some cases, the maternal body is described as being in a perverse relationship with the fetus, enacting a kind of fetal gender masquerade. In one example, the umbilical cord lay draped between the thighs of the female fetus, looking in the sonogram like a penis, the fetal body itself taking on the function of gender masquerade.

The authors identify both the maternal body and fetal body as causal agents in the production of artifactual genitalia—aberrant "noise" in the visual display that must be placed in the background or erased. Designated "false determinations," these cases are attributed not to problems in interpretive methodology, but to problems in fetal and maternal behavior. A certain agency is attributed to the maternal body—the female body, in their view, is a force with the power to subvert the truth of the image. By inserting itself

into the wrong place in the image field, the maternal body jams the sonographic codes of gender and sexual representation.

Ultrasound continues to rely on more conventional codes of visual culture. Just as the viewer of televised football "knows a well-executed touchdown pass when he sees one," so the ultrasound technician apparently
"knows" fetal sex when he or she sees it. Clearly, even the most elite areas of
medical imaging research are continually restructured from within through
such interlacing of popular and scientific spectatorial modes. As Donna
Haraway has explained, the cultural and material authority of biomedicine's
productions of bodies and selves is vulnerable and dynamic, and constituted
through multivalent discursive strategies and social forms.[10] If the voice of
patients and medical subjects is not heard in the process of constructing
medical meanings, at least ruptures in the apparently seamless logic of the
sonogram's visual proof can be identified; and symptomatic moments of
transgression can be located within these institutional attempts to make
the fetal image perform within normative models of gendered appearance
and sexual behavior.

Technological Media Activism in Medical Countercultures

There has been a widespread movement toward collective revisionings of
the monolithic set of high-tech instruments and strategies in medicine and
health culture. Some of the most influential health-care activism in recent
years has taken the form of video and public art works. The politics of AIDS,
reproductive rights, and breast cancer, for example, have been transformed
through public service announcements, documentaries, demonstration-
performances, site-specific installations, educational interactive-media
kiosks, and found-image mixed-media work. While some of these works
appropriate medical images or repurpose medical imaging technologies,
others use more broad-based media technologies such as video and computer imaging to create texts that directly challenge the construction of
medical technology as an elite culture.

Media activist Kathy High's videotape Underexposed: Temple of the Fetus (1992)
is particularly relevant to my discussion of obstetrical ultrasound. High's tape
is, overall, a condemning analysis of the field of reproductive technologies.
The tape weaves together scripted narratives and faux and actual interviews

with medical specialists, social workers, and women who have undergone genetic and reproductive counseling or therapy. It concludes with a real interview with sociologist Jyotsna Gupta, who poses the question, "do [women] really need [reproductive] technologies?" Gupta answers her own question by arguing that these technologies will lead only to "more commodification of our lives and further industrialization of biological processes, forcing women into the margins of reproduction."

A scene from the tape documenting a medical procedure called transvaginal ultrasonographic-guided follicula aspiration, or egg "harvesting," a technique in which eggs are removed from the female body in order to be fertilized in the laboratory, in vitro, demonstrates the place of imaging in reproductive technologies. There are two imaging systems in operation: an ultrasound monitor is placed at the foot of the examining table, and another monitor displaying a fiber-optics image of the eggs still in vivo is suspended above it. The doctor's gaze is divided between the two, rarely glancing in the direction of the body of the woman on whom he operates. This scene could demonstrate, as it does for Gupta, how women are quite literally marginalized in reproductive technologies. However, as Rayna Rapp has noted, totalizing critiques like this leave women with few strategical options for action in an already technologically complex society.

A more empowering narrative about the uses of reproductive technologies, which resists participation in schemes of social control, is depicted earlier in High's tape. Annie and Susan, a lesbian couple played by performance artists Annie Sprinkle and Shelley Mars, prepared to inseminate Annie, via the turkey-baster method, with sperm that they've purchased from a certified physician for eighty dollars a hit. Is this one of those utopian fantasies about the promise of new technologies? We later see Susan and a very pregnant Annie in one of the tape's mockumentary-style interviews with Kate, a fictional television news reporter. Susan relates to Kate the fact that some states have on the books laws preventing access to donor sperm by lesbians (that is, those who identify themselves as such to their doctors). Temple of the Fetus pushes the envelope of reproductive policy by modeling its possible uses to break with normative models of sexuality and family. While this segment of High's tape precisely revises medicine's visual culture, it is a strong example of how one medical technology can be appropriated and repurposed to progressive ends. This scene not only opposes the use of high technology with the low-tech process of donor insemination, but culturally rethinks the technologies through which medicine builds gendered, sexual, and familial identities and relationships. Annie and Susan's doctor has in fact violated mandated medical procedure by giving them sperm to take home. While their option of self-treatment may seem to be a casual fact here, in other medical contexts there is much more at stake with home self-treatment.

Carl M. George's short film, DHPG Mon Amour, for example, documents a normal day at home with Joe Conover and his lover David, hanging out on the patio and in the kitchen, gardening, cooking—and preparing and administering David's complicated thrice-daily AIDS drug treatment. David must be hooked up to an IV through an infusor port attached to his body to receive DHPG gancyclovir. As we see Joe and David go through the steps of the process, we hear their voice-over narration, recorded as they watched the footage at home. The language of the film is insistently proactive; it is laced with messages like "we just wanted to let people know that AZT is not the only fucking drug" and that you can take on the complicated task of home self-treatment, even though most doctors would consider the risks and the inconvenience too great to be worth the trouble. But their relentless positivity is continually juxtaposed with evidence of the tremendous difficulty of their circumstances. Joe relates that, though we are hearing David explain the steps of his complicated procedure while we watch them demonstrated on the screen, David is in fact blind—he has CNV retinitis—a condition that might have been avoided had he been placed on DHPG a little earlier. At the point in the film when David sinks the needle into his body through the port attached to his chest, Joe says in voice-over, "I hope none of this film shocks anybody because doing this right now is not a hassle in our lives, it's keeping David alive—and here goes."

DHPG Mon Amour is a visual lesson in the fact that the management of medical technologies need not be off-limits to patients, and that agency and authority is not always at the expense of high-tech treatment. Indeed, in DHPG Mon Amour, the "home movie" genre functions like an imaging tech-nology insofar as it reconfigures the relationship between David and his prosthetic treatment apparatus into one that is healthy and positive, rather than debilitating and demeaning. Moreover, Joe and David directly confront the fact that spectators may be repulsed by images like the close-up shot of David's body being hooked up to his IV. Their matter-of-fact voice-over encourages viewers to see these images as evidence of the pleasures of asserting one's own autonomy in the techniques of survival. Indeed, the image construct of David hooked up to his treatment technology is a powerful condensation of both the tremendous potential and the nightmarish threat of the cyborg figure in contemporary Western biopolitics.

Repurposing Medical Images and Imaging Systems in Gallery Installation Art

In an installation entitled *Examinations: Words Most Commonly Used in Medical Settings*, artist Molly Blieden replicated the basic elements of the medical examination room. A monitor displaying words that one might expect to hear in the course of a medical exam is positioned above an examination table. This set, though reminiscent of the egg-harvesting scene on High's tape, disrupts and reorders the logic of the gaze. The monitor is placed on the ceiling, tilted to correspond directly with the hypothetical patient's line of sight. (Some of us might recall that, in the course of a gynecological exam, there are few places to rest one's eyes except on the ceiling.) The words posted on the video monitor are terms taken from the American Medical Association's *Manual of Style*, such as *observe, enlarge, reduce, record* — significantly, words that underscore the centrality of observation in the examination process. Because these words appear on the screen backwards, they can be read correctly only in their reflection, which appears in a mirror embedded in the head of the examining table.

Blieden's installation reorders the spatial and visual logic of the examination room to situate the patient, rather than the physician, as the authorial subject of medical knowledge and the gaze. It also metaphorically transforms the clinical cubicle from a site that renders the patient's body docile and vulnerable to a space where the patient may become the locus of a reflexive critical interrogation of medical discourse.

Swiss artist Alexander Hahn's *Urbs Turrita* (1992), a two-channel video work displayed on three stripped television tubes positioned on the gallery floor, similarly subverts the visual logic of medical representation. A montage of brain scans — MRIs — that Hahn has manipulated and colorized appears in his monitors. Hahn scanned the images into his computer and altered them using a program called Image. Significantly, Image is a medical imaging application commonly used by medical technicians and doctors, not gallery artists. Hahn's access to Image is significant to a discussion of where agency and authority is located in the cultures of medical technology.

Image is a program distributed by the National Institutes of Health (NIH). The explosion of new imaging devices and systems throughout the eighties created a tremendous amount of confusion—not only were doctors confronted with competing modalities (ultrasound, PET, MRI), they were faced with the fact that there was no single standard technique or procedure for producing and interpreting images. The NIH recognized the need for a standardized system among their own laboratories, and released a single program for free among their own researchers, distributing it on the internet, replete with source code. Image provided, among other things, standardized colorization and spatial encoding systems, data analysis techniques, and display modalities. Hahn simply downloaded Image and used it to modify the MRIs in his installation. His process demonstrates the degree to which the apparently elite and specialized codes of high-tech medical imaging have by economic necessity become public property, available for free.

Hahn's altered MRIs comment precisely on the status of the high-tech body image as "portraiture" within public culture. In this frame, we see MRIs positioned against what appears to be a domestic space—there is a wooden floor, a shuttered window. The settings for the MRIs are taken from paintings by Caspar David Friedrich. Through computer manipulation, Hahn removed the female figure that occupies the room in the original painting, replacing her with a magnetic resonance "portrait" of the body. Here Hahn has eliminated the domestic portrait and put in its place an image of a television monitor whose encasing body is stripped away. On this tube within a tube, the MRIs also function as an artifact of the natural body, marking the presence of the human subjects, which have been eliminated from the frame. The MRI stands in for the human subject, stripped of all markers of cultural identity. What is the gender and race of the subject imaged in the magnetic resonance cross-sections that appear on the screen? What is this person's state of health? Placed outside the medical context, the image is emptied of its specific ties to health and identity.

On one level, there is a certain utopian agenda at work in this piece. It

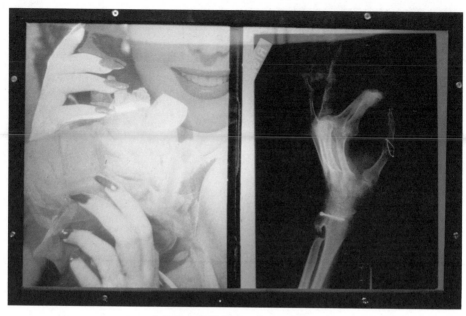

A. D. Satterfield, *Systemic Onset*, 1990.

indicates the potential for a technological dissociation of image and identity, image and behavior. But if it suggests that the domestic subject may be stripped from the scene of history, the current claims around magnetic resonance imaging suggest that MRI, like ultrasound, will in fact facilitate the reinscription of historical notions of gender, sexuality, and race, and it will make this inscription in previously unmarked regions of the body, such as in the soft tissue of the brain.

While Hahn's magnetic resonance portraits are stripped of their history and culture, the X-ray collages of Anne Duncan Satterfield directly address the issue of the artist's own body in the manufacture of her work. Satterfield's work documents the treatment she has received for rheumatoid arthritis. In the series titled *Systemic Onset*, we see X-rays of Satterfield's arthritic hands juxtaposed with collages of popular cultural images of the female hand as icon and fetish. The unnatural construction of the female hand as an icon of female sexuality—colorized, excessively bejeweled, and endowed with decoratively polished nails—is foregrounded; the "natural," healthy female hand bears little relation to the prosthetically aided and optically stripped appendage.

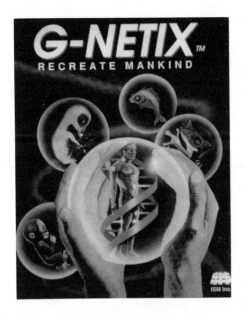

Artist Michael Joo draws directly on bodily remnants as they are used in medical science as artifacts visually encoded with markers of racial identity. In his wall installation *Yellow, Yellower, Yellowest* (1991), Joo provides a commentary on the encoding of identity through color. Shifting the focus from skin color to bodily excretions, Joo presents a display in which three beakers of preserved urine are assigned name plates with corresponding designations of tone that also function as designations of identity as defined through cultural mythology and history. Joo's piece comments on the tendency in science toward the inscription of racial and sexual identity in regions and entities previously unmarked (the blood, the urine, the lymph), the color of bodily excretions symbolizing the designation of racial identity more familiarly associated with skin color. This displacement parodies the cultural displacements that occur in science when the focus shifts from exterior to interior, from surface to plane, or from skin to bodily fluids. Joo's *Yellow, Yellower, Yellowest* comments both profoundly and humorously on the scientific compulsion toward the fabrication of markers of biological and cultural difference in the smallest structure and function of the body.

The installations discussed here for the most part appropriate the high-tech medical image in order to redirect its cultural function. In his interactive computer program, *Portraits of People Living with AIDS*, computer graphics artist Hazen Reed takes on a technology commonly found in medicine in the context of patient education. This kind of medical interactive initiative is exemplified in Dartmouth Medical School's recent "educationals" targeted at men contemplating prostate cancer treatment, and women considering breast cancer treatment options. In these programs, interactivity is limited to selecting educational sequences on various topics, and the audience address is hopelessly didactic and patronizing. Reed, an independent media artist, set out to counter this didactic approach by rendering more subtle and varied, and decidedly nondidactic, "portraits" of four different AIDS patients. Each portrait is presented in a format designed to correspond to the tastes, interests, and lifestyles of the individual represented. For example, in one sequence Richard, a painter, talks about his artwork in the familiar television interview format, with the head shot framed by a virtual gallery space created in the computer screen. Richard's talking head is surrounded by reproductions of his artworks hung on the virtual gallery walls. Click on a piece of artwork and Richard's voice is interrupted, then the user moves directly to a close-up of the painting. The user thus is able to "move" through the space of the gallery, experiencing various points of view on Richard's artwork while hearing his narrative about it. The user can then contribute her or his own remarks on the paintings in a computerized bulletin-board space.

Conclusion

Medical culture's anxiety over the management of its field of imaging has resulted in its becoming vulnerable to intervention and reconfiguration. This intervention is taking place, in part, through technological agents—the alien concepts, formidable techniques, and impossibly complex image-rendering processes that constitute medicine's volatile field of vision. But on this field, like that of the medical image itself, the social body is constructed, not simply through institutional discourses and professional competition, but through public culture's historical refunctionings of bodily regimes and optical paradigms. Interventions in elite technological culture are thus a crucial means through which health and the body may be reconfigured in postmodern culture. Medicine's proliferation of visual management strategies demands an equally prolific and diversified set of critical counterstrategies from a range of positions inside and outside the field of medicine. Perhaps the most crucial areas of medical imaging are those implicated in the task of reinscribing historical narratives of institutional agency and those generating technological countercultures within institutional discourses.

at last going   there would be a
battle, an   liged to labor to
make h   ance an omen
that   of the earth.
     f vague and
     and fire. In
     d imagined
     s. But awake
     es of the past.
     hought-images
     on of the world's
     wars, but it, he
     nd had disappeared

     oked upon the war in his
     some sort of a play affair. He
     a Greeklike strug   would
be   en were better
and religious education had effaced th
or else firm finance held in check the

He had burned several times to er
shook the land. They might not be
seemed to be much glory in them. I
conflicts, and he had longed to see it
for him large pictures extravagant in
deeds.

But his mother had discouraged him. She   look

Tim Rollins + K.O.S., *The Red Badge of Courage*, 1992.

Eric Santner

POSTMODERNISM'S JEWISH
QUESTION: SLAVOJ ŽIŽEK AND THE
MONOTHEISTIC PERVERSE

1

There is an old Jewish joke about a zoology course at a distinguished university in which the students were requested to write a term paper on the subject of elephants. The French student writes a paper with the predictable title,
"On the Sexual Habits of the Elephant"; the German student submits a teu-
tonically comprehensive "Introduction to the Bibliographic Sources for the
Study of the Elephant"; the American student submits a paper on the topic
of "Breeding Bigger and Better Elephants"; and, finally, the Jewish student
chooses as his theme—what else?—"The Elephant and the Jewish Question."

The joke presupposes, of course, the listener's acceptance of common
stereotypes of national and ethnic character traits: a French preoccupation
with sex, German industriousness and *Gründlichkeit*, American pragmatism
and entrepreneurial ambitiousness, and finally, a certain Jewish self-absorption,
or the Jewish obsession with the fate of the Jews. Being a Jewish joke,
there is, of course, a peculiar asymmetry in the list. The Jewish national character trait stands out as something of an anomaly in the context of the list
provided by the joke. For one could say that, according to the joke, what
marks the Jew as a Jew is a preoccupation with the dilemmas and difficulties
of being marked as having a national character trait in the first place. The Jew
is typecast as one for whom the very experience of being typecast constitutes
his type, for whom the phenomenon of types and stereotyping is, as it were,
his typical problem. To be Jewish is to be that exceptional type in whom the
principle of typing and stereotyping is, to use an Hegelian locution, reflected
into itself, and makes its appearance as a particular element in the list.

I found myself recalling this joke at a recent Modern Language Association
panel entitled "Mourning and Melancholia in the Post-Holocaust." The panel
was conceived on the premise that at least some of the central concerns, preoccupations, and debates in postmodern theory gain their maximal urgency
when seen as, or placed in dialogue with, efforts to work through what is
arguably the core trauma of modern history: the implementation of the

so-called "Final Solution." Such a premises pushes one to reconceptualize that strange postmodern phenomenon, the debate on "p.c.," so that "p.c." in the last resort, may best be understood not as political correctness, but rather as an ethical call to the psychic and cultural labor of remembering and working through historical trauma. Thus, by engaging intellectually, affectively, imaginatively, with the horrific details, as well as the sheer and brutal facticity of the "Final Solution," individuals and collectivities could develop a certain cognitive and psychic resistance to the totalitarian temptation. The postmodern preoccupation with undoing all forms and residues of "essentialism" —the modern drive for ethnic cleansing—derives much of its moral energy from the historical experience of Nazism and the "Final Solution." Postmodern anti-essentialism would thus always refer back to a concrete historical experience, would always include an engagement with memory. Michel Foucault concisely formulated this nexus of historical and theoretical concerns in his preface to Gilles Deleuze and Félix Guattari's *Anti-Oedipus*: "…the major enemy, the strategic adversary is fascism.…And not only historical fascism, the fascism of Hitler and Mussolini—which was able to mobilize and use the desire of the masses so effectively—but also the fascism in us all, in our heads and in our everyday behavior, the fascism that causes us to love power, to desire the very thing that dominates and exploits us."[1] In recent years there have been a number of provocative attempts to articulate and develop the links between intellectual, mnemonic, and political responsibility, links that together could constitute the foundations of a properly postmodern ethics. Slavoj Žižek's contribution to such an ethics— informed by Lacanian psychoanalysis, German Idealist philosophy, close readings of popular culture, and analyses of political ideologies—underlines the extent to which postmodern thought has been engaged in the effort to rethink modern anti-Semitism. In Žižek's work, postmodern theory, including the theory of the visual field, is, among other things, a renewed meditation on the "Jewish Question."[2]

2

Žižek's analysis of Jewish theology and anti-Semitism arises from a theory proposed in the writings of Louis Althusser, Jacques Lacan, and Pierre Bourdieu, among others. This theory of the constitution of subjectivity proposes that the subject exists by way of a primordial interpellation issued in the name of the big "Other" of the symbolic community. One is, throughout one's life, invested by the community and its institutions—including, of course, the micro-institution of the family—with symbolic mandates; one is addressed with terms and titles in which we are obliged to recognize ourselves, if we want a place in the socio-symbolic network. For the socio-symbolic community to maintain its consistency, its capacity to generate "reality effects," the subject's complicity in sustaining the community's authority must remain unconscious. As Bourdieu has put it, "the language of authority never governs without the collaboration of those it governs, without the help of the social mechanisms capable of producing this complicity, based on misrecognition, which is the basis of all authority."[3] In the Lacanian terms favored by Žižek, if acts of nomination are to be effective, the "big Other" must be kept ignorant of its own "desire," it must not "know" that it lacks any existence independent of the subject's subjugation to it.

Žižek proposes that Jews have been the object of racism par excellence not because of any positive attributes of Jews as an historical people, but rather because the structure of belief in Jewish monotheism realizes in a pure way the hysterical dimension of socio-symbolic complicity. In Jewish monotheism, Žižek argues, the "desire of the Other," the vicious circle of complicity at the core of all symbolic power, is encountered for the first time in sublime and traumatic splendor:

> is not the Jewish God the purest embodiment...of the desire of the Other in
> its terrifying abyss, with the formal prohibition to "make an image of God"
> —to fill out the gap of the Other's desire with a positive fantasy scenario?...
> The fact that Jews perceive themselves as the "chosen people" has nothing to
> do with a belief in their superiority; they do not possess any special qualities;
> before the pact with God they were a people like any other, no more and no
> less corrupted, living their ordinary life—when suddenly, like a traumatic
> flash, they came to know (through Moses...) that the Other had chosen them.[4]

It has been, Žižek suggests, the genius of the Jews to persist in this experience of the desire, or void, of the Other. It is their genius to refuse the temptation of the logic of sacrifice, which secures for the faithful the fantasy that this desire could be appeased and the consistency of the Other thereby established as a visually verified, dependable support:

> Sacrifice conceals the abyss of the Other's desire, more precisely: it conceals the Other's lack, inconsistency, "inexistence," that transpires in this desire. *Sacrifice is a guarantee that "the Other exists":* that there *is* an Other who can be appeased by means of the sacrifice.... [By] *the very act of sacrifice, we (presup)pose the existence of its addressee* that guarantees the consistency and meaningfulness of our experience—so, even if the act fails in its proclaimed goal, this very failure can be read from within the logic of sacrifice as *our* failure to appease the Other. Insofar as this abyss of the Other's desire emerged in all its violence with the Jewish religion—i.e., insofar as the fundamental position of the Jewish believer is that of a perplexed…What does He want of me?…it was unavoidable for it to break with the logic of sacrifice: sacrifice would mean that we translated God's desire into a demand that can be appeased by means of sacrifice.[5]

This Lacanian rereading of Jewish theology—mediated in large measure by Freud's highly speculative reflections on trauma, neurosis, and religion in *Moses and Monotheism*, and, one suspects, by Schönberg's opera *Moses and Aron*—provides the background for Žižek's understanding of anti-Semitism, especially in its modern, National Socialist version. Žižek claims that, the paradox of sacrifice is that the "illusion…finds its clearest articulation in the anti-Semitic concept of the Jew: the Nazi has to sacrifice the Jew in order to be able to maintain the illusion that it is only the "Jewish plot" which prevents the establishment of the "class relationship," of society as a harmonious, organic whole."[6] Or, as Žižek argues elsewhere in much the same vein:

> "Jew" is a fetish which simultaneously denies and embodies the structural impossibility of "Society": it is as if in the figure of the Jew this possibility had acquired a positive, palpable existence—and that is why it marks the eruption of enjoyment in the social field.…The thesis…that "Society doesn't exist," that the Social is always an inconsistent field structured around a constitutive impossibility, traversed by a central "antagonism"—this thesis implies that every process of identification conferring on us a fixed socio-

symbolic identity is ultimately doomed to fail. The function of ideological fantasy is to mask this inconsistency…and thus to compensate us for the failed identification….The "Jew" is the means, for Fascism, of taking into account, of representing its own impossibility….The whole Fascist ideology is structured as a struggle against the element which holds the place of the immanent impossibility of the very Fascist project; the "Jew" is nothing but a fetishistic embodiment of a certain fundamental blockage….Society is not prevented from achieving its full identity because of Jews: it is prevented by its own antagonistic nature, by its own immanent blockage and it "projects" this internal negativity into the figure of the "Jew." In other words, what is excluded from the Symbolic (from the frame of the corporatist socio-symbolic order) returns in the Real as a paranoid construction of the "Jew."[7]

At the "origin" of every social space one finds a void filled by a foundational act that establishes the conditions of intelligibility and the necessity of that space. Such foundational acts, even when they inaugurate a reign of law, are in essence, acts of violence. Walter Benjamin's name for violence that marks the advent of any social order was *rechtssetzende Gewalt*; it is the violence that establishes the framework, the rules by which it can be determined which acts of violence may be deemed criminal in the first place. "At the beginning of the law," Žižek claims,

> there is a certain "outlaw," a certain Real of violence which coincides with the act itself of the establishment of the reign of law: the ultimate truth about the reign of law is that of an usurpation, and all classical politico-philosophical thought rests on the disavowal of this violent act of foundation. The illegiti-mate violence by which the law sustains itself must be concealed at any price, because this concealment is the positive condition of the functioning of law: it functions insofar as its subjects are deceived, insofar as they experience the authority of law as "authentic and eternal" and overlook "the truth about the usurpation."[8]

Ultimately, the rule of law has the structure of a vicious circle, which, according to Žižek, must undergo what Freud called *Urverdrängung* (originary or primordial repression) if a socio-symbolic order is to reign. Primordial repression could thus be said to represent the truth of the social contract; a truth one must forget in order to enjoy the symbolic status of a subject able to enter into contracts, social or otherwise. Since the advent of modernity or what Žižek calls, following Martin Heidegger, "modern-age subjectivity,"[9] originary repression is no longer what it used to be, or, as Žižek writes, "today…the substitution of Name for Thing is losing its edge…."[10] The paradoxical knowledge of what it is forbidden to know is what Žižek, following Lacan, calls *jouissance*, or enjoyment. It is the "knowledge" that characterizes the position of the psychotic and causes the meltdown of his reality. The psychotic has, in a sense, forgotten how to forget the tenuousness of his obligation to the Other. He is plagued by a knowledge that compels him to maintain a distance from the symbolic order and not be duped by it, lured into complicity. His behavior is the extreme limit of the refusal to play the social game, a radicalization of the narcissistic disengagement lamented by social critics in the 1970s.[11] This forbidden knowledge of *jouissance* can become a determining factor in the visual field, particularly in visual displays of the wounded body.

Žižek's argument would seem to be that modern anti-Semitism makes a certain sense, because Jewish theology is implicated in the coming to self-consciousness of the psychotic risk dwelling in the heart of the human condition.[12] Jewish theology, Žižek suggests, opens the door to a psychotic space in us; but Jews manage to persist in an hysterical compromise, refusing the consolations of the fetish as well as avoiding the fall into the madness of cynical reason. "The basic position of a Jewish believer," Žižek says, "is…that of Job: not so much lamentation as incomprehension, perplexity, even horror at what the Other (God) wants with the series of calamities that are being inflicted upon him."[13] The story of Job is seen in turn as an elaboration of the case of Abraham for whom, despite the concreteness of God's demand that he sacrifice his son, still it "remains quite open to what he really wants with it: to say that with this horrible act Abraham must attest to his infinite trust and devotion to God is already an inadmissable simplification."[14] The Jews are precisely those who do not search for imaginary solutions, let alone final ones, to the question of the desire of the Other, which *is*, in a sense, for Žižek, the "Jewish Question," the question introduced by the Jews into the history of civilization.

One must feel uneasy with the above association of Jews and hysteria. It is worth remembering that psychoanalysis came into its own by way of the study and treatment of *female* hysteria, a fact that for Žižek enjoys a certain degree of self-evidence. There is a reason, he argues, why

> psychoanalysis began with the study of hysterical symptoms, why its "native soil" was the experience of female hysteria: in the last resort, what is hysteria if not precisely the effect and testimony of a failed interpellation; what is the hysterical question if not an articulation of the incapacity of the subject to fulfill the symbolic identification, to assume fully and without restraint the symbolic mandate?[15]

In a patriarchal society, women are more chronically exposed to failures of interpellation. Such failures make pulpable the "nonexistence" of the Other as a consistent and functioning symbolic support. But this "native soil," this peculiar homeland of neurosis, was, in the nineteenth century, also seen as a Jewish one;[16] and Žižek urges us to consider that this association is founded not merely on the historical experience of Jews in their host societies, but rather on the very structure of Jewish monotheism. We need thus to understand the anomalous position of the Jew—to return to the joke. The Jew is the one for whom the dilemmas of being typed constitute his type, not merely as the result of being positioned historically as the Other by various host cultures, but also as a function of the (hysterical) structure in which he finds himself vis-à-vis his God and the ethical rigors of his faith. Only by attending to the structural features of Jewish monotheism can one avoid the impasses of historicism; only then can one begin to analyze the vehemence and persistence of anti-Semitism in settings even where Jews are absent.[17] For Žižek, hysteria defines the human subject as a being-of-language, as the being who is from the start addressed as if he knew why he occupies the place he does in the symbolic network, a place that necessarily fills him with symbolic mandates he can never fully justify or fulfill.[18] Hysteria is, at bottom, the deep discomfort—Freud's word was *Unbehagen*—that arises from such feelings of obligation and failure to fulfill. The dis-ease inherent in the functioning of symbolic power comes to self-consciousness with Jewish monotheism. Zizek both appropriates and reverses, by way of a dialectical shift, the misogynist and anti-Semitic arguments made by Otto Weininger at the turn of the century in his notorious book *Sex and Character*. Yes, Žižek, like Weininger tells us, women and Jews are predisposed to hysteria. But not because of any inbred intellectual or ethical inferiority, as Weininger and other nineteenth-century thinkers claimed; rather because women and Jews have no access to culturally sanctioned fantasies and fetishes enjoyed by those in positions of hegemony, which allow them to avoid encountering the lack, the inconsistency of the Other.[19]

Žižek's reading of cultural history gets more complicated still. It is ultimately the Jews who, for him, introduce into civilization the possibility of assuming a (psychotic) distance from the symbolic order. It is the Jew, in other words, who presents the possibility of slipping from the position of hysterical subject, whose anxieties are still ultimately addressed to the big Other, into a psychotic identification with the object that materializes the Other's inconsistency. Žižek criticizes Jewish theology not for introducing the hysterical question into civilization—if anything, Žižek wants to claim that this was at some level the supreme cultural achievement of Judaism and that all anti-Semitism is grounded in the refusal or inability to come to terms with the sublime monumentality of this very achievement. Rather, Žižek proposes that Jewish monotheism is *not pathological enough*, that it does not go far enough toward embracing the psychotic risk at the heart of its own revolutionary restructuring of the ethical imagination; it does not, perhaps cannot, go far enough in mobilizing the "perverse" resources produced by its own set of prohibitions and injunctions.[20]

3

Žižek saw his analyses of modern anti-Semitism as part of a larger project of articulating the contours of a postmodern ethics. Such an ethics implied a kind of mnemonic imperative with regard to historical trauma, and in particular, the trauma of the Holocaust. At the end of his book *For they know not what they do*, Žižek suggests that this ethical attitude is best understood in conjunction with the psychoanalytic concept of the drive; indeed every ethical attitude can be correlated with the structure of a particular psychopathology:

The *hysterical* ethical imperative is to keep desire alive at any price: apropos of every object which could satisfy it and thus threaten to extinguish it, the hysterical reaction is a "This is not *that!*" which sets the desire again in motion. The object of the *obsessional* desire is the Other's *demand*: his imperative is to guess it and comply with it at any price. The obsessional...sacrifices himself, works all the time for the Other, in order to prevent the appearance of the Other's desire. The imperative of a *pervert*, on the contrary, is to work for the Other's *enjoyment*, to become an object-instrument of it....Beside these three ethics of hysterical desire, obsessional demand, and pervert enjoyment there is, however, a fourth ethical attitude, that of the *drive*....[That is] the ethical compulsion which compels us to mark repeatedly the memory of a lost Cause. The point is *not* to remember the past trauma as exactly as possible: such "documentation" is a priori false, it transforms the trauma into a neutral, objective fact, whereas the essence of the trauma is precisely that it is too

Film still from *Kafka*, 1991, directed by Stephen Soderbergh.

horrible to be remembered, to be integrated into our symbolic universe. All we have to do is to mark repeatedly the trauma as such, in its very "impossibility," in its nonintegrated horror, by means of some "empty" symbolic gesture.[21]

For Žižek, a key exemplar of this anamnestic imperative is Claude Lanzmann and the aesthetic procedures he employs in his documentary film *Shoah*. In *Shoah*, Lanzman:

> renounced in advance every attempt to reconstruct the "reality" of the Holocaust; by means of numerous interviews with survivors, with peasants who today live on the site of Auschwitz, by means of shots of desolated remnants of the camp, he *encircled* the impossible place of the Catastrophe. And this is how Lacan defines drive: the compulsion to *encircle* again and again the site of the lost Thing, to *mark* it in its very impossibility—as exemplified by the embodiment of the drive in its zero degree, in its most elementary, the *tombstone* which just marks the site of the dead.[22]

In this postmodern, post-Holocaust ethics of the drive one identifies with and remains open to the traumas of history in order to gain a non-cynical distance on the present. Curiously, perhaps, it is a Jewish filmmaker and intellectual dealing with the core trauma of modern Jewish history who exceeds the limits of the ethical universe opened by Jewish monotheism. For Žižek, the secret to the so-called progress of postmodern over modern ethics and aesthetics lies in his understanding of the differences between Jewish and Christian theology, and, in turn, his understanding of Hegel's revision of Kant:

> Hegel's reproach of Kant (and at the same time of Jewish religion) is…that it *is Kant himself who still remains a prisoner of the field of representation*. Precisely when we determine the Thing as a transcendent surplus beyond what can be represented, we determine it on the basis of the field of representation, starting from it, within its horizon, as its negative limit: the (Jewish) notion of God as radical Otherness, as unrepresentable, still remains the extreme point of the logic of representation.[23]

It is Hegel's assumption of a perspective "more Kantian that Kant himself"[24] which allows him to recognize the crucial dialectical dimension of the Christological conception of God's incarnation in Christ.

> In Kant, the feeling of the Sublime is evoked by some boundless, terrifying imposing phenomenon (raging nature, and so on), while in Hegel we are dealing with a miserable "little piece of the Real"...God who created the world is Jesus, this miserable individual crucified together with two robbers.... Herein lies the "last secret" of dialectical speculation: not in the dialectical mediation-sublimation of all contingent, empirical reality, not in the deduction of all reality from the mediating movement of absolute negativity, but in the fact that this very negativity, to attain its "being-for-itself," must embody itself again in some miserable, radically contingent corporeal leftover.[25]

The postmodern ethics of the drive delineated by Žižek "leans on an identification with just such a corporeal leftover or partial object, an identification prefigured by the (Christian) saint who "occupies the place of the *objet petit à*, of pure object, of somebody undergoing radical subjective destitution."[26] For Žižek, the Christian saint *repeats* the fundamental theological gesture of Judaism, as the subject made destitute by the call to the order of subjectivity. If I have understood Žižek correctly, that is what it means to "enjoy your symptom": to identify, in an active mode with the uncanny object which serves to materialize the traumatic dimensions of subjectivity and therewith the *state of emergency* of the socio-symbolic order.[27] Such a perspective places squarely—and obsessively—in the foreground of its attention and concern the caesural dimension in and through which the subject emerges, is established, but also thrown into crisis, suspended.[28]

Read too simply, Žižek's work might be understood as one of the oldest gestures of Christian anti-Semitism, namely the claim that the Jews got stuck at an earlier stage of cultural, psychological, and moral development, and that they remain a people who cannot move beyond their outdated covenant and its representational practices. To the extent that such a claim does appear in Žižek's work, it is crucial to emphasize once again how it runs counter to expectations. Žižek does not suggest that Judaism's ethical rigor and representational asceticism introduce disequilibrium into an organic, functioning

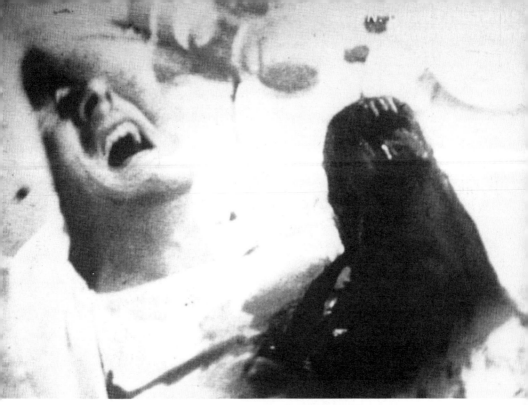

Film still from *Alien*, 1979, directed by Ridley Scott.

society otherwise in harmony with itself. Rather, Jewish monotheism, he argues, is not disturbing enough, not radical enough in its embrace of trauma and abjection, that it maintains too *external* a relation to the social pathologies produced by the felicitous functioning of symbolic power and exchange. There are still other complications in Žižek's account of the resources of monotheisms.

Christianity can be, for Žižek, an attempt to mask the anxiety of inter-pellation, to "gentrify" the encounter with the inconsistency of the Other. Christian love and sacrifice can figure as elements of a fantasy-scenario allowing the subject to avoid the Real of his or her desire.[29] Furthermore, Žižek's two key examples of postmodernist sensibilities turn out to be modernist Jewish writers: Franz Kafka and Benjamin. But, what turns out to be postmodern about both Kafka and Benjamin is that they are each seen as moving beyond the "modernist" limits of their Judaism.

Of Kafka's *The Trial* and, in particular, of Josef K.'s encounter with the obscene dimension of the Court (K.'s argument before the court is interrupted by a public act of sexual encounter), Žižek says the following:

> Kafka's sensitivity to this "trespassing of the frontier that separates the vital domain from the judicial domain" depends upon his Judaism: the Jewish religion marks the moment of the most radical separation of these domains. In all previous religions, we encounter a place, a domain of sacred enjoyment (in the form of ritual orgies, for example), whereas in Judaism the sacred domain is evacuated of all traces of vitality and the living substance is subordinated to the dead letter of the Father's law. Kafka trespasses the divisions of his inherited religion, flooding the judicial domain, once again, with enjoyment.[30]

With regard to Benjamin, the understanding of repetition in history, which he developed in *Theses on the Philosophy of History*, is the clearest formulation of the "ethics of the drive" so crucial to Žižek's conception of contemporary cultural and political options. But Žižek links Benjamin's thesis with the Kierkegaardian idea of historical repetition as the act of becoming a Christian: the identification with Christ, not as Master, but as the "humiliated originator of a scandalous act."[31] Žižek seems to say that although Jews have been positioned historically within their host societies as an "exception," a queer remainder, Jewish theology lacks the imaginative resources that could support the mad decision to identify with this position or to produce a politics based on such an abject identification.[32]

4

It is in his relation to Wagner and, in particular, to Wagner's final opera, *Parsifal*, that the most concentrated expression of Žižek's complex relationship to Judaism and to theology itself can be discovered. That Žižek would be drawn to *Parsifal* is no surprise considering how the opera weaves together late nineteenth-century ideological fantasies about women and Jews with larger political and theological questions concerning authority and mercy, suffering and redemption.[33] The opera's feature that focuses his attention is the famous wound burning in the thigh of the Fisher King Amfortas. The uncanny nature of this wound, received upon succumbing to the lures of Kundry, embodiment of Woman and Wandering Jew, condemns him to a state of eternal suffering, allowing him neither to die nor to administer his duties as King of the Grail Society. The crisis that forms the dramatic point of departure of the opera is that the social and liturgical conditions for effective ritual discourse—for its capacity to produce reality effects—no longer obtain. "The mystery of performative magic," Bourdieu has noted, relies on that "alchemy of *representation*...through which the representative creates the group which creates him."[34] It is this alchemy that is in crisis in the opera, a crisis materialized in the Fisher King's wound.[35]

It is only in Hans Jürgen Syberberg's film version of the opera that the crucial dimension of the wound finds its proper mise-en-scène: Syberberg externalizes the wound, places it on a pillow outside the body as a vagina-like, bleeding organ, as a fragment of libidinal life-substance, as that which will not allow Amfortas to die.

For Žižek this life-substance represents not so much a primal preverbal realm of pure animal instinct, but rather the disruptive leftover of the hystericizing interpellation itself; it is a surplus produced by the intervention of language and symbolic power into the animal realm: "The trap to be avoided here...is to conceive this pure life-drive as an entity subsisting prior to its being captured in the symbolic network: it is, on the contrary, the very mediation of the symbolic order which transforms the organic 'instinct' into an unquenchable longing which can only find solace in death...The Symbolic itself opens up the wound it professes to heal."[36]

Žižek shares Wagner's Judaic association to this woundedness, this surplus *jouissance*. For Wagner, the disequilibrium embodied in the wound is the stuff of the Wandering Jew, represented in the opera by Kundry, who, through a kind of metaphysical unsafe sex, infects Amfortas with her disease, her congenital restlessness. She has the nature of a kind of black marketeer, a messenger and a go-between for others, but with no indigenous realm herself. She has no access to autochthonous existence.[37] The crucial difference between Žižek and Wagner is, of course, that while Žižek is constantly searching for more productive ways to inhabit the states of emergency of sociopolitical existence, Wagner longed for their final overcoming, their final solution. *Parsifal* stages a fantasy of redemption from the symptoms of a modern subjectivity marked as feminine and Jewish; Žižek, on the contrary, proposes an ethico-aesthetic attitude whereby one would mobilize

Film still from *Parsifal*, 1983, directed by Hans Jürgen Syberberg.

constructive identifications with those very symptoms.

Thus Žižek finds Syberberg's film version of the opera to be more Wagnerian than Wagner. For a moment in the second act when, upon kissing Kundry, Parsifal suddenly remembers Amfortas's suffering, Syberberg replaces the male actor with a woman, who continues, like the actor before her, to lip-synch the male tenor voice. This is the moment when Parsifal enters the realm beyond phallic identification; a transition and transmutation occur, supported by an act of compassion in its turn "founded on the identification with the *real* of Amfortas's suffering, [that is] it involves the *repetition* of Amfortas's pain in the Kierkegaardian sense."[38]

As Žižek narrates the historical unfolding of the logic of the signifier, the "Jewish Question" is first raised as the Jewish expression of perplexity in the face of the faceless God, an anxious bewilderment on the part of Jews as to

Gregory Crewdson, *Untitled*, 1994.

what God wants with them. The abjection resulting from failing to assume fully the symbolic mandates enunciated in the name of the Other (God), is still addressed to the Other's overwhelming authority; the Other's inconsistency is taken upon oneself. In the perverse, Wagnerian scenario, the Jewish question finds its final solution; the tensions it introduces are relieved once and for all by the invention of a pure redeemer. Here, abjection is offered as a sublime spectacle of Otherness, that heightens the effect of final purification. One suspects that such a strategy was behind the famous exhibition of "Degenerate Art" put on by the Nazis in Munich in 1937 and recently reconstructed at the Los Angeles County Museum of Art. Here, too, abjection, materialization of the Other's inconsistency, is taken upon oneself, but now in the person of the redeemer, who promises to absorb and purify it without remainder. Paradoxically, in this perverse scenario, monotheism's surplus is made to disappear.

Žižek's ethics of the drive can, finally, be understood as an attempt to approach this perverse remainder of the "Judaic" crisis from a different perspective.[39] Rather than seeking answers or final solutions, he *repeats* the Jewish question—indeed, one might say, he compulsively repeats it—but with an interest now in deploying the abjection and the disequilibrium it introduces into the psychic economy. This deployment becomes a resource for mobilizing deeper levels of compassion for and identification with those who find themselves at dis-ease in society.[40]

That Žižek believes Jewish theology precludes a critical mobilization of ethical resources suggests that he himself remains captivated by a Christian fantasy about Jewish moral and religious underdevelopment. Yet among his crucial contributions to contemporary ethics is his insistence on their theological dimension—a dimension we avoid at our peril.

Film still from *Close Encounters of the Third Kind*, 1977, directed by Steven Spielberg.

Scott Bukatman

THE ARTIFICIAL INFINITE:
ON SPECIAL EFFECTS AND THE SUBLIME

All my modes of conveyance have been pictorial.
— Charles Dickens, "Some Account of an Extraordinary Traveler" (1885)

Introduction

In the eighteenth and nineteenth centuries, as new technologies and social formations displaced the haptic in favor of the visual as a source of knowledge about an increasingly complicated set of lived realities, popular culture offered a surfeit of spectacular forms, which compensated for the lack of touch with what might be termed a hyperbole of the visible. An apparently direct address toward the spectator depended upon techniques of perspectival composition, trompe l'oeil, a hiding or de-emphasis of the frame, an often overwhelming scale, and a mimesis of the natural. Historians tend to agree that underlying the fascination with such displays was an anxiety regarding urban growth, technological development, and social change. The spectacle was a simulacrum of reality, but spectators weren't fooled by these illusions—by paying admission, the customer indicated a comprehension of the terms of the exhibition. Some pleasure, however, clearly derived from responding to these entertainments *as if they were real*. Visual spectacle provided reassurance in the form of a panoptic power—the human subject was, after all, capable of perceiving and comprehending the new conditions of physical reality through the projection of an almost omnipotent gaze out into the represented world.

The cosmic displays of science fiction cinema, produced by technologically advanced optical effects, surely derive from a similar drive for scopic mastery. The overwhelming perceptual power granted by these panoramic displays addressed the perceived loss of cognitive power experienced by the subject in an increasingly technologized world. In acknowledging anxiety while ultimately producing a sense of cognitive mastery, these entertainments frequently evoked the rhetorical figures of the sublime. The nature of popular, commercial entertainment suggests that this was actually a tamed sublime and not truly awe-inspiring, transcendental visions; nevertheless, the sublime became an important mode for these mareoramas, landscape paintings, stereoscopic views, and science fiction films.

The stock scripts and relatively wooden performances of science fiction cinema shouldn't distract one from the articulations of meaning located in the mise-en-scène as well as the state-of-the-art technological spectacle on display.[1] While there are relatively few director-auteurs in science fiction film, cinematic style (as well as authorial consistency) can be located in the fields of art- and effects-direction. The special-effects work of Douglas Trumbull is particularly distinctive and sustained in its evocation of the sublime, and this essay will concentrate on sequences from his films. Trumbull supervised the Stargate sequence of 2001: A Space Odyssey (1968) and produced the luminous alien spacecraft for Close Encounters of the Third Kind (1977). He worked in conjunction with "visual futurist" Syd Mead on Star Trek: The Motion Picture (1979) and Blade Runner (1982). Beyond his work as an effects designer, Trumbull directed two features, Silent Running (1972) and Brainstorm (1983)—both interesting in themselves—while developing his 65 mm, 60 fps Showscan exhibition system. Finally turning away from Hollywood and a system that was, as he put it, "multiplexing itself to death," Trumbull turned to "special venue" productions, developing multimedia technologies for theme parks or World's Fair exhibitions. The popularity of simulation rides in a surprising range of settings has provided new opportunities for Trumbull to experiment with the kind of experiential cinema that has been his forte since the 1960s. The attention to spectacle and the simulative conditions of theme parks and fair exhibitions recall the early history of the cinema as well as the history of precinematic phantasmagoria.

In Trumbull's effects sequences, the sublime is elicited around a massive technological object or environment: the Stargate (2001), the mothership (Close Encounters), V'ger (Star Trek), and the city (Blade Runner). Inspiring the sensations characteristic of sublimity, technology alludes to the limits of human definition and comprehension.[2] The special effect unfolds before the human gaze and becomes susceptible to the encompassing control that inheres in the very act of seeing. Trumbull's sequences, however, are different from other effects work in their ambivalence: they are neither

Film still from *Blade Runner*, 1982, directed by Ridley Scott.

unabashedly celebratory (*Star Wars* [1977]) nor darkly condemning (*Alien* [1979]). As with the panoramas and other displays of the last two hundred years, Trumbull's effects are rooted in an ambivalent relation to new technologies; like those other forms, Trumbull's effects too often depend upon new technologies to succeed.

Concerning Visuality

The ability to cognize is often dependent upon the concurrent ability to envision and thereby conceive, and this can be equally true for both quantitative information and abstract conception. Therefore, debates over the place and meaning of observation and visual representation within culture take on a crucial importance. This is generally, although not unanimously, regarded to be a period of information proliferation, thus less information comes to the subject via direct sensory, bodily experience and more, far more, arrives in mediated, representational forms. If, as some cultural theorists would have it, mediation is immediately tantamount to manipulation, then the proliferation of mediated experiential modes will indeed produce a vapid, inertial society of spectacles and simulations. On the other hand, if visuality comprises a more complex and open phenomenon, then the range of observer positions will be less circumscribed and possibly less debased. The relation between visual experience and cognition, then, always an active topic for philosophical debate, becomes increasingly crucial as a means of understanding the places available to the subject in this heavily technologized and electronically mediated culture.

Jonathan Crary's extended essay *Techniques of the Observer* has proven its value in the fields of art history, cinema studies, and cultural studies. This analysis of paradigmatic shifts in the construction of "observation" is set against the context of electronic culture; his opening question—"How is the body, including the observing body, becoming a component of new machines, economies, apparatuses, whether social, libidinal, or technological?"[3]—straddles historical and contemporary moments. The model Crary constructs is grounded in the process of modernization, under the conditions of which the observer "is made adequate to a constellation of new events, forces, and institutions that together are loosely and perhaps tautologically definable as 'modernity.'"[4] Classical models of vision collapse, along with "their stable space of representations. Instead, observation is increasingly a question of equivalent sensations and stimuli that have *no reference to a spatial location*."[5] Crary's emphasis is less on changing spatial conceptions than on the implications of a culture founded upon a new relation between visuality and experience, a relation that now "depends on the denial of the body, its pulsings and phantasms, as the ground of vision."[6]

Representation begins to have less to do with the world "out there" than with the physiological conditions of vision, conditions that can now be simulated. Thus the experience of a three-dimensional image is no longer any guarantor of "reality," but is more a physiological sleight-of-hand. Crary brilliantly argues that a range of aesthetic techniques generally lumped under the heading of *realism* "are in fact bound up in nonveridical theories of vision that effectively annihilate a real world."[7] The absence of spatial verifiability uproots signs from an ostensibly stable field of meaning, whereupon meanings and values can be exchanged more freely.

The separation of the visual and the haptic then resulted in an over-emphasis on the former. The "empirical isolation of vision" permitted its "quantification and homogenization" while, at the same time, the objects of visual contemplation were "sundered from any relation to the spectator's position within a cognitively unified field."[8] A veritable explosion of visually based toys, displays, and environments appeared, as if to compensate for the diminished role played by the senses. These objects and environments, however, were irreducibly situated within the increasingly centralized and disciplinary conditions of industrial capitalism. Where some might see the construction of a "transcendent subject" no longer limited to a single set of spatiotemporal coordinates, Crary, following Foucault, sees a model grounded in systems of surveillance and control, in which the observer becomes, almost literally, "a component."[9]

Crary emphasizes the kineticism that emerged in the nineteenth century. Visual experience was "given an unprecedented mobility" that was "abstracted from any founding site or referent." Crary tracks this mobility into the field of representation, noting that "the traveling artist's kinesthesia demanded and elicited a new and complexly fluid state of mind. Locomotion was consonant with the experience of mobile and mutable aspects or shifting effects."[10] This analysis is likewise consonant with that of some others who link the emergent kinesis of the Machine Age to a set of epistemological reconfigurations and adaptations on the part of the mobile observer. In the nineteenth century, travel and tourism by the middle class increased. Vision was put into motion around the rise of railway travel, with its new emphasis on what Wolfgang Schivelbusch has dubbed "panoramic perception."[11] The replacement of the slow, horse-drawn coach by the speeding train shifted the rider's attention from the foreground to middle- and backgrounds. The windowed and enclosed train put the world behind glass and effectively filtered out auditory, olfactory, and haptic sensations of the world beyond the window, forcing a reliance on sight as the sole source of information.

Crary's sociology differs significantly from that of Schivelbusch, however. While for Crary, "panoramic perception" would demonstrate the severing of visuality from the body, Schivelbusch describes a *reconfiguration* of the body in relation to the shifting nature of spatial apprehension. Despite their common suspicion of industrial capitalist culture, Schivelbusch remains committed to a phenomenological perspective that is less concerned with judging than with *mapping* alterations in lived experience. Whatever it is that Schivelbusch is describing, it is *not* a removal of the bodily experience from the field of industrial development—the velocity that produces a panoramic view is also the velocity that cripples and pulverizes bodies, whether in crashing railway carriages or across the fields of wartime carnage. Panoramic perception (even in its simulacral, cinematic variation) remains a most definitely embodied phenomenon.

It is the absence of a phenomenology that weakens Crary's work, and that absence tends to schematize some of his most provocative arguments. The body, as an experiential field, disappears from his consideration, repressed, as surely he claims it was in the past.

While vision may be detached from the body of the observer, it is constantly reattached to an at least partially illusory body. There *is* a being at the center of the panorama, enjoying the view. The body isn't at the center of Paris, it's at the center of an exhibition, a display—still, it's at the center of *something*. As at Disneyland, where real motion and simulated motion are intricately combined, the actual position of the observer's body becomes a means of support for illusionistic position.

Why is the body constantly being recalled into being, by amusement park rides or panoramic addresses? Undoubtedly, Crary could argue that the loss of the body is the precondition for creating that equivalence of signs and values that obtain when vision is decorporealized, "liberated" from direct physical verification, and so the support described here would serve as an ersatz re-embodiment to further ground the ideological operations of industrial capitalism. Indeed, every moment of potential liberation Crary describes is immediately recontained by the disciplinary society:

> But almost simultaneous with this final dissolution of a transcendent foundation for vision emerges a plurality of means to recode the activity of the eye, to regiment it, to heighten its productivity and to prevent its distraction. Thus the imperatives of classical modernization, while demolishing the field of classical vision, generated techniques for imposing visual attentiveness, rationalizing sensation, and managing perception.[12]

This is not the whole story. Indeed, Crary provides some clues to a world beyond his monolithic historical read. He acknowledges the existence of oppositional modes, but argues that they only become "legible against the more hegemonic set of discourses and practices in which vision took shape."[13] However, a reading of this "set of discourses" as all-determining perhaps should be resisted.

When Crary discusses "techniques for imposing visual attentiveness, rationalizing sensation, and managing perception," he becomes aligned with the very tradition he critiques. Can the study of visuality from the contemporary academy's own predilection for rationalized sensation and managed perception be liberated? Barbara Stafford offers a different set of terms with which to understand visual culture. While her theoretical models are less elaborated than those of Crary, she describes a pervasive shift from a culture grounded in visuality and physical experience to one dominated by textuality and instrumental reason.

Stafford's histories reveal the diversity of visual culture in the eighteenth century. If research into the physiology of perception "objectified" the viewer, this objectification was often a prelude to further revelations or discoveries of natural law. Such "rational recreations" as automata, kaleidoscopes, miniatures, illustrated texts for children, and even the phantasmagoria of magic lantern presentations served as forms of "phenomenalized instruction," according to Stafford, erasing "the dualism between mind and body, art and craft, science and technology."[14] Stafford emphasizes the construction of "an informed and performative gaze"[15] operating within a field of "sensationalized knowledge."[16] As for the illusionism attendant upon most of these phenomena, Stafford notes that these were "licit effects"[17]; their principles were to be revealed and explained to the audience or observer. Yes, the world and the observer were inscribed within a field of knowledge and therefore within the disciplinary apparatus that Foucault correctly describes, but this is not the sole aspect of visuality that needs to be acknowledged (as Crary likely would concur).

So the constant address to the body, which marks the panorama and, later, the amusement-park attraction, is not simply a writing of the body into an expanding field of signification, it is *also* a means of inscribing new, potentially traumatic phenomena and perspectives onto the familiar field of the body. They are holdovers from a time when, Stafford writes, "spatial and kinesthetic intelligence were not yet radically divorced from rational-linguistic competence and logical-mathematical aptitude."[18] Empirical positivism may have suffered at the hands of the perceptual skepticism exercised by eighteenth-century British philosophy, but enough faith in "direct" and "unmediated" experience survived to be flattered at the fairground.

If this is an argument for the validity of an "embodied knowledge," it comes not from a belief in the existence of some empirically verifiable "truth," but from the conviction that knowledge grounded in the conditions of physical experience permits a necessary accommodation—perhaps it could be called an *adaptation*—to a new set of lived conditions. Crary's emphasis on the separation of observation from spatial referent, following the macroscopic, strategic model upon which Foucault's historiography depends, might be countered with Michel de Certeau's emphasis on the range of interventionist *tactics* available to the subject within these broader structures, tactics that are the very stuff of individual adaptation to the strategies of centralized power structures. While the incorporation of the body into a range of primarily visual entertainments constitutes for Crary a *colonization* of that body, it represents a *compensation* for the declining centrality of sensory experience; a valid (that is, *useful*) means of recentering one's experience of a decentered world. If this was, in some ways, complicit with dominant ideological agendas, it is also, irreducibly, a necessary means of being in the world.

Corporeal Mappings

Now the sense of displacement or disorientation produced by the environment of the industrial city gave rise to new entertainments, which produced a cognitive and *corporeal* mapping of the subject into a previously overwhelming and intolerable space. Panoramic perception became a fundament of the Machine Age, a function of new architectures of steel and glass; it defined the arcades and department stores of consumerist abundance, as well as a set of spectacular forms that reinforced the new dominance of an epistemology of vision. Telescopes, microscopes, maps of continents, geological periods, and human anatomy further extended the reach of human perception, as Stafford notes:

The extension of vision permitted a new form of travel. Opaque depths were opened up, becoming transparent without the infliction of violence. The veil of the invisible was gently and noninvasively lifted. The eye could easily voyage through and beyond the densities of a plane, or silently journey beneath the stratified level.[19]

Travel provided the metaphor for a broad evocation of a spatiotemporal continuity wedded to a utopian dedication to "progress"; Susan Buck-Morss writes that "Railroads were the referent, and progress the sign, as spatial movement became so wedded to the concept of historical movement that these could no longer be distinguished."[20] Journeys to new heights, new perspectives, and new worlds became the substance of such recreations as the packaged tour, the panorama, the scenic garden, and the World's Fair. In popular literature, Jules Verne took his readers aloft in a hot-air balloon to go *Around the World in Eighty Days* and fired them from a cannon to bring them *From the Earth to the Moon.* As Buck-Morss notes, new modes of conveyance became linked to new fields of knowledge and new possibilities for human advancement.

Here, then, was the start of at least one thread of what we have come to refer to as the Information Age, as an abundance of physical data was fitted to the epistemological desires and requirements of the public consciousness. Spectacular displays depended upon a new mode of spectatorial address— essentially, *you are there* (even though you're not)—linked to new technologies of visual representation. Of course, these presentations can, in their turn, be traced to the geometric specificities of perspectival composition, which situated the observer in relation to the scene observed: now the spectator was provided with panoptic views of the inside of the human body, astronomical phenomena, and newsworthy events. Panoramas of exotic ports evoked an illusory immersion in faraway places:

The panorama struck a responsive chord in the nineteenth century. It satisfied, or at least helped to satisfy, an increasing appetite for visual information. A revolution in travel had made the world seem smaller. The growth of a literate middle class and the burgeoning newspaper industry meant that many more people were aware of a greater number of happenings over a larger area of the globe. It is not surprising that people should desire visual images of a world of which they were becoming increasingly aware through the printed word. The panorama supplied a substitute for travel and a supplement to the newspaper.[21]

Bodily experience and cognitive understanding were thus supplemented, or replaced by a reliance on vision within a simulacrum of the real.

Most popular were panoramas of one's own city. One was positioned at the precise center of a 360-degree space that had, until now, been imperceptible and overwhelming in its entirety. If the visual was now released from the confirmation of haptic experience (a fundament of the Information Age), then the visual would become a hyperbolically self-sufficient source of knowledge and information for the general public, as well as for the scientist. The panorama and its successor, the diorama, would eventually incorporate simulated motion, lighting, and sound effects, platforms to rock or even move the audience, photography, and even, in the case of Hale's Tours, cinema. Such attractions have made an important return: Trumbull has developed the "Ridefilm Theater," a simulator-theater system, which features a fifteen-passenger motion base encompassed by a 180-degree spherically curved screen. High-resolution images are projected with synchronized movement to produce a remarkable sense of immersion in a complex technological space.

Special Effects

A too-easy historicism has tended to divide cinematic representations into naturalist and anti-naturalist categories (Siegfried Kracauer's realist versus formalist debate). Within this dichotomous schema, special effects hark back to the imagistic manipulations of Georges Meliès, but it should be clear that even the supposedly naturalistic Lumière brothers were purveyors of spectacle and novelty. Cinema is, of course, a special effect, and that is how it was regarded by its initial audiences. The illusion of motion, with its consequent sensations of temporal flow and spatial volume, provided enough innovation for spectators already familiar with a range of spectacular visual novelties. If cinema's unique blend of spatiotemporal solidity and metamorphic fluidity was largely assigned to the representation of narrative, the effect(s) of the medium nevertheless remained central to the spectatorial experience.

Writings on early cinema by both Tom Gunning and Miriam Hansen describe a "cinema of attractions"—an "unabashed eclecticism" that was figured in a direct address to the viewer. "[T]his is an exhibitionistic cinema,"[22] Gunning claims, while Hansen, following Jean Mitry, writes that "The frontality and uniformity of viewpoint is clearly the mark of a presentational—as opposed to representational—conception of space and address."[23] The presentational mode ultimately yielded to a more univocal narrational system that stabilized space and introduced "the segregation of the fictional space-time on the screen from the actual one of the theater or, rather, the subordination of the latter under the spell of the former."[24]

Nevertheless, Gunning argues that the fascination of the attraction "does not disappear with the dominance of narrative, but rather goes underground, both into certain avant-garde practices and as a component of narrative films, more evident in some genres (e.g. the musical) than in others."[25] The genre of science fiction often exhibits its spectatorial excess in the form of the special effect, which is especially effective at bringing the narrative to a spectacular halt. Science fiction participates in the presentational mode through the prevalence of optical effects that in fact reintegrate the virtual space of the spectacle with the physical space of the theater.

Special effects redirect the spectator to the visual (and auditory and even kinesthetic) conditions of the cinema, and thus bring the principles of perception to the foreground of consciousness. This idea is at the center of Annette Michelson's superb analysis of 2001: A Space Odyssey.[26] The expansion of the visible field to cineramic proportions, the removal of perceptual clues to verticality and other conditions of physical orientation, the sustained evocation of bodily weightlessness, the imposition of the rhythms of respiration and circulation on the soundtrack all contributed to the profound redefinition of haptic experience undergone by the voyagers in the audience. If 2001 is more radical in its affect than other works of narrative cinema, visual effects remain central to it and all science fiction. "If we think of what it is that science fiction 'does,'" writes Brooks Landon, "surely we must acknowledge that its frequently mentioned 'sense of wonder' derives from 'a new way of seeing.'"[27]

The optical effects of the contemporary cinema are thus only a more recent manifestation of spectacular technologies of vision, which combine large-scale display with direct spectatorial address to create an immersive and apparently immediate sensory experience. Trumbull's work inherits from an entire history of visual displays, including "Renaissance" and aerial perspectives, panoramas, landscape paintings, dioramas, and the cinema (the cinema of attractions).

Sublime Space and Science Fiction

The presentational mode described by Gunning and Hansen exceeds the logics of narrative and exaggerates the poetics of spectacle, and thus bears a relation to certain conceptions in poetry and painting of the sublime—especially the sublime as figured in American art of the nineteenth century.[28] The classical conception of the sublime, as described by Longinus in relation to spoken rhetoric, emphasizes its power to enthrall and elevate the mind of man; in a famous passage, Longinus celebrated its unambiguous glory through his own little special-effects sequence, writing that "our soul is uplifted by the true sublime; it takes a proud flight, and is filled with joy and vaunting, as though it had itself produced what it has heard."[29] Joseph Addison and Edmund Burke were largely responsible for transforming the sublime from Kantian doctrine to aesthetic strategy. The field of the sublime was comprised of the majestic, the awe-inspiring, and the literally overpowering: it spoke the languages of excess and hyperbole to suggest realms beyond human articulation and comprehension. The sublime was constituted through the combined sensations of astonishment, terror, and awe that occur through the revelation of a power greater, by far, than the human. Those commingled sensations result from the rhetorical construction of grandeur (either grandly large or small) and the infinite. The object of sublime rhetoric is often not all available to vision or description: uniformity (the similarity of all parts) and succession (a sense that the object extends on and on) characterize this "obscurity." The sublime initiates a crisis in the subject by disrupting the customary cognized relationship between subject and external reality. It threatens human thought, habitual signifying systems, and, finally, human prowess: the mind is hurried out of itself by a crowd of great and confused images, which affect because they are crowded and confused.[30] The final effect is not a negative experience of anxious confusion, however, because it is almost immediately accompanied by a process of appropriation of, and identification with, the infinite powers on display. The phenomenal world is transcended as the mind moves to encompass what cannot be contained.

As telescopes provided tantalizing glimpses of worlds beyond our own, astronomy provided a new and exalted ground for the rhetoric of the sublime. In 1712 Addison wrote of the infinitude of the heavens in language typical of the mode:

> When we survey the whole earth at once, and the several planets that lie within its neighbourhood we are filled with a pleasing astonishment, to see so many worlds, hanging one above another, and sliding round their axles in such an amazing pomp and solemnity. If, after this, we contemplate those wild fields of ether, that reach in height as far as from Saturn to the fixed stars, and run abroad almost to an infinitude, our imagination finds its capacity filled with so immense a prospect, and puts itself upon the stretch to comprehend it. But if we rise higher, and consider the fixed stars as so many vast oceans of flame, that are each of them attended with a different set of planets, and still discover new firmaments and new lights that are sunk further into those unfathomable depths of ether, so as not to be seen by the strongest of our telescopes, we are lost in such a labyrinth of suns and worlds, and confounded with the immensity and magnificence of nature.[31]

Here, in a sense, the cosmic trajectories of 2001 are prefigured not only in the evocation of astronomical *scale*, but in the description of successive levels of macrocosmic order that signal the limits of our abilities to comprehend the vastness of the universe.

The universe is without end, it confounds us, but the rhetoric of the sublime paradoxically permits an understanding of these sensory and conceptual limits (the rhetorical threat posed by the sublime is finally, then, not really that much of a threat). In the twentieth century, the genre of science fiction has continued this representational tradition. The precise function of science fiction, in many ways, is to *create* the boundless and infinite stuff of sublime experience, and thus to produce a sense of transcendence beyond human finitudes (true to the form of the sublime, most works produce transcendence of, and acknowledgment of, human limits). Indeed, science fiction

is characterized by a spatiotemporal grandeur revealed by its titles alone: *A Space Odyssey*, *When Worlds Collide* (1951), *The Star Maker* (1939); also consider the titles of early science fiction magazines: *Astounding*, *Amazing*, *Thrilling Wonder Stories*, *Weird Tales*. The conclusion of Richard Matheson's *The Incredible Shrinking Man* (1956) links the micro- and macro-cosmic in an infinite continuum of religious transcendence. Science fictional objects are sublimely obscure: the city of Trantor in Isaac Asimov's *Foundation* series covers an entire planet—one of the boundless cities of the genre—and there is the spaceship that begins *Star Wars*: too large for the screen—or our consciousness—to hold. Science fiction is immediately and deeply bound to the tropes of the sublime. Burke's "artificial infinite" is echoed in *2001*'s story "Jupiter and Beyond the Infinite": rhetorical allusions to the unrepresentable forms of infinity.

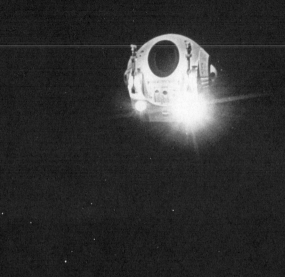

Film still from 2001: *A Space Odyssey*,
1968, directed by Stanley Kubrick.

Landscape Effects

The figures of sublime rhetoric were developed and understood primarily
with reference to poetic language, and were first related to the register of the
visual arts only with suspicion. With the unintentional influence of Burke,
however, painting became a site for the instantiation of the sublime. The
representation of natural phenomena — mountains, sky, flora — became
the means of meditating upon the magnificence of their Creator (and the
magnificent powers of reason that could ruminate upon that magnificence).

The landscape sublime is rooted in an activity of contemplation, in the
attempt to grasp what, fundamentally, cannot be grasped. The breadth of
Nature proves ideal for stimulating the dynamic cognitive processes that exalt
the mind. The artworks most closely associated with the sublime, therefore,
are often detailed, scrupulous revelations of nature's grandeur — but less

from an impulse toward mimesis than from a wish to encourage specific spectatorial behaviors. For landscape painting to inspire dynamic contemplation, however, duplication of external form is not enough. Many artists, J.M.W. Turner and Frederick Church among them, provided a kind of viewing instruction in the depiction of a frequently tiny figure fixed in contemplation of the very wonders that the painter chose to embellish.[32]

Spectacular and monumental elements, all encompassed by a dynamic spectatorial gaze, are easily found among the plethora of special-effects sequences in the history of the cinema, especially in the films with effects by Douglas Trumbull. A Trumbull sequence is less the description of an *object* than the construction of an *environment*. The work privileges a sense of environmental grandeur: the wide-screen effect becomes an enveloping thing, such as the roiling cloudscapes that presage the appearance of the mothership in *Close Encounters*, the gorgeous and monstrous Los Angeles of *Blade*

Film still from *2001: A Space Odyssey*, 1968, directed by Stanley Kubrick.

Runner, or the amorphous, infinite interiority of the starship V'ger in *Star Trek*. The Stargate sequence in 2001 features scarcely any objects; it emphasizes instead a continuum of spatiotemporal transmutations.

Trumbull's effects are grounded in a phenomenologically powerful spatial probing, and emphasize the spectatorial relationship to the effect/environment.[33] To some degree all special effects are so inscribed: the effect is designed to be seen, and frequently the narrative pauses to permit the audience to appreciate (or groove on) the technologies on display (what, in a somewhat different context, Laura Mulvey once referred to as "erotic contemplation"). However, Trumbull's sequences are different. Where John Dykstra's work in *Star Wars* or *Firefox* (1982) is all hyperkinesis and participatory action, Trumbull's work is especially contemplative.

Further, and regardless of the director involved, the extended effects sequences typical of Trumbull's films frequently include an explicit, pronounced spectatorial position within the diegesis: the cutaways to an astronaut's frozen features, Spielberg's typically slack-jawed observers, the crew of the Enterprise, or the disembodied eye that holds the infernal city reflected in its gaze.[34] Dykstra's work on *Star Wars* is not so inscribed: the passage of the first, impossibly enormous spaceship is witnessed by the audience, but there is no spectator within the diegesis (the same holds for the climactic explosion of the Death Star). Trumbull stages an extended encounter with the sublime by including the presence of the diegetic spectator, rehearsing (and hyperbolizing) the filmic spectator's own response.

Through the prevalence of such temporally distended special-effects sequences, science fiction clearly participates in the presentational mode of cinematic discourse. While audiences may use a diegetic human figure as a guide through the immensities of alien space, these characters do not serve to deflect the spectator's own experience of the action.[35] The passage into the kinetic lights and amorphous shapes of the Stargate sequence in 2001 is directed right at the viewer. The close-ups of David Bowman, the astronaut, do not reintegrate us into a fictional (representational) space, neither do they situate Bowman as a psychologized subject to focus audience identification. The cutaways to human observers in Trumbull's sequences re-establish scale and re-emphasize the Otherness of the sublime environment. They do not mediate the experience through the psychology of characters who are, uniformly, stunned into a profound passivity. The fictive and the theatrical spaces are collapsed, as the diegetic and cinematic spectators are, in a metaphorical sense, explicitly united (Michelson has argued that 2001 is predicated upon just such a phenomenological confusion between astronaut and spectator[36]). The presence of diegetic spectators, then, here actually enhances the presentational aspect of the cinema, while also evoking the sublime.

America (and Beyond the Infinite)

In the nineteenth century, America revealed its obsession with the relation between nature and human power and human destiny in prose, paint, and politics. A rhetoric of progress mingled with the sense of a people chosen by God and history, privileged to engage with and tame a New World that still seemed to bear the fresh touch of its Creator. The vast reaches of the American West seemed to test the will of the nation's new citizens and the emerging technologies of industrial capitalism were extraordinarily suited to the colonization and economic exploitation of these territories. Alan Trachtenberg has written that "the American railroad seemed to create new spaces, new regions of comprehension and economic value, and finally to incorporate a prehistoric geological terrain into historical time."[37] (This powerful spatiotemporal collapse echoes Buck-Morss's contention that spatial movement analogized historical progress.)

In an oft-quoted section of *Nature* (1836), Emerson—who also could be somewhat delirious about train travel—narrates a state of mind characteristic of the transcendental sublime:

> Standing on the bare ground,—my head bathed by the blithe air and uplifted into infinite space—all mean egotism vanishes. I become a transparent eyeball; I am nothing; I see all; the currents of the Universal Being circulate through me; I am part and parcel of God....In the wilderness, I find something more dear and connate than in streets or villages. In the tranquil landscape, and especially in the distant line of the horizon, man beholds somewhat as beautiful as his own nature.[38]

Emerson's debt to Kant is evident in his version of the sublime as exaltation, and in his description of the ego's dissolution, which is ultimately recuperated in the beauty of human nature.[39] His "transparent eyeball" anticipates those infra-diegetic, but impossibly positioned, spectators that populate Trumbull's effects sequences, and provides a strikingly direct gloss on Trumbull's evident transcendentalist bias.

The landscape took on a centrality in American painting during this period, which became "immersed in nature."[40] On the union of sublime aesthetics and transcendental philosophy, one critic has written, "the sublime experience was transformed into a new mode of landscape expression; the traditional sublime setting was augmented by the transcendental sublime sensibility, a sensibility that found its roots in man's internal perception of time and space."[41] This mix of the sublime and the transcendental found its clearest expression in the genre of Luminist painting, which emphasized impersonal expression, horizontality, minute tonal gradations, intimate scale, immobility, and silence. And, of course, the Luminist work is defined by its

Film still from *Close Encounters of the Third Kind*,
1977, directed by Steven Spielberg.

representation of light: a cool, hard, palpable light (not diffuse), spread across a glassy surface. "The linear edges of reality are pulled taut, strained almost to the point of breaking."[42]

Luminism was not the only means of evoking the sublimity of the American landscape. The monumental paintings by such nineteenth-century figures as John Singleton Copley, Thomas Cole, Church, Albert Bierstadt, and others constructed a visual rhetoric of the sublime far removed from the solitude and silence of the Luminists, although there were numerous shared concerns.[43] "The landscape painter must astonish his audience by the immediacy of his effects," Andrew Wilton writes.[44] While much of this immediacy was achieved through the hyperbolized detail of the rendering, the scale of the works also served to overwhelm the sensibility of the spectator. These representations of exotic landscapes in the American West or South America were too large and too detailed to be "taken in" with a single glance; the spectator's gaze had to be put in motion to assimilate the work. Furthermore, this especially exhibitionistic mode of representation was often exhibited like a fairground attraction. In its creation of a dynamic, kinetic spectatorial gaze, as well as in its mode of exhibition, the monumental landscape painting takes a place alongside such contemporaneous "phantasmagoria of progress," in the words of Buck-Morss, as the diorama and magic-lantern show.

The paintings of Church are particularly appropriate to consider alongside Trumbull's effects. The astonishing, bold color experiments (special effects) that Church unleashed in depicting his twilight skies and volcanic eruptions were the result of new technologies in cadmium-based pigment production. These effects were put in the service of atmospheric and astronomical phenomena: not just the sky, but also the sun and moon, a meteor, and the aurora borealis. One critic has pointed to the promise of revelation that underlies the dramatic scenography and monumental scale of Church's later paintings.[45] Another writes of Twilight in the Wilderness (1860) that "The painting defies simple categorization as a 'luminist' work of art, but there can be no doubt that the subject of the picture is, literally, American light, symbolic of the new world Apocalypse. It is a compelling work of art which combines two aspects of the sublime, the traditional interest in nature as object and the transcendental concern for nature as experience, through color, space, and silence."[46] The dual contexts of Luminism and "great pic-

Frederick Edwin Church, *Twilight in the Wilderness*, 1860.

tures" provide a further context for understanding the Stargate sequence. The passage through the Stargate is a voyage "beyond the infinite": a movement beyond anthropocentric experience and understanding. Through slitscan technology, Trumbull created a set of images that were little more than organized patterns of light—the very stuff of cinema. Light, with its implications of revelation and blinding power, is also the very stuff of the sublime:

> Light is…the alchemistic medium by which the landscape artist turns matter into spirit….In American art especially, light has often been used in conjunction with water to assist spiritual transformation, either dissolving form, as in some of Church's large South American pieces, or rendering it crystalline, as in the works of [Fitz Hugh] Lane. In the former, light is more closely attached to what we generally call atmosphere, and has a diffusive, vaporous quality. In the latter, light itself partakes of the hard shiny substance of glass. In all instances, the spirituality of light signals the newly Christianized sublime. In the large paintings by Church and Bierstadt light moves, consumes, agitates, and drowns. Its ecstasy approaches transcendence, but its activity is an impediment to consummating a complete unity with Godhead.[47]

In 2001, light's transformative power illustrates, embodies, and enacts the supercession of the human (and the human's rebirth as a super-human; a Star Child). The *sturm und drang* of the Stargate sequence is clearly different from the Luminism of Lane, but I would argue that the sequence involves both topoi of light, moving from the diffusion and mutability of the first section to the color-tinted, crystalline silence of the landscapes at the end. Light "moves, consumes, agitates, and drowns," but there is nevertheless a stillness that subtends the sequence's last minutes. Here the landscape becomes more concrete, but commensurably more barren, and the sky and sea blend as the horizon disappears. The penetrating camera movements persist, but are now overwhelmed by the quietude of these enormous and empty worlds. Luminism produces a sense of distance from the aestheticized landscape, unlike the sense of the immersion; nevertheless, a similarity abides in their suspended temporalities.

"While Church's handling of composition and paint only peripherally borders on Luminism," John Wilmerding writes on Church, in terms applicable to the Stargate sequence, "the sense of vast stillness verg[es] on an imminent crescendo of light and sound."[48] The "imminent crescendo" directs us to the function of sound here and in other sequences. While most are accompanied by tumultuously loud sound effects or scoring, language is, in every instance, *absent*. Again, there is a conflation of two tropes found in the American landscape sublime: the evocation of Apocalypse ("sublimity overwhelms with a deafening roar") and the quietude of Luminism ("the spectator is brought into a wordless dialogue with nature").[49]

Techno Encounters

Mark Seltzer has astutely proposed that "Nothing typifies the American sense of identity more than the love of nature (nature's nation), except perhaps the love of technology (made in America)."[50] To the American paradigm that opposed nature's might and human will, American painters, poets, essayists, and novelists added the newly unleashed forces of technology to produce what Leo Marx has labeled "the rhetoric of the technological sublime."[51] The anxiety surrounding the new prominence of technology has received much attention since the Industrial Revolution, and its representation has hardly been limited to science fiction.

Thomas Cole, *The Course of Empire: The Savage State*, 1833–36.

In nineteenth-century America, technological anxiety was transformed by a sense of destiny. "Above all, the rhetoric conveys that sense of unlimited possibility which seizes the American imagination at this remarkable juncture."[52] This rhetoric of unlimited possibility does not, however, mask some residual anxieties, as a surfeit of landscapes featuring decimated woodlands and smoke-obscured vistas demonstrates: "The new significance of nature and the development of landscape painting coincided paradoxically [!] with the relentless destruction of the wilderness in the early nineteenth century."[53] As Rosalind Williams notes in her study of subterranean environments in the nineteenth century, "Technological blight promotes technological fantasy."[54] The presence of the sublime in science fiction—a deeply American genre—implies that our fantasies of superiority emerge from our ambivalence regarding technological power, rather than nature's might (as Kant originally had it). The might of technology, supposedly our own creation, is mastered through a powerful display that reveals anxiety but recontains it within the field of spectatorial power.

What Buck-Morss refers to as the "phantasmagoria of progress" (panoramas, world's fairs, and the like) are visual displays that concretized metaphors of progress to provide some means of contending with the complexity of what Walter Benjamin called a "new nature." By this, she contends, Benjamin meant:

not just industrial technology but the entire world of matter (including human beings) as it has been transformed by that technology. There have been, then, two epochs of nature. The first evolved slowly over millions of years; the second, our own, began with the Industrial Revolution, *and changes its face daily*. This new nature, its powers still unknown, can appear ominous and terrifying to the first generations confronting it, given "the very primitive form of the ideas of these generations" who have yet to learn to master, not this nature itself, but humanity's relationship to it.[55]

The sublime is thus figured in these spectacles as an idealist response to significant and continuing alterations in lived experience. Hence the sustained reappearance of the sublime in popular, technologically based entertainments. Then and now, the language of consumption and the display of spectacle grounds the spectator/visitor, and hides the awful truth: that an environment *we made* has moved beyond our ability to control and cognize it. Therefore the experience of technology is both alien and enveloping in Trumbull's effects sequences. The simultaneous fascination with, and fear of technology's beauty, majesty, and power reveals a necessary ambivalence, and through this ambivalence, the sublime becomes a crucial tool of cognitive mapping.

Technology has come to comprise an environment, a second nature "with its own attendant pleasures and hazards."[56] Nature is displaced by technology in 2001, *Close Encounters*, and *Silent Running*, and this displacement is complete in *Star Trek* and *Blade Runner*. Buck-Morss notes that the new space of the Crystal Palace, a space permitted by new technologies of glass and steel architecture, "blended together old nature and new nature—palms as well as pumps and pistons."[57] Technology permits a containment of nature in the Crystal Palace and in the crystalline domes of *Silent Running* (the garden in the machine, perhaps). But the appearance of nature has become little more than nostalgia for a pastoral ideal. If the rhetoric of the technological sublime in nineteenth-century letters was characterized by the appearance of "the machine in the garden," then, as we leave the twentieth century, we would have to note that the machine *is* the garden.[58]

A clue to the significance of this shift can be found in Thomas Weiskel's emphasis on the distance between our experiential realm and those of the eighteenth and nineteenth centuries:

To please us, the sublime must now be abridged, reduced, and parodied as the grotesque, somehow hedged with irony to assure us we are not imaginative adolescents. The infinite spaces are no longer astonishing; still less do they terrify. They pique our curiosity, but we have lost the obsession, so fundamental to the Romantic sublime, with natural infinitude. We live once again in a finite natural world whose limits are beginning to press against us and may well crush our children.[59]

In the absence of *nature*'s grandeur, technology constitutes a new ground for human definition and for our obsession with infinite power and possibility.

Recent theorists of the postmodern have emphasized the moment's techno-cultural underpinnings and the rise of invisible networks and decentered fields of power that characterize electronic and nuclear technologies. The aesthetics of John Pfahl's series of photographs (from the early 1980s) of power plants in their "natural" settings are troublingly, shockingly ambivalent: nuclear (and other) technology becomes truly aweful—somehow simultaneously coexisting with nature, dominated by nature, and dominating over-all.[60] The startling rise of mediating electronic technologies has precipitated a crisis of visibility and control. If cultural power now seems to have passed beyond the scales of human activity and perception, then culture has responded by producing a set of visualizations—or allegorizations—of the new "spaces" of technological activity. Most science fiction remains unflaggingly conservative in its language and iconography, but it still remains the genre most committed to narrating the ambiguities that mark the technological contours of contemporary culture.

The ambivalent relation between technological and human definition is evident in the mothership sequence in *Close Encounters*. First, one must note the sky in the film's night scenes—abundant stars allude to the infinite reaches of space: as we know, "theorists of the sublime attached much importance to the associational significance of the sky, and usually placed the night sky full of stars at the head of their list of its sublimities."[61] For landscape painters, clouds also afford the opportunity to depict "the storm cloud, with its obvious propensities for sublimity,"[62] and *Close Encounters* provides strikingly exaggerated clouds; substantial yet strangely liquid, and far more animated than the dumbfounded characters themselves.

The star-filled skies presage the appearance of the mothership. The ship's design was inspired, according to Spielberg, by the sight of an oil refinery — the sublime is thus constituted around an anxious technological object (recalling Pfahl's contemporaneous reactor shots). Additionally it might be noted how nature, in the form of Devil's Tower, dwarfs the humans who nestle against it until the mothership, in its turn, dwarfs nature. The complex relationship between nature and technology is also manifested in the first appearance of the mothership, which emerges from behind the mountain; that is, *from the earth*, instead of from the improbably starry sky. The scale of the ship further indicates the subjugation of nature by the power of technology — Spielberg wanted it to be so big it would blot out the stars. Finally, while the ship is defined by brilliant and beautiful light, it is also distinguished by the black shadows that swallow the observers: for all its beauty, the mothership is a dark, visually negative force. Burke noted the same dialectic between light and its absence in Milton's descriptions of God: "Dark with excessive light thy skirts appear."[63]

Artificial Infinities

Artificial infinities abound in science fiction: generation ships, outer space, cyberspace, boundless cities, cosmic time, galactic empires, 2001's mysterious monolith, the endless underground cities of the Krell in *Forbidden Planet*. Rosalind Williams has written about the craze for artificial environments that punctuated the fancies of the nineteenth century, noting that these industrial fantasies have continued unabated into the present era "in the form of retreats into personal or collective environments of consumption—the artificial paradises of the shopping mall or the media room, for example. This is a journey further inward, a retreat from technology into technology."[64]

Trumbull's accomplishment is the articulation of the tension between anxiety and identification, as we strain to assimilate the imagined infinities of technological power. Such tension is exemplified in the opening sequences of *Silent Running*, as a lush, natural forest is slowly revealed to exist within the hyper-technologized spaces of a vast spacecraft— nature is now enclosed and redefined by the experience of the technological, as "man's traces"[65] become increasingly more evident until they finally overwhelm. The ending is even more complex: the drones are left to care forever for the forests as they drift through deep space. The spaceship explodes in a, well, *sublime* pyrotechnical display (a new sun). The drones tend to the forest in a series of interior shots. Then the drifting, domed biosphere is seen in its entirety, slowly receding in the visual field. Culture (the ship) is superseded by nature (the pure light of the explosion); then the natural (forest) is contained by the technological (dome), which in its turn is contained by the cosmological (space).

The archetype of the artificial environment is, of course, the industrial city, revisited and hyperbolized in *Blade Runner*. The oil refinery motif of *Close Encounters* has become more pronounced as the entire city is now explicitly figured as an anxious technological object. There is no more nature, only its simulacra in the form of synthetic animals and humans and no escape from the encompassing technological landscape. Williams argues that "in the late twentieth century, our technologies less and less resemble tools—discrete objects that can be considered separately from their surroundings—and more and more resemble systems that are intertwined with global systems, sometimes on a global scale."[66] In *Blade Runner*, as the hovercar glides above and through the city, we indeed "take a proud flight" and attain a position of conceptual mastery over the complex and superbly synchronized urban scene. The film provides two fields of vision—the physical reality beyond the windshield and a graphic display of what must be an electronic traffic corridor along which the car is gliding. Each view explains the other as urban space, and maps the other to produce an intertwined global system.

The phantasmagoria of progress involves a sustained immersion within an artificial environment that *suggests technology's own ability to incorporate what it has generally excluded*. If the disappearance of nature is seen as a consequence of a burgeoning technosphere, then utopian technologies will incorporate Arcadia (Crystal Palace, Futurama, *Silent Running*). If technology is seen as a dehumanizing force that leads to an impoverishment of spirit, then utopian technologies will permit a new emergence of spirituality and cosmic connectedness (Enterprise, virtual reality). It even might be argued that cinema is the very paradigm of an artificial, technological environment that has incorporated utopian fantasies of nature, kinetic power, spiritual truth, and human connection.

Conclusion

Trumbull's effects are not the sole staging for sublime experience in electronic technoculture—it is evident that the rhetoric of the sublime made a somewhat massive return in recent years. Jean Baudrillard's kinetic cyberblitz, the techno-mysticism of the magazine *Mondo 2000*, the transcendent possibilities envisioned in William Gibson's cyberspace trilogy, a new attention to its rhetoric within philosophy and the academy, and millennial fantasies of various stripes are all markers of the renewed relevance of the sublime.

The reasons for its return are not difficult to fathom. The sublime came to prominence in the eighteenth century in response to the increasing secular rationalization of modern life,[67] and was later coopted as a mode of accommodation to the power of industrial technology. The late twentieth century presents an historically analogous time of technological development and expansion, and so it isn't at all surprising that this rhetoric should recur to ground an understanding of an ostensibly new phenomenon. Just as Gibson's cyberspace recasts the new "terrain" of digital information processing in the familiar terms of a sprawling yet concentrated urbanism, the sublime becomes a means of looking backward in order to recognize what's up ahead.

But there's something else going on. The sublime not only points back toward an historical past, but also holds out the promise for self-fulfillment and technological transcendence in an imaginable near future. Under the terms of the sublime, technology is divorced from its sociological, rationalist underpinnings to become a technology without technocracy, a technology beyond the scope of human control. Inevitably the *fact* of technological progress, and thus accommodation, becomes the single valid response. The sublime presents accommodation that is both surrender and transcendence, a loss of self only leading—*back? forward?*—to a renewed and newly strengthened experience of the self.

Thomas Weiskel's revisionist approach to the Romantic sublime represents an understanding of this characteristic ambivalence as a repressed content: namely, the playing through of an Oedipal scenario. On some level, then, the return of the sublime represents a throwback to fantasies of masculinist dominance, and to this interpretation Trumbull's endless penetrations into vast unknown regions seem to lend themselves. "I think we may infer," Weiskel writes, "that the 'imminent danger' [Burke] to which we are exposed and

Film still from *Close Encounters of the Third Kind*, 1977, directed by Steven Spielberg.

from which we are then released in the sublime moment is an unconscious fantasy of parricide."[68] There are elements of this scenario in each of Trumbull's sequences as the human—character *and* cinematic spectator—is first overwhelmed before being granted some measure of cognitive control. The destabilizing function is then subverted and recontained by the narratives of some of these films: Spielberg's parricidal anxiety becomes especially evident when *Close Encounters*'s omnipotent aliens emerge from the "mothership" resembling the doe-eyed Third World waifs of a Margaret Keane painting. Human superiority is (re)assured in relation to these diminutive *and neutered* figures. *Star Trek*'s new captain literally mates with the female manifestation of V'ger in a transcendent, trans-species union that nevertheless somehow remains comfortably heterosexual.

The sublime's rhetoric of confrontation and mastery smacks of phallocentric bias, while the landscape sublime's predilection for the "virgin landscapes" of South America and the North American West aligns it all too neatly with the colonialist usurpation that called itself manifest destiny. Its mystical overtones no longer jibe with a secularist culture which remains deeply suspicious of spiritual value. Despite these condemnations, however, any number of theorists and artists have attempted to rescue the sublime, finding in its confrontational power an ethos of exploration and self-discovery that meshes with this sense of Trumbull's effects work.

Patricia Yaeger has specifically challenged the masculinist modalities of sublime rhetoric. The sublime preserves a sense of the Other, or "alienness," even in the face of cognitive assimilation, and it can encompass the intimate as well as the grandiose. The Other need not be "obliterated or repressed," but can be preserved in a newly dialectical Self-Other relation. Yaeger argues that one can locate a desire to *merge* with the Other in the sublime moment, and thus the Oedipal struggle for control may be a feint that masks more primordial (and less gendered) desires.[69]

In *Agon*, Howard Bloom connects sublimity to questioning traditions of Gnostic thought. Like the sublime, "Gnosis is more than or other than rational," Bloom writes. "And yet this need not be considered either a mystical or a visionary experience, since in Gnosis the knowledge is neither of eternity nor of this world seen with more spiritual intensity. The knowledge is of *oneself*."[70] The confrontation leads back to a confrontation with a self that is neither fixed nor given, but which comes into being through the act of interrogation. Bloom refers to Gnosis as "performative knowledge," a knowledge that can only emerge via experience. Further, the experience of "the Sublime moment proper" opens a "gap of negation or disjunctive generation of meaning."[71] The sublime thus depends upon a disruption followed by a performative adaptation, which yields a dynamic knowledge of a dialectically constituted self. Yaeger and Bloom might be approaching the sublime from different directions, but for both the trope offers something more than phallocentric reassurance.

Bloom has devoted some attention to the sublimity of science fiction and fantasy: "What promises to be the least anxious of literary modes becomes much the most anxious, and this anxiety specifically relates to anterior powers."[72] Again, ambivalence—"the eddies between the polarities of bondage and freedom"—structure the experience of the text. The sublime enacts an ambivalent relation to authority, while the *technological* sublime enacts a conflict between a humanity ever more tenuously linked to nature while ever more imbricated with the "anterior powers" of technocultural structures. If a positive value can be assigned to the return of the sublime in science fiction cinema, then it lies in a rhetoric of scopic destabilization that yields a new subject position with regard to the source of technological anxiety. Unlike *Star Trek*, 2001 does not "explain" its ultimate trip, and so denies its viewers the firm ground provided by cognitive comprehensibility. In 2001, director Stanley Kubrick and Trumbull have emphasized and fore-grounded the phenomenological instability that has always been more or less present in science fiction cinema. If science fiction seems anchored (or mired) too often in rationalist cant, then the "performative knowledge provided by inventive special effects moves the spectator beyond the rational to a space beyond the infinite. Despite the recontainments and reassurances that are the functions of these films' narratives, scopic instability and cognitive accommodation remain fundamental to, and implicit in, our experience of the works.

Novak describes another moment when advanced technology was employed to (re)present advanced technology: "The most exciting visual encounters with the railroad were those that took place through the media-tion of yet another machine—the camera. The photographer, having already accommodated one machine within his artistic perspective, had much less difficulty than painters in accommodating still another."[73] As with the privi-leged views provided by panoramas, elevations, photographs, and the cinematograph, special effects encourage engagement with a reality that seems to defy engagement. Through the "magic" of special effects, a contem-porary rhetoric of technological sublimity is produced by technological means. Cinematic *affect* is rooted in cinematic technology, but *effects* empha-size those underpinnings—if cinema is rooted in illusions of light, for example, then optical effects endow light with an overwhelming physicality. Science fiction cinema uses state-of-the-art effects to "accommodate still another" realm of machinery. The effects put machinery in motion, offering technology up to dynamic contemplation (and in the Ridefilm theaters machinery in motion puts the spectator in motion as perception is now supplemented by bodily experience).

However, one must acknowledge (at least briefly) the recurrent fantasies of sexuality and power at work within many of these texts. The mythology of the frontier is clearly evoked in narrative, image, and technique, as a penetration of sublimely mysterious and fluid interior spaces become the

Film still from *Star Trek: The Motion Picture*, 1979, directed by Robert Wise.

precondition for masculinist mastery (*regeneration through cyberspace*). But this overdetermined phallocentric, um, thrust should not blind us to the overwhelming need to map ourselves into the anxious spaces of, first, industrial, and now, electronic culture. Cognition, one hopes, does not necessarily imply domination; and while the science fiction narrative often speaks to militaristic male fantasies, the spectator's immersion in a technologized environment presented by the wide-screen special-effects sequence retains phenomenological validity and importance. To invoke a Transcendentalist, Thoreau's admiration of the Native American was grounded in their relation to nature—"Perception, rather than domination or calculation, is his forte."[74] Relations between perception, cognition, knowledge, and power are neither

NB: Does special effect provide engagement with technological culture + an inclusion of virtual

288

simple, nor absolute, and the phenomenological status of these phantasma-goria of progress merits an attention that moves beyond simply classifying such spectacles as masculinist, colonialist, or consumerist.

But we should remember Gunning's argument that "effects are *tamed* attractions." The reflexivity of special effects (a technology of technology; a cinema of cinema) indeed encourages some sense of identification and mastery. The effect is possessed of its own hypnotic grandeur: it is designed to inspire awe, but always within a reassuring sense of play (note the number of fan magazines devoted to effects extravaganzas). Rapture replaces terror in most of these artificial infinities. There is, ultimately, a denial of human limitations that connects to science fiction's overall denial of sexuality, mortality, and fleshy bodies (what Vivian Sobchack has described as "the virginity of astronauts").[75]

Special effects, in the cinema and in their extension to virtual reality systems, are but the latest in a series of popular cultural entertainments that emphasize what Stan Brakhage has referred to as the "adventure of percep-tion." Despite their emphasis on perceptual mastery and the magisterial gaze, these recreations significantly balance sensory pleasure and cognitive play. The effects sequences of science fiction cinema are significant for what they say, as well as for what they do not say, about our complicated relationship to complex technologies at this precarious historical moment. This ambivalence permeates the culture of visuality. As Miriam Hansen wrote with regard to the development of cinema's moving camera, "The mobilization of the gaze promises nothing less than the mobilization of the self, the transformation of seemingly fixed positions of social identity. This mobilization, however, is promise and delusion in one."[76]

A two-ton cast of Actress Marie Wilson's leg is unveiled by a Los Angeles hosiery shop.

DISCUSSION

Edward Ball Ralph Rugoff described the esoteric collections of the Museum of Jurassic Technology, and you described the performative nature of the cabinet of curiosities. Do you recognize qualities in the MJT that you see in the cabinet of curiosities, and if so, what would they be?

Stephen Bann Obviously, there are several senses in which the performative can be understood. There's a sense in which the performative element resides in certain kinds of images. It resides, for example, clearly in Susan Stewart's image of Peale lifting the curtain. In the MJT the performative element is certainly there, though Ralph did not speculate as to any kind of motivation or psychological reason for its presence. It is clearly a performative display that only can be understood in relation to the specific, though unfathomable, intentions of one particular person.

Ralph Rugoff The dialogue between the enunciator of the cabinet of curiosities and its viewers seems to be a negotiation process—i.e., what this exhibit means is open to dialogue.

Stephen Bann Ralph, you talked about the Gene Autry Museum as having mutually irreconcilable viewpoints—the victor or the victim?—and the viewer can adopt either one, but you said that the MJT instead represents a shifting or fusion of horizons rather than viewpoints. I consider the cabinet of curiosities to belong to that second pattern as well. It embodies neither the religious nor the scientific viewpoint, but instead it negotiates and shifts between the two.

Marina Warner Something that arose for me from what you were saying is that in New Zealand there are museums that are monuments to the fallen. There's a convergence of national mourning with the national collection. A museum set up by a colonial power creates a Jurassic Technology–style narrative, false and indeterminate.

David Freedberg There is quite a lot of material about popular responses to relics in the twelfth century. Interestingly enough, Meyer Schapiro wrote a remarkable piece on aesthetic attitude in Romanesque art in which he deals with both learned and popular responses. There are remarkable precedents for museum labels, guidebooks, and acoustic guides in museums today. For example, little pamphlets were issued as guides to treasures containing relics and other vestiges of saints. I was struck by Bargraveana because it is, of course, a reference to seventeenth-century French books ending in *ana*. They're an interesting textual parallel to objects.

We've talked a lot about Freudian notions of mourning and loss, but there is a curious absence here of references to what seems to be the key Freudian term, fetish, which rarely refers to the ultimate perception of loss and the sense of the possibility of restitution of that loss. Perhaps these concepts are more useful in a discussion of cabinets of curiosity than the rather broad notion of mourning.

Stephen Bann I don't want to use the fetish because it is understood by anthropologists and to a certain extent by psychoanalysts as a fixation of a desire or an obsession, whereas what seems more important here is the generative power of the object in negotiation, in dialogue with the observer or spectator, and, indeed, the displayer as a mediator. One cannot escape that definition of the fetish as that which both displaces and arrests narrativity or generative power. What is unique about the Erasmus account—even though it is seen from a kind of rationalist point of view—is the clear analysis of displacement. The bones can't be seen; however, the gold casket drawn up out of the wooden one is seen. The individual jewels are not after all the relics, but they are labeled, described, and associated with the "great ones of the earth," as Louis XVI of France said of Canterbury. This is an extraordinarily precise description not only from the point of view of response but also from the point of view of performance.

Susan Stewart I don't think that mourning and fetishism are unrelated terms. Because of the specificity of mourning and the specificity of the substitutions that are referents, it's a term that can be used more rigorously in historical argument, whereas the fetish reifies the process, not the referent.

Peter Wollen Do you have any comments on the shifting balance between private and public?

Stephen Bann It was precisely the historical circumstances of the British Civil War and Bargrave's exile from civil society that made it possible for his private pursuits to take on public significance. He became a memorialist of a society that no longer existed. Then, with the Restoration, he could display its public face once again. Perhaps today there are analogous historical circumstances that would make that shifting between the public and the private possible, or necessary. The museums we're discussing are associated with individuals. Over the last ten or fifteen years museums—the massive museums, like the Louvre or the Metropolitan—have been forthrightly attacked for alienating their public, for simply being repositories of booty stolen from original possessors. It's a reading that makes it important to recontextualize individual or eccentric obsession and nonideological construction.

Ralph Rugoff While the MJT is largely the work of a single individual, it is presented as a public institution without an individual persona attached

Allan McCollum, *Lost Objects*, 1991, as installed in the Carnegie Museum of Art.

to it. There's the attempt to borrow some of the authority of a state institution, but it's really an act of imposture.

Susan Stewart For Peale there was no connection of individuality to his museum except in the tragic circumstances when he couldn't get state support for his museum. He saw himself in a line of museologists who had founded national museums. His notion of knowledge is not tied to the artifact. Most of the objects in the museum were gifts, and he was much more interested in displaying nature. Any cultural items were there as examples of nature.

Marina Warner I wonder if you could give some account of how the word curiosity changes from what is essentially a negative principle, certainly in Catholicism, to what becomes a positive principle. And certainly this relates strongly to women's roles in the cabinets of curiosities phenomenon because it's probably, I think, the first area of museology that women entered, mainly in Protestant countries. It always struck me that when Dutch women took up making cabinets of curiosities, it was because Protestantism did not actually indict the female principle of curiosity as strongly as in Catholic thinking.

Stephen Bann The particular translation of Erasmus's colloquies that I was using not only translates *Animigrateo* as curiosity, but also translates *comme antium* as the coming and going of tourists; Pomian's created two spectacular anachronisms. I couldn't possibly go into the development of the word *curiosity* and *curiosis* to the extent that he did; but the term has a sheaf of meanings that evolved during the sixteenth and seventeenth centuries, somewhat like the word *virtuoso*. For example, when John Evelyn visits Bargrave in 1672, he says he "visited Dr. Bargrave, the great *virtuoso*."

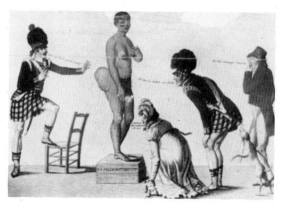

I've thought to myself that the statement was patronizing, but I'm not really sure. *Virtuoso*, of course, now means someone who plays an instrument in a technically accomplished way.

Lynne Cooke Are these visitors to Canterbury proto-tourists, or is there another moment when the

Fred Wilson, *Guarded View*, 1991.

pilgrim without an endpoint becomes someone who's looking for spectacle?

Stephen Bann In the sixteenth century, when preaching was thought to be the primary business of the church, buildings like the chapter house were used for preaching. But in the seventeenth century they tried to envision a situation in which the axis of the main building could be used for preaching. So, there certainly were some people who were there to *observe* the beauty, but there were others trying to present the semblance of a religious service.

Marina Warner Curiosity led to the formation of spectacle. Curiosities can be thought of in relation to other types of cabinets of display, like anatomical museums, which brings up not only issues of who the *collector* is but also the issues of private and public in terms of *spectatorship*.

Audience I was struck by Ralph's description of himself as a human exhibition, which raises the question for me of the ownership of collection

and the display of human curiosities. During the French Revolution when
the guillotine was operating and an exhibitionary complex occurred with
Madame Tussaud's Museum, the Louvre opened, and the collections,
including Barnum's living exhibitions in America, Tom Thumb, and the
Ripley's Believe It Or Not Museums. Contemporary artists such as James
Luna, Coco Fusco, and Guillermo Gomez-Peña are recuperating the exhibition of human beings in order to disrupt complacent museum viewership,
by returning the gaze.

Ralph Rugoff There is a difference: in much performance art the performer's body usually represents a more general idea, perhaps a specific type
of body, but not an individual person. Of course, a stuffed human being
could represent an even more specific individual than one layered with readings as presented by a performance artist. And obviously a stuffed figure can
represent an historical figure if it's someone like say Jeremy Bentham, who
is stuffed. Susan, would you like to say something about him?

Susan Stewart Well, not so much about Bentham, but Peale was much
more interested in the typical case of the species within a natural system.
Therefore the aberration was not of interest. Interestingly though, P. T.
Barnum eventually acquired much of Peale's collection. The foundation of
one's individuality and one's ability to reciprocate and countenance speech
was bound to their typicality, for him. Ironically, the person on display as an
aberration does become a type, and is then silenced. Peale held the curiosity
collection, or what is called now a freak show, in contempt. And yet, it
occurred at the same moment that commercial interests took over civic interests, and commercial interest marketed novelty. Novelty and aberration
became synonymous. Whereas, for Peale, novelty was an object of knowledge
that expanded the system's knowledge.

Audience There's a whole backwards trompe l'oeil history of human
bodies on exhibit in cases of the historical reconstruction of villages such as
Williamsburg, where the live people are not freaks but supposedly typical
milk-churners. I was wondering if Susan had more to say about Peale's interest in the idea of human bodies imitating other human bodies.

Susan Stewart I think Peale would have been contemptuous of the idea
of deception or simulation in a historical reconstruction. He felt that his
portraiture was a material trigger for the citizenry to reference noble ideas.

Ralph Rugoff Isn't embalming, if not exactly reconstruction, a repairing activity? Peale is clearly not showing *nature*, he's showing *embalmed nature*, which is a fetishized nature.

Susan Stewart Well, I don't know if it is fetishized. My own concepts of emotion or sentiment are disjunctive with what is going on with Peale. He saw his taxidermy as being a continuation of his skills in repairing saddles. He used the same skills in working with leather as he did in working with human skin. It's something Lillian Miller has said about his relationship to the corpse— it is a material object—but of course we associate it with great power.

Ralph Rugoff But it's hard to really believe that someone can only imagine a corpse as a material object and not as the site of loss and anxiety about one's own death.

Susan Stewart There's an exaggerated relation between the conscious and unconscious in this history.

Peter Wollen This is just an aside on taxidermy, but I recently read a biography of Darwin and I was struck that he'd learned taxidermy as a student from an African in Edinburgh. He spent his whole life stuffing things. Taxidermy

Hiroshi Sugimoto, *Ostrich / Warthog*, 1980.

was then clearly connected with the problem that refrigeration had not yet been invented, and it was necessary for the preservation of *specimens*. Is the implication that the shift from the aberrant to the typical is also the shift from the cabinet of curiosities to the modern museum?

Lynne Cooke Jean-Hubert made a distinction between memory and history and demonstrated how recent artists have acted as curators both of their own work and the work of others. Do you see in this impulse an attempt to get memory back into readings of history? This is linked to Alfred Parr's choice of the upstate New York area for the dioramas—an area that would be familiar and is reliant on memory for the individual to deal with issues of history.

Ann Reynolds The museum attempted to construct a false memory for the majority of its audience, which was based on some sort of rural notion about nature that they could tap into through a leisure relationship with location. It's appropriate to think about it that way.

Jean-Hubert Martin I made this distinction between history and memory because one is absolute rule; codified history relies on supposed scientific knowledge, and the memory is subjective, to put it succinctly. Artists have had an important role since the sixties in changing this pseudoscientific attitude. Most art history justifies but cannot explain creation. It's important that scientists themselves doubt science today.

David Freedberg I was very struck by Lisa Cartwright's suggestion that new medical images, because they are more ambiguous, somehow offer greater scope for interpretation. The first and most authoritative Greek medical writer, Galen, was extraordinarily hostile to images. He said images are too ambiguous—medicine can only be written in words. When he set up his system of classification, the great botanist Linneaus also said no icons, no images: if you want precision, you use words. I am interested in your disinterment of the uses of images and, then, your critique of the dangers of the construction of images.

Lisa Cartwright I wasn't quite trying to suggest that there is a danger in using images, but that there is precisely an ambiguity in the image leading perhaps toward an opening up of the tasks of images.

David Freedberg Well, I thought one of the striking features of your talk involved the problems that arise from the overvaluation of the ultrasonic

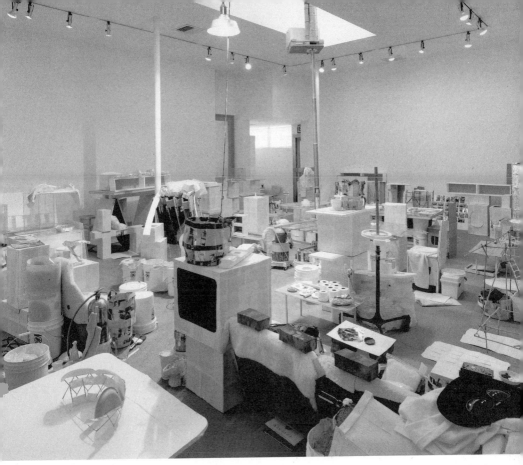

Jason Rhoades, *Swedish Erotica and Fiero Parts*, 1994.

image. In scientific literature, from Linneaus onward, there is this skepticism about the value of image-making. The discussion of this suspicion and fear of mimesis enters the realm of morality, ethics, and so on.

Marina Warner The odd thing about the quarrel about representation is that ambiguity is not targeted until much later. Instead, the *persuasiveness* of the simulation is targeted. From Plato onward, the argument was about how people were deceived by the truthfulness of the image, rather than the legibility of the image.

Lisa Cartwright Many of the images Ludmilla and I are looking at straddle an area between image and text that can't be regarded as simply pictorial images. The graphic image that's produced through ultrasound is then translated into the conventions of the photographic image. If there is a danger, and I'm not sure there is, it's in the reading of an image within particular pictorial conventions.

Ludmilla Jordanova It seems to me the role of instrumentation is important here. Anybody who's ever looked down a microscope is aware of what Lisa is talking about. The ambiguity that results from intervening instrumentation is heightened because the information is translated and encoded in one form and produced in another as a photographic image. That sense of interpreted space, which is constantly monitored, is a significant part of modern science. So, it seems to me that Lisa was talking about the notion of *practice*.

Susan Stewart Lisa's images reminded me of the representation of wounds in painting, where the skin of the paint is foregrounded and the interior presents an exterior surface. Part of our frustration about the unintelligibility of the image seems related to that.

Marina Warner I was struck by looking recently at Grünewald's crucifixion. The idea of actually seeing the interior might be connected to the change of symptomatic signs on the exterior body to do with illness. Of course, illness is internal these days. You rarely see it on the outside anymore. The symptom has been internalized, partly accounting for the need for the interior scrutiny.

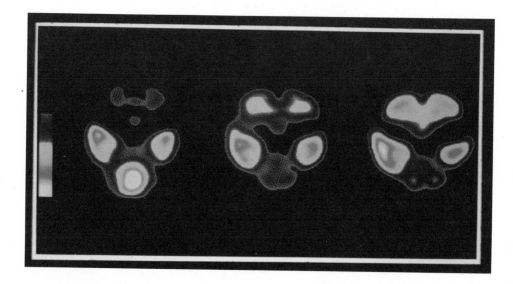

Lisa Cartwright Ultrasound technology emerged at about the same time as modernist painting and the concern with the surface. But an understanding of contemporary medical technologies in terms of techniques for looking into the body is a bit mistaken. For example, a technology like magnetic resonance imaging carves up the body through a series of one-dimensional planes, and that's not so much looking into the body. In fact, concepts of interior/exterior no longer operate. A concern with painting's surface expresses a certain anxiety around the disappearance of the body surface at that particular historical moment.

Stephen Bann We expect the ultrasonic images to be intelligible, or we expect them to be like something else and to represent a certain form of knowledge. Bargrave's cabinet includes one particular object he referred to as an artificial model of the human eye. Made of ivory and consisting of about twelve separate pieces nesting within each other, it doesn't look anything like a human eye. The object represents a tested knowledge: when Bargrave was in Padua he participated in two eye-dissections of a woman and a man to discover whether or not his ivory model corresponded to the real eye. It was a matter of empirical testing. I wonder whether one issue raised here hasn't been that regimes of intelligibility and mimesis become confused. Marina, for example, raised the possibility that Tussaud's Sleeping Beauty might well have been a medical model, whose innards had been taken out and replaced by a beating heart.

Marina Warner The scrutiny of unintelligible marks in forms like sonograms also have a religious fantasy dimension; of course, there's a phenomenon of the accidental photograph showing Christ's face or the Virgin Mary, for example. They're the objects of cult and veneration resulting from the deciphering of technologically produced random marks. In that case the technology, like a camera, replaces craft for the production of verisimilitude and is thought of as reliable. A technical instrument thus somehow produces the miracle.

Susan Buck-Morss How helpful is the *sublime* for critical understanding?

Scott Bukatman How relevant is the category of the sublime, how useful is it, what can we do with it? Jean Baudrillard, Paul Virilio, J. G. Ballard, Frederic Jameson, and even Donna Haraway again and again have evoked some huge totalizing narrative, which bears explicit relations to the sublime.

Peter Wollen Almost all the people you just mentioned have an exquisite interest in science fiction. Haraway has written on the cyborg; Jameson has written considerably about science fiction, especially that of Philip K. Dick.

Scott Bukatman There's an eerie overlap between Virilio and Ballard. Their rhetorics are similar.

Stephen Bann If one draws analogies, as you were plausibly doing between the landscape tradition—whether it's the American Luminist tradition, J.M.W. Turner, or, arguably, Caspar David Friedrich—is there not a drive toward using the mechanisms of picture making in order to supersede the traditional perspectival construction or single viewpoint construction? Turner, for example, increasingly used the circular format more and more toward the end of his life. Is the single viewpoint a precondition of the type of special effect you are referring to?

Scott Bukatman While Turner played with a sense of multiple perspectives, or at least a breakdown of a centered perspective, it seems to me that the spectator, in gazing over the surface of the painting, is locked within his or her own perspectival experience. Douglas Trumbull's sequences are more explicitly marked for the spectator. The rectangular format is pretty much inherent in the technology, so there is that difference. But the notion of a dynamic gaze, the gaze put in motion, seems to be similar. The American landscape painters weren't as concerned with perspectival breakdown as Turner. I've become dissatisfied with the position that the representations of electronic culture are new, and what that means. So, I've begun to dig into art history to ground current representations more fully.

Susan Buck-Morss Kant's sublime can never be direct or sensory, as in the realm of the representation of the sublime. For example, Cecil B. DeMille's sets in The Ten Commandments are straight out of the nineteenth-century panoramas. But, Kant would have been against this visual materialization of the transcendent.

Scott Bukatman In fact, William Gibson's cyberspace is precisely an attempt to map the economy in order to provide a graphic metaphor of the circulation and organization of capital, which are also susceptible to readings in terms of the sublime. Gibson has provided one mapping of the overlap of political economy and this encompassing, imperceptible, bigger-than-us force.

Susan Buck-Morss When you showed clips of Blade Runner, you asked us

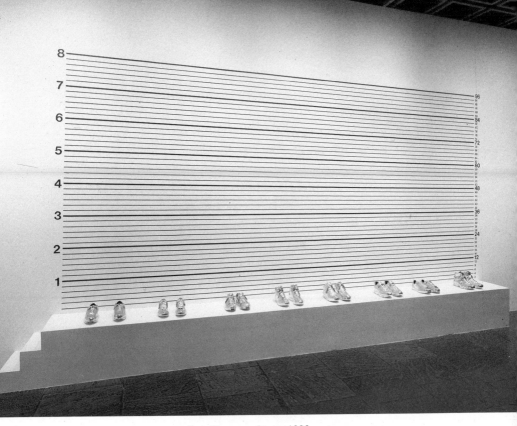

Gary Simmons, Lineup, 1993.

to ignore the narration, but I found it to be very important since it was the one time the character describes the people in the city, their pigeon language—a mixture of Japanese and American or something else. It seems that mixture, that culture, has potential.

Scott Bukatman Without the narration, you actually hear the mixed languages yourself. Also, importantly, cyberspace is a limited metaphor for circulation of capital in the present economy. I don't think it's an adequate metaphor, but that is its function. It's a theme-park reduction of the material Susan presented in the graphs, for example.

Giuliana Bruno I want to introduce one other element to the discussion of spectacle mapping. Ed Ball spoke about spectacle in relation to questions of ethnicity and formations of cultural identity. I was wondering about gender in relation to the spectacle in motion. Some of you have hinted at the idea of desire. How do we speak about, for example, women in that respect? It seems to me that the flâneur, the tourist, the immobilized gaze suggests for the female subject possibilities for exploring and exiting territory. Susan showed pictures of women in families. I'm always a little wary of the criticism of spectacle on that basis because it seems to enclose the female subject in a nonexploring territory, as opposed to a transitory state.

Edward Ball I'm tired of the sublime. I would subtract some of the thrall from the experience of spectacle and Otherness. One of the meanings of the phrase "woman as spectacle" in feminist film theory is exactly the construction of feminine sexuality as a kind of sublime Otherness. Clearly there's a real problem with the maintenance of this construction in a heterosexist media landscape. For me the answer is to step away from the sublime and even stop talking about it. I'm always fatigued when I sense the thrall of media critics talking about the technological megastructure.

Simon Leung Just as the gaze is not a sensory experience, as in the sublime, it is at the same time a type of demand. Although there is no longer a demand for any authenticity from the Other, we seem to be collectively demanding the Other to perform hybridity.

Edward Ball In fact, I disagree with you. There are two opposing demands. On one hand, there is a demand for cultural authenticity. But I don't think there's a demand for hybridity. One must be more black in the presence of a white person.

Simon Leung I think the demand is not a black or white situation especially in the age of what we call the multicultural or multinational perspective. It's not a matter of performing authenticity or performing hybridity per se, but it's a matter of performing authenticity and hybridity to better serve the purposes of, for instance, the flâneur.

Edward Ball Another demand is for assimilation to the white metaculture, and I agree with you here, there is a demand for the gestures of authenticity within the system of that white metastructure. The flâneur, though, is a marginal figure.

Simon Leung I'm not critiquing your implications of hybridity. But what is the nature of the demand for something not authentic? There seems to be an intrinsic relationship between demands for authenticity and the performance of hybridity.

Susan Buck-Morss I'm not just tired but I'm scared of a return to authentic traditions, whether Islamic, Russian, or European. It's a matter of politics. I don't want to participate in that. I want to fight against it with a strategy that glorifies the hybrid. It's a political position, not just an aesthetic trend.

Audience A Balzac text plays on *le capital* and *la capital* and perhaps we're talking about capital meaning "the head." Part of what is at stake here is multicultural identity: on what are different cultures going to be founded; what is going to be the common link that binds one person to another? That crisis is linked to the end of a certain moment of capitalism. One has talked about the crisis of the chronicled failure of Communism, but the question is, what is happening at the end of the century with cutting off the head of capital— what sort of community is based on that? That capitation or decapitation is linked to a figure of castration, in Freud or in Helene Cixous's work on decapitation and castration. I've been troubled by the facility with which Žižek substitutes Lacan's woman for the Jew. Lacan is very clear that this is a structure about the woman, and Žižek cheerfully globalizes this. But the woman is always singular—there's no community of women. The Jew is always plural, the Jew is always a race, the Jew is always defining a community. Also troubling is that Žižek has made the Jew the figure of all racism. Eric, you seem to follow him on that point. Could you comment on that and the moment of decapitation?

Eric Santner He does say anti-Semitism is an example of racism, but it's the exemplary example of racism. The way he understands the position of the Jewish believer vis-à-vis the Jewish god is such that the Jewish believer is compelled to feel the nonjustified dimension of the address of the big Other of authority. The experience of the nonjustified, the nongroundedness, the violence of the symbolic mandate of your community; for Žižek that means you automatically experience the breathing space. And he calls this the hysterical question: why am I what you are saying that I am. By asking that question you have experienced the dimension of the object, that is, what is not subsumed by that symbolic mandate. He clearly thinks that in the West, in Judeo-Christian societies, Jews have been privileged to have elaborated a theology on that experience. There's an exemplary experience of the structure of symbolic power; authority commands belief and the belief in authority produces a surplus, which could ultimately challenge that belief. To a certain extent it's a question of diasporic existence versus existence within an embodied nation state. But you're right, he's not interested in Jews as discrete human beings. Tackling the problem of anti-Semitism without Jews forces an engagement with a structural dimension of that racism. It's not just based on empirical encounters.

Audience I appreciated your discussion of the other side of the concept of sublimity, in a sense, Eric. What you've outlined here certainly resonates with the work of Sander Gilman who, in *Jewish Self-Hatred*, chronicled a history of German literature where the Jewish language or self-expression in language was made to reveal a kind of state of languagelessness. On the other hand, you accept the presence or absence of religious sacrifice as distinguishing Jewish monotheism from other religions. In the text *Sacrifice: It's Nature*

Cindy Sherman in her studio, 1994.

and *Function*, by Henri Hubert and Marcel Mauss, although Jewish sacrifice or its presence or absence is not the primary concern, the absolute sort of presence or absence of sacrifice as a practice vis-à-vis "archaic Jewish religion" or other forms of religion is not so absolute as it seems Žižek would have it. Obviously their study is empirically grounded in historical documentation. Your acceptance of Žižek seems fundamental to your whole theory of sacrifice.

Eric Santner Sander Gilman's work is more focused on the way in which the Jew as perverse object in the host culture is produced by the host culture's revulsion toward the Jew, and that has nothing to do with anything structural in Jewish monotheism. He's talking about how a host culture produces its Other through discourse and imagery. I'm more interested in the structural dimensions of theological systems and the ways in which those structural dimensions suggest choices made by cultures to determine what is abject.

Peter Wollen Modernism had begun with the birth of the counterculture, which became codified as a form of high culture. At the beginning of the century, the fantasy of the counterculture was to "harmoniously hold bodies in ritual touch with nature." But it was a fantasy that became more out of touch with any historical reality and, in fact, became complicit with the Holocaust in many ways. In the sixties, the counterculture reappeared as an important force within the art world—and the body with it in the form of performance art. This obsession with the fragmented, abject, or pathetic body might be a final uttering of the twentieth-century counterculture, in relation to both a broader history and the specific history of the art world.

Eric Santner I am struck by this preoccupation at the conference with body parts. Does anyone else have other ideas about where this obsession comes from? There's nothing special about this historical moment that's suggesting this obsession.

Jean-Hubert Martin Do you have a body?

Eric Santner Yes, but it's interesting that within the topic of visual display, people are cutting off fingers and body parts of saints. It's not the obvious thing of one simply having a body to be obsessed with displaying the body as relic.

Jean-Hubert Martin There have been many writings recently about the body in art.

Eric Santner There's a lot more to it than simply just empirical chains of associations—I need objects, I have a body, I'll show the body.

Stephen Bann Peter introduced the subject of gymnastics, a notion of the expressiveness of the body, and we are also talking about open wounds that have failed to heal. It seems implicit that we are brought back to religious sacrificial ritual.

Giuliana Bruno Perhaps this might be a cyclical return to fin-de-siècle culture. At the turn of the century, there was an insistence on treatises that mapped the body, by dividing it into parts and putting it back together: physiognomy, phrenology. The work of Cesare Lombroso, for example, certainly had an importance in art history. The Italian art historian, Giovanni Morelli, populated art historical books with body parts. The anatomical museums are yet another example of similar preoccupations. It also has something to do with tourism and touring the spectacle.

Eric Santner There does seem to be some need to find bodily materializations of states of emergency, whether they're institutional states of emergency like the museum, or of larger political structures. In *The Body in Pain*, Elaine Scarry identifies the inner lining in political states of emergency and moments of ideological fatigue.

Audience The notion of ruins and wounds seem to have something in common. The ruin is kind of a wound of memory.

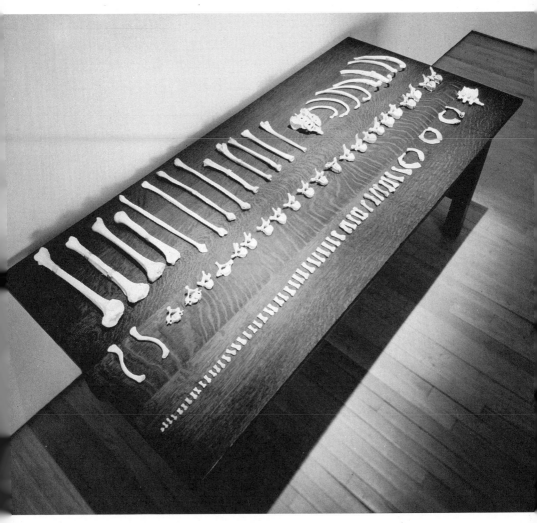

Jenny Holzer, *Untitled*, 1994.

NOTES

Stephen Bann

Translations from the French by the author.

1. See M. F. Hearn, "Canterbury Cathedral and the Cult of Becket," *Art Bulletin* 74, no. 1 (March 1994), pp. 19–52. The author explicitly makes the point that no serious consideration previously had been given to the fact that Canterbury Cathedral developed architecturally as a specific response to the need to accommodate both the monastic foundation and the visiting pilgrims. See also the fascinating contemporary analysis of an early guide to the shrine of Loreto in Pierre-Antoine Fabre, "En quête d'un lieu: Remarques sur Le Pélerin de Lorette de Louis Richeome," in *Genius Loci*, ed. Judith Barry, et al. (Paris: La Différence, 1993), pp. 185–206.

2. Norman Bryson, *Word and Image: French Painting of the Ancien Regime* (New York: Cambridge University Press, 1981), p. 3.

3. Ibid., p. 5.

4. Louis Marin, *Des pouvoirs de l'image: gloses* (Paris: Editions du Seuil, 1993), p. 224.

5. Ibid, pp. 224–25.

6. Erasmus, "*Peregrinatio Religionis Ergo,*" in *Colloquies*, trans. Craig R. Thompson (Chicago: University of Chicago Press, 1965), p. 295.

7. Ibid., p. 308.

8. Much interesting work has been done in recent years, notably by David Freedberg, on the phenomenon of iconoclasm in Northern Europe.

9. Erasmus, p. 292.

10. Ibid., p. 288.

11. Krzysztof Pomian, *Collectors and Curiosities: Paris and Venice 1500–1800* (Cambridge, Mass.: Basil Blackwell, 1990), p. 64.

12. Richard Culmer, *Cathedral Newes from Canterbury* (London, 1644), p. 7.

13. John Bargrave, *Pope Alexander the Seventh and the College of Cardinals with a Catalogue of Dr. Bargrave's Museum*, ed. J. C. Robertson (London: Camden Society, 1867), pp. 130–31.

14. Ibid., p. 118.

15. Ibid., p. 117.

16. Ibid., pp. 123–24.

17. Ibid., p. 133. For further discussion of Bargrave's collection, see Stephen Bann, *Under the Sign: John Bargrave as Collector, Traveler, and Witness* (Ann Arbor: University of Michigan Press, 1994).

Susan Stewart

I would like to thank the Getty Center for Art History and the Humanities, Los Angeles; the Center for Literary and Cultural Change at the University of Virginia, Charlottesville; and the Dia Center for the Arts, New York, where preliminary versions of this essay were read.

1. See *Plato's Meno*, ed. R. S. Buck (Cambridge: Cambridge University Press, 1961). For discussion of Daedalus, see, especially, pp. 408–11. I have discussed the theme of animation more generally in *On Longing: Narratives of the Miniature, the Gigantic, the Souvenir, the Collection* (Baltimore: Johns Hopkins University Press, 1984, and Durham: Duke University Press, 1993). A suggestive parallel to the case considered here is Annette Michelson's study of the iconography of Lenin's death, "The Kinetic Icon in the Work of Mourning: Prolegomena to the Analysis of a Textual System," *October* 52 (Spring 1990), pp. 16–51.

2. The relation between countenance and oblivion is outlined in Emmanuel Levinas, *Totality and Infinity: An Essay on Exteriority*, trans. Alphonso Lingis (The Hague: Martinus Nijhoff, 1961).

3. Peale's biography and the material history of the Peale family's activities have been exhaustively researched by Peale's lineal descendent, Charles Coleman Sellers, and by Lillian B. Miller. The major groups of the Peale Family papers are held at the American Philosophical Society and the Historical Society of Pennsylvania in Philadelphia. Additional materials used in this essay are located at the American Philosophical Society Library and the Library Company in Philadelphia. See also *The Selected Papers* of *Charles Willson Peale and His Family*, ed. Lillian B. Miller (New Haven: Yale University Press, The National Portrait Gallery and the Smithsonian Institution, 1983–88); Charles Coleman Sellers, *Charles Willson Peale* (New York: Charles Scribner's Sons, 1969); Charles Coleman Sellers, *Mr. Peale's Museum: Charles Willson Peale and the First Popular Museum of Natural Science and Art* (New York: W. W. Norton, 1980); Charles Coleman Sellers, *Charles Willson Peale with Patron and Populace: A Supplement to "Portraits and Miniatures by Charles Willson Peale" with a Survey of his Work in Other Genres*, vol. 59, pt. 3 in *Transactions of the American Philosophical Society* (Philadelphia: American Philosophical Society, 1969); Charles Coleman Sellers, *Portraits and Miniatures by Charles Willson Peale*, vol. 42, pt. 1, in *Transactions of the American Philosophical Society* (Philadelphia: American Philosophical Society, 1952); *Catalogue of an Exhibition of Portraits by Charles Willson Peale and James Peale and Rembrandt Peale* (Philadelphia: Pennsylvania Academy of the Fine Arts, 1923); *Charles Willson Peale and His World*, ed. Edgar P. Richardson, Brooke Hindle, and Lillian B. Miller (New York: Harry N. Abrams, 1983); James Thomas Flexner, *America's Old Masters: First Artists of the New World* (New York: The Viking Press, 1939), pp. 171–244; *New Perspectives on Charles Willson Peale: A 250th Anniversary Celebration*,

ed. Lillian B. Miller and David C. Ward (Pittsburgh: University of Pittsburgh Press and the Smithsonian Institution, Washington D.C., 1991).

4. Charles Willson Peale, *Discourse Introductory to a Course of Lectures on the Science of Nature with Original Music Composed for, and Sung on, the Occasion: Delivered in the Hall of the University of Pennsylvania, November 8, 1800* (Philadelphia: Zachariah Poulson, Junior, 1800), p. 34.

5. Richardson, et al., p. 101. See Sellers, *Mr. Peale's Museum*, p. 19. Peale's skill at mounting skins on woodwork stemmed from his apprenticeship as a saddler.

6. Zebulon Pike had given two grizzly cubs, male and female, to President Jefferson who in turn gave them to Peale for the museum zoo. One severely injured a monkey and later entered the Peale kitchen in the Hall basement. Peale contained the animal and shot it. He later killed the mate and mounted the two. See Sellers, *Mr. Peale's Museum*, pp. 206–07. Peale himself recounts the story in his *Autobiography*, p. 373.

7. For surveys of Deism, see *Deism, Masonry, and the Enlightenment*, ed. J. A. Leo Lemay (Newark: University of Delaware Press, 1987); Peter Byrne, *Natural Religion and the Nature of Religion: The Legacy of Deism* (London: Routledge, 1989); Kerry S. Walters, *The American Deists: Voices of Reason and Dissent in the Early Republic* (Lawrence, Ka.: University of Kansas Press, 1992); Kerry S. Walters, *Rational Infidels: The American Deists* (Wolfeboro, N.H.: Longwood, 1992).

8. See "Profession de foi du Vicaire savoyard (1762)," in *Rousseau: Religious Writings*, ed. Ronald Grimsley (London:

Clarendon Press, 1970), pp. 107–200. Peale mentions that he is reading Rousseau's *Confessions* in his *Autobiography*, p. 12.

9. See Anthony Ashley Cooper, Third Earl of Shaftesbury, *Characteristics of Men, Manners, Opinions, Times* (1711), ed. John M. Robertson, vol. 1 (Indianapolis: Bobbs-Merrill, 1964), pp. 268–69, who holds the belief in future rewards and punishments to be immoral, and Benjamin Franklin, letter to Ezra Stiles, 9 March 1790, in Walters, *The American Deists*: "the soul of Man is immortal, and will be treated with Justice in another Life respecting its conduct in this" (p. 105).

10. See James Thomas Flexner, *The Light of Distant Skies: History of American Painting, 1760–1835* (New York: Dover, 1969), p. 12.

11. Peale also copied West's copy of Titian's *Venus*. See *Charles Willson Peale: Artist in Revolutionary America, 1735–1791*, vol. 1 of *The Selected Papers of Charles Willson Peale and His Family*, ed. Lillian B. Miller (New Haven and London: Yale University Press, 1983), p. 87.

12. Sellers, *Mr. Peale's Museum*, p. 101.

13. The most important essay on this painting is Phoebe Lloyd's "A Death in the Family," *Philadelphia Museum of Art Bulletin* 78, no. 335 (Spring 1982), pp. 3–13. Lloyd connects the painting to European mourning portraits and the conventions Peale may have drawn from Charles LeBrun's 1649 tract on the depiction of the emotions, *Traité des Passions*. She adds a detail which links the painting back to the artifice of *Elisha Restoring the Shunamite's Son*: "The telltale indication that Peale did not observe his

wife from life is to be found in the whites of the eyes visible below the rolled up iris, after the example of LeBrun. This glance is nearly impossible to hold, especially with the head held straight" (pp. 3–5). An interesting parallel to the separation of Rachel's figure from the foreground can be found in Peale's complex *Self-Portrait with Angelica and a Portrait of Rachel* (1782–85), where the portrait of Rachel, slightly larger than the scale of the other two figures, is positioned beyond the picture plane. David Steinberg relates the structure of this work to "images of supernatural aid to the artist in the moment of creation," connecting the pun between *Angelica* and *angel* as the daughter reaches to guide her father's hand. But such an interpretation of divine intervention would seem to be contrary to Peale's Deism, unless perhaps it can be read as a playful allusion or parody. See David Steinberg, "Charles Willson Peale: The Portraitist As Divine," in *New Perspectives on Charles Willson Peale*, ed. Miller and Ward, pp. 131–44, 132. John Adams was "prodigiously" affected by the picture of Rachel mourning when he saw it on August 20, 1776. See *Selected Papers*, ed. Miller, vol. 1, p. 382n and *Adams Family Correspondence* (June 1776–March 1778), vol. 2 of *The Adams Papers*, ed. Lyman Butterfield, et al., series 2, (Cambridge, Mass.: Belknap Press, Harvard University Press, 1963), p. 103: "Yesterday Morning I took a Walk, into Arch Street, to see Mr. Peele's [sic] Painters Rooms. Peele is from Maryland, a tender, soft, affectionate Creature…He showed me one moving Picture. His wife, all bathed in Tears, with a Child about six

months old, laid out, upon her Lap. This Picture struck me prodigiously." In the same letter Adams says Peale's head "is not bigger than a large Apple…I have not met with any Thing in natural History much more amusing or entertaining than his personal Appearance."

14. Richardson, et al., p. 66.

15. Sigmund Freud, "On Transience," in *Freud, Character, and Culture*, ed. Philip Rief (New York: Collier, 1963), pp. 148–51.

16. "An Essay on Vital Suspension," medical brochure (London, 1741), pp. 7–11.

17. Peale himself records several incidents of ambiguous death in his account of Rachel's death in his *Autobiography*. He writes: "The custom of burying the dead too soon, has often been found a dreadful consequence. There once lived in Maryland a Mr. Chas. Carrol who very narrowly escaped being buried alive. He was supposed to be dead, and was laid out in the usial [sic] manner and persons employed to set up with the corpse—among them was a schoolmaster who had lived in the family. At a late hour when they had become inebriated, or as we might say, drunk, the schoolmaster said, our friend there used to love a drop while living, suppose we should now give him some grog, they poured it down his throat and it produced motions of life and he lived some years after this event. A Dr. Corson revived his daughter with a glass of madeira when she was supposedly dead of yellow fever" (pp. 135–36).

18. See John McManners, *Death and the Enlightenment* (Oxford: Clarendon Press, 1981), for a survey of French eighteenth-

century practices regarding death; Margaret M. Coffin's *Death in Early America* (Nashville: Thomas Nelson, 1976), is an anecdotal account of a variety of folkloric customs regarding death, mourning, and burial; see also *Death in America*, ed. David E. Stannard (Philadelphia: University of Pennsylvania Press, 1975), especially Philippe Aries's survey "The Reversal of Death: Changes in Attitudes toward Death in Western Societies," pp. 135–58, which sees the eighteenth century as the turning point in the historical movement toward the denial of death and suppression of mourning characteristic of modern society. Yet Peale explicitly rejected common mourning customs of his day. In his *Autobiography*, he wrote "If we are free agents to act as our best reason shall direct, then to [not] follow any custom which we deem absurd or even useless, must be laudable" (p. 137). The ambivalent status of the corpse is given much attention in chapters 5–7 of Charles Brockden Brown's 1799 novel on the yellow fever epidemic in Philadelphia: *Arthur Mervyn or Memoirs of the Year 1793* (Boston: S. G. Goodrich, 1827).

19. *Selected Papers*, ed. Miller, vol. 2, part 1, pp. 14–15.

20. Ibid., p. 21 n. 4. She continues: "Only one incident of the exhibition of an embalmed body is known, that of the English philosopher Jeremy Bentham (1748–1832), who, toward the end of his life, suggested that people have themselves exhibited after death so that their remains would become a statue, or 'auto-icon.' On his death, Bentham's corpse was mummified, dressed, and placed in a chair for display at the University of London." Among the miscellaneous papers relating to Peale's Museum at the American Philosophical Society Library is a document attesting to the authenticity of two mummies sold to the museum. Dated July 28, 1825, from Trieste and signed N. Mireoville, the note claims the mummies were collected in Alexandria by the signer and shipped from Trieste on an Austrian vessel and later sold to a W. B. Hight, from whom Peale may have purchased them.

21. Ibid., p. 21 n. 4.

22. Flexner, *America's Old Masters*, pp. 195–96.

23. *Selected Papers*, ed. Miller, vol. 1, p. 380.

24. Charles Willson Peale, letter to Joseph Brewer, Philadelphia, 15 January 1783, in *Selected Papers*, ed. Miller, vol. 1, pp. 382–83. Peale had four children by this time: Raphaelle, Angelica Kauffman, Rembrandt, and Titian Ramsay. His worries about his mother-in-law's will may stem, writes Miller, from financial difficulties. Questions of inheritance in fact haunt Peale all his life, since his early trip to study with West marked his final understanding that he would not, as he had hoped, be receiving an inheritance from England. Further, he learned, during the time of that sojourn, of the true, disgraceful circumstances of his father's emigration to America. Phoebe Lloyd in "A Death in the Family" sees this period as a key to the ways in which Peale concentrates on "making the most of a loss," including the altered mourning portrait of Rachel and Margaret, throughout his career (see p. 5).

25. See Richardson, et al., p. 88.

Issues of trompe l'oeil often appear in the discourse around Peale. See, for example, *Life, Journals, and Correspondence of Reverend Manasseh Cutler*, ed. William Parker Cutler and Julia Perkins Cutler (Cincinnati: Robert Clarke, 1888). In his account of a journey to New York and Philadelphia in 1787, Cutler tells of how he visited Peale with Dr. Gerardus Clarkson. As they entered Peale's studio, they saw "a gentleman...standing with a pencil in one hand and a small sheet of ivory in the other and his eyes directed to the opposite side of the room, as though he was taking some object on his ivory sheet." They decide that Peale must be busy and they retreat to wait. But in turning around, they meet Peale, who shows them that the "gentleman" is a sculpture of himself, life-sized, in wax. Cutler remarks "To what perfection is this art capable of being carried? By this method our particular friends and ancestors might be preserved in perfect likeness to the latest generation. We seem to be able in some degree to disappoint the ravages of time, and prevent mortality itself, the common lot of man, from concealing from us in its dreary retreats our dearest connections" (pp. 259–60). Peale writes in his *Autobiography*: "If a painter... paints a portrait in such perfection as to produce a perfect illusion of sight, in such perfection that the spectator believes the real person is here, that happy painter will deserved to be caressed by the greatest of mortal beings" (p. 338).

26. Flexner, *The Light of Distant Skies*, p. 140.

27. See *Psychiatric Dictionary*, ed. Leland E. Hinsie and Robert Jean

Campbell, 4th ed. (New York: Oxford University Press, 1970), p. 205.

28. Peale describes the moving pictures in his *Autobiography*, pp. 79–83. The presentation of *Pandemonium*, after Milton's description, is accompanied by a note that "Before the scene opened the following words were sung with musick": "To raise by art the stately pile/ we will essay our skill/...Yet great the task to make the glow/ that burning sulphur does bestow/ Yet great the task to make the glow/ That burning, that burning sulfur/ Does bestow..." (p. 81). In the American Philosophical Society copy of the typescript, a 1785 notice of the exhibit of moving pictures is inserted between pp. 79–81.

29. Charles Willson Peale, letter to Benjamin West, 17 November 1788, in *Selected Papers*, ed. Miller, vol. 1, p. 544.

30. Charles Willson Peale, *Discourse Introductory to a Course of Lectures on the Science of Nature with Original Music Composed for, and Sung on, the Occasion*, p. 48.

31. Ibid., pp. 39–40.

32. Ibid., pp. 6–7.

33. Ibid., p. 47.

34. Sellers, *Charles Willson Peale and His World*, p. 305.

35. Charles Willson Peale, letter to Elizabeth DePeyster Peale, 28 June 1801, in *Selected Papers*, ed. Miller, vol. 2, part 1, p. 335.

36. Charles Willson Peale, letter to Andrew Ellicott, 12 July 1801, in *Selected Papers*, ed. Miller, vol. 2, part 1, pp. 343–44.

37. Charles Willson Peale, letter to Benjamin West, 16 December 1807, in *Selected Papers*, ed. Miller, vol. 2, part 2,

pp. 1052–54. This letter is discussed briefly in an article in the *Pennsylvania Magazine of History and Biography* 9 (1885), pp. 130–32. At the left of the tent, standing with arms folded, is Peale's fellow naturalist Alexander Wilson (author of *American Ornithology*). Climbing a ladder in the foreground is John Masten, the farm's owner. Peale himself stands with arm extended, holding a large drawing of the bones. Next to him, from left to right, are Mrs. Hannah Peale in Quaker cap, possibly Mrs. Rembrandt Peale, and members of the Peale family: Rembrandt, Sybilla, who is pointing up to heaven to explain God's plan for the universe and the meaning of the discovery to her little sister Elizabeth, Rubens (with glasses) and Raphaelle. James Peale stands between the two poles at midpicture. In the group to the right of Wilson, Peale's deceased second wife, Elizabeth DePeyster, scolds her youngest son, Titian Ramsay II; her sister and brother-in-law, Major and Mrs. John Stagg, stand behind her. Other relatives are behind the green umbrella and the two younger Peale boys, Linnaeus and Franklin, push a log into the pit with a long pole.

38. Rembrandt Peale, *An Historical Disquisition on the Mammoth, or Great American Incognitum, an Extinct, Immense, Carnivorous Animal, Whose Fossil Remains Have Been Found in America* (1803), in *Selected Papers*, ed. Miller, vol. 2, pp. 544–81.

39. Peale's statement is in the *Autobiography*, pp. 428–29. See also Sellers, *Mr. Peale's Museum*, p. 246. It is interesting to note that Manasseh Cutler's journal of his 1787 visit also draws an analogy between Peale and Noah. See *Life, Journals, and Correspondence of Rev. Manasseh Cutler*, ed. Cutler and Cutler, p. 261.

40. Mario Praz, *Conversation Pieces: A Survey of the Informal Group Portrait in Europe and America* (University Park: Pennsylvania State University Press, 1971), pp. 209–23.

41. Charles Willson Peale, letter to Rembrandt Peale, 11 September 1808, in *Selected Papers*, ed. Miller, vol. 2, part 2, p. 1136. By the time the picture was finished, St. George had died in 1778; Peale's mother had died in 1791; his young daughter Eleanor (here on his mother's lap) had died in 1772 in infancy; Rachel had died in 1790; Margaret had died in infancy in 1788; Peale's sister Margaret Jane had also died in 1788; and the family's old nurse, on the right, Margaret Durgan had died in 1791.

42. Several times in his career Peale was called upon to paint memorial portraits of dead or dying children. See *Selected Papers*, ed. Miller, vol. 1, p. 415. It is a theme we see not only in the relation between Titian's death and the museum's establishment, but also in the controversies surrounding the life and death of Raphaelle Peale. In his thorough analysis of *The Artist in His Museum*, Roger B. Stein adds a note that poses a somewhat ironic reading of Peale's citation of Luke 15 ("For thy brother was dead, and is alive again, and was lost and is found") in his 1812, "An Essay to Promote Domestic Happiness." Stein sees the quote as an admonition to Peale's own prodigal son, Raphaelle. Raphaelle died in 1825 after years of physical and mental instability probably brought on by arsenic poisoning as a result of taxidermic work. (See

Stein, "Charles Willson Peale's Expressive Design: The Artist in His Museum," in ed. Miller and Ward, *New Perspectives on Charles Peale*, pp. 167–218, p. 217 n. 95.) For an account of Raphaelle's poisoning, see Phoebe Lloyd, "Philadelphia Story," *Art in America* 76 (November 1988), pp. 154–71, 195–203. Further, there is an uncanny echo between the passage from Luke and the 1783 breakdown, for it is Raphaelle who cannot be remembered at the time. And it is obviously Raphaelle's drinking and tumultuous marriage, which are the thinly veiled referents of passages on the "hideous form of drunkenness" which makes "the proud form of man... degraded below the brutes," described in Peale's *An Essay to Promote Domestic Happiness by Charles W. Peale* (Philadelphia: Philadelphia Museum, 1812) Library Company copy, p. 4. The meaning of the Luke passage can also be taken to refer to the position of St. George in *Peale Family Group* where Peale's painting situates himself and James in conversation and positions of observation in relation to the dead, but here revived, St. George. And the theme of the lost brother recurs as well, of course, with the traumatic aftermath of the Battle of Trenton— James's disfigurement and Charles's inability to recognize him.

43. See *Selected Papers*, ed. Miller, vol. 2, part 2, p. 1136.

44. Charles Willson Peale, letter to Rembrandt Peale, 23 July 1822.

45. It is suggestive to consider that in his last years Peale in fact seemed to undertake a repetition or review of his earlier work. In January of 1821 he began a large historical work on a theme directly in contrast to the Deist tenets on miracles and revealed religion, *Christ Healing the Sick at the Pool of Bethesda*. The work returned to the issues of miracles and Peale's legacy from West. West had treated the subject, even though Peale was working on an adaptation from a print by Christian Wilhelm Ernest Dietrich. In 1823 Peale made a new version of the *Staircase Group*. In this now-vanished piece, eight feet by six feet, he showed himself full-length, descending a short flight of steps with a palette and maulstick in hand and his saddler's hammer in the foreground. His movement is the opposite of the earlier staircase group, inverting the generations and inverting the direction of movement. His painting room and the Museum could be seen behind him. He wrote in his *Autobiography*, "I mean to make the whole piece a deception if I can... The frame is to be a door case with 2 steps and in the painting two other steps, and with my left foot on the lower step and the other behind as coming downstairs. This may be truly emblematical of his desending [sic] in life, with his pallet and pencils in his left hand and the mallstick in his right. Behind an easel with your Mother's portrait and her child asleep, from the idea of a picture which he painted early in his life, and which was much admired, so much that a poet wrote the following verses on it" (pp. 452–53). Peale characteristically talks of himself in the third person. In this passage he conflates the two pictures: the now-lost portrait of Rachel holding a sleeping Margaret, finished about 1771 (see Lloyd, "A Death in the Family," p. 3)

and the funerary portrait called *Rachel Weeping* to which he appended his verses. He forgets himself, rather slyly, as he forgets the pictures in time. "The steps will certainly be a true illusion, and why not my figure? It is said that Apelles painted grapes so natural that the birds came to pick them, that he then painted a boy to protect them, but the birds still came to take the grapes"—Peale recorded in a letter to Rubens of August 25, 1823, that Thomas Sully was fooled by the new *Staircase* painting, thinking the bottom step was a real step as in the first *Staircase* group. See Sellers, *Charles Willson Peale and His World*, pp. 409–11.

Ann Reynolds

During the discussions at this conference, several participants proposed various reasons for the constant return to the topic of displayed bodies, body fragments, and disease in various presentations. I did not offer my own response then—it seemed more personal than the others—but I have always regretted my silence. Until I moved to Texas in 1991, I lived in New York and attended most of Dia's "Discussions in Contemporary Culture." This symposium on visual display reminded me of all of the individuals now deceased or dying from AIDS, whom I'd seen and heard at these conferences over the years. This essay is dedicated to the memory of Eugene Santomasso, a mentor and beloved friend.

1. "U. S. Gives Go Signal For Superjets," and "Your Read and Study Guide," *My Weekly Reader* 48, no. 4 (5 October 1966), pp. 1, 8.

2. The designers also reveal their indifference to visual appearances by mistakenly switching the captions for the images of the two jets reproduced with the article.

3. "Packaged Power" and "Your Read and Study Guide," *My Weekly Reader* 48, no. 6 (19 October 1966), pp. 1, 8.

4. "Where the Buffalo Roam," *My Weekly Reader* 48, no. 7 (26 October 1966), p. 1.

5. "Your Read and Study Guide: 'Where the Buffalo Roam,'" *My Weekly Reader* 48, no. 7 (26 October 1966), p. 8.

6. John Kennedy, "Philanthropy and Science in New York City: The American Museum of Natural History 1868–1968" (Ph.D. diss., Yale University, 1968), pp. 226–32.

7. Ibid., p. 231. Kennedy notes that this was the conclusion drawn in a survey taken by the Council of the Scientific Staff in March 1936, n. p., Archives of the American Museum of Natural History, New York.

8. Kennedy, p. 232.

9. Ibid., p. 234.

10. Ibid., p. 238.

11. Parr was an oceanographer and the former director of the Peabody Museum of Yale University. The scientists of the AMNH were disappointed by his appointment because they did not consider oceanography to be a museum science, and some of the staff believed that Parr was not appropriately impressed by the natural stature of the AMNH or the prestige of his position. Many also did not approve of his well-known advocacy of new, unorthodox exhibition methods that disregarded the pre-existing traditions and strengths of individual institutions

and collections (Kennedy, pp. 239–40). In a letter to Kent Leavitt dated October 10, 1947, the AMNH's president, F. T. Davison, noted that Parr developed his basic ideas for new exhibition halls long before he came to the AMNH and "he brought them with him to the museum" (Archives of AMNH).

12. Kennedy provides a useful summary of the AMNH's commitment to evolutionary studies and taxonomic zoology, Parr's opinions on this history, and his ignorance of the revolutionary developments occurring within these areas during the very period he called them moribund fields. (See Kennedy, pp. 241–44.)

13. In a letter to the museum's president dated February 5, 1942, A. P. Osborn stated that the trustees established the Plan and Scope Committee in January 1942 to develop a new "philosophy of purpose" for the AMNH (Archives of AMNH). This committee reported to the director, but Parr also took over as the committee's chair in March, three months before he officially became the museum's new director; he skillfully used the committee's meetings to draft new policies sympathetic to his goals.

14. Minutes from the meeting of the Administrative Committee on Plan and Scope (9 March 1942), n.p., Archives of AMNH.

15. The Plan and Scope Committee's review was initiated approximately one month before the opening of the North American Mammals Hall on April 8, 1942, the last traditional habitat group hall to be built in the museum.

16. For a slightly more in-depth discussion of my interpretation of this process see my "Reproducing Nature: The Museum of Natural History as Nonsite," *October* 45 (Summer 1988), pp. 109–27.

17. George H. Sherwood, "The Story of the Museum's Service to the Schools," *Natural History* 17, no. 4 (July–August 1927), p. 332.

18. "The Habitat Group" (6 May 1942), p. 1, Archives of AMNH. Although the author of this text is not indicated, Parr attributes it to Dr. Clark Wissler in a memo concerning exhibitions for the Plan and Scope Committee (July 1942), p. 8, Archives of AMNH. Wissler may have based his contribution to the Plan and Scope review on his own, earlier survey of the museum's needs, begun at the request of the Council of the Scientific Staff in 1940 and completed sometime in 1942. For a brief discussion of the history and purpose of Wissler's survey, see Kennedy, pp. 233–34. Parr later wrote several articles on the history and general premises of habitat groups. See, for example, "The Time and Place for Experimentation in Museum Design," *Curator* 1, no. 4 (1958), pp. 36–40; "The Habitat Group," *Curator* 2, no. 2 (1959), pp. 107–28; and "Dimensions, Backgrounds, and Uses of Habitat Groups," *Curator* 4, no. 3 (1961), pp. 199–215.

19. "The Museum's Visitor" (6 May 1942), pp. 1–2, Archives of AMNH.

20. Alfred Parr, letter to Clark Wissler (12 March 1942), n.p., Archives of AMNH.

21. Untitled document, (ca. 12 March 1942), n.p., Archives of AMNH.

22. Ibid.

23. Ibid.

24. Alfred Parr, letter to Dr. Edwin H. Colbert (9 September 1942), pp. 1–2, Archives of AMNH. Parr responded to Colbert's suggestion that an introductory hall present the birth of the solar system and the earth. Parr states: "Nothing could possibly be further from the common everyday experience of man than the birth of the solar system and the earth which your plan would offer as the first exhibit."

25. Ibid., p. 1.

26. Ibid., p. 2.

27. Alfred Parr, letter to Dr. William K. Gregory (8 October 1942), p. 1, Archives of AMNH. According to Parr's January 15, 1951, proposals to the council meeting for the general rules for the planning and execution of exhibits, such "interdisciplinary" halls would also give him even greater control over the museum's future: "It shall be the duty of the director to serve in the capacity of special executive for such interdepartmental exhibition projects, with responsibilities corresponding to those resting upon the chairman in case of the exhibition activities of a single department." Archives of AMNH.

28. Memo concerning exhibitions, Plan and Scope Committee (ca. July 1942), pp. 7–8, Archives of AMNH. Parr was probably the author of this memo.

29. Alfred Parr, "Towards New Horizons," *American Museum of Natural History Annual Report* 78 (July 1946–June 1947), p. 16. In "Purposes and Progress Report of the Director," *American Museum of Natural History Annual Report* 82 (July 1950–June 1951), p. 9, Parr described the new hall's pedagogical approach this way: "The new hall also departs from previous tradition in that it attempts to deal with the totality of nature from the geological past of the landscape to its present-day life, and in that it introduces the history and effects of human settlement as part of the history of nature."

30. "The Hall of Local Landscape" was one of the hall's working titles.

31. Alfred Parr, letter to Mrs. Paul Moore (13 January 1943), p. 1, Archives of AMNH.

32. Alfred Parr, "Hall of the Local Landscape" (25 September 1946), p. 1, Archives of AMNH.

33. Alfred Parr, letter to Moore, p. 1.

34. Kennedy, pp. 246–48.

35. Ibid., p. 249.

36. The hall was named in memory of the father of the hall's major financial backer and trustee of the museum, Frederick M. Warburg. He contributed sixty thousand dollars, the cost of the individual exhibits. Felix Warburg, the hall's namesake, was a Jewish immigrant born in Germany in 1871; he became a U. S. citizen in 1894. He was also a financial backer and trustee of the museum before his death in 1937. Warburg Correspondence, Archives of AMNH.

37. See, for example, John O'Reilly, "Warburg Hall of Museum to open on May 15," *New York Times*, 4 May 1951; "Pine Plains Folk View Exhibit Here," *New York Times*, 15 May 1951; and the museum's two press releases, dated May 4 and May 15, 1959, Archives of AMNH.

38. O'Reilly calls the meandering or serpentine layout of the displays "a drastic departure from the conventional type

of rectangular museum hall," but neither he nor any of the other commentators who discuss this aspect of the hall's design elaborate on its educational effects.

39. Most of the depictions of spatial recession in the hall's displays also echo the visitor's progressive movement through the meandering layout of the hall. For example, the recession of the space depicted in "An October Afternoon Near Stissing Mountain" from right to left encourages the viewer to move from left to right and then on to the next display in the hall. The only exceptions are the large displays, which contain numerous miniature habitat groups; in these, the spacial recession often counters the general flow of traffic so that the viewer must pass by the display twice to take in both the series of miniature groups and the overall effect of the display.

40. Parr, letter to Gregory, p. 1.

41. Ibid.

42. The topographical map is now mounted vertically on the wall diagonally opposite the initial habitat group. In this location, the map is barely noticeable. In an article on the new hall, Louis Bromfield noted that the hall also included an automobile road map of the area, "one of the modern touches and an extremely intelligent one." (Louis Bromfield, "Build a Healthy Acre," Natural History 60, no. 6 [June 1951], p. 259.) It is not clear from the surviving documentary photographs where this map was located or how it was installed. It also no longer remains in the hall, unless Bromfield is calling the topographical map a road map since it includes roads as well as topographical features.

43. Bromfield (ibid., pp. 254, 256) noted that after the initial habitat group, the landscape is "broken down into detail, as if bit by bit the spectator were taking apart the landscape and examining it under a heavy magnifying glass or even a microscope....The spectator goes underground and becomes a field mouse, chipmunk, mole, or yellow jacket." Since this article appeared in the AMNH's own magazine, Natural History, Parr probably approved of Bromfield's descriptive assessment of the viewer's experience. Bromfield also gave the dedication address at the hall's opening ceremonies.

44. Unlike My Weekly Reader's disassembly of the buffalo-hunt diorama, these cases dissect a particular geological and biological situation and not just the illusionistic devices of the habitat group itself.

45. In a July 1942 memo on exhibitions for the Plan and Scope Committee, p. 5, Archives of AMNH, the author, probably Parr, noted that the average viewer missed a great deal in the old halls because "it is extremely irritating to have to look away from the group and hunt through a label to find out what one wants to know...[the visitor] prefers to move on rather than to examine the labels to find out what he has looked at." He proposed using soundtracks of music and narration to link information and images together since the narrator could tell viewers what they were looking at while simultaneously guiding them visually through every aspect of individual displays. Approximately three years later, Parr chose brighter colors for the hall's walls than those used in the old habitat

halls. These colors were keyed to the display labels and to the natural colors of many of the specimens in the cases so that the entire hall would appear as a unified system of images and information and not just a dark gallery with illuminated and colorful pictures. Alfred Parr, "Through the Past Towards the Future," *American Museum of Natural History Annual Report* 76 (May 1945), p. 36. These colorful formal analogies between objects, images, and texts were one of Parr's more visually directed and less costly solutions to the problem of balancing education and entertainment.

46. Parr, "Hall of the Local Landscape," p. 1.

47. For example, see Parr, letter to Moore, p. 1. F. T. Davison also identified the hall's public as "city children" in his report on the state of the museum in the *American Museum of Natural History Annual Report* 81 (July 1949–June 1950), n.p.

48. Parr, letter to Moore, pp. 1–2.

49. Parr was already looking for this audience in his 1942 survey of the museum visitor. In the same letter in which he discusses how to accurately measure the educational efficacy of the museum's existing halls, he also suggests that the survey-takers "get names of visitors, particularly visitors of affluent appearance." (Alfred Parr, letter to Wissler, Archives of AMNH.)

Kennedy notes that despite Parr's efforts, he never did win back many wealthy urban donors to the AMNH because his new exhibition halls did not speak to them as the habitat groups had in the early part of the century (p. 252). Perhaps this was because in the 1920s

and '30s, donors contributed many of the specimens to the halls through safaris and hunting expeditions organized by the museum. The displays in halls like the Warburg Hall contained more mundane specimens that did not need to be collected in such glamorous ways, and they were never the property of wealthy donors, not even momentarily. Parr did attempt to include the property of one of the private donors, Clarence Hay, in the Forestry Hall, completed in 1958, by replicating part of Hay's New Hampshire estate in a habitat group. For more information on this aspect of the Forestry Hall's design, see Milton Mackaye, "Big City's Primitive Forests," *Saturday Evening Post* (13 September 1958), p. 69.

50. In the introduction to the Warburg Hall guidebook, the authors, Henry K. Svenson and Farida A. Wiley, claim that both city dwellers and farmers need to better understand the complexities of the landscape, but their own point of departure, although never stated directly, is clearly that of the urban sightseer. Their text begins with a description based, in part, on the hall's initial habitat group: "A steady procession of automobiles goes out from New York City every weekend. At intervals along the parkways there are lookout areas thronged with sightseers who stop to enjoy the landscape, with its views of mountains, lakes, farmlands, and woodlands. The landscape varies during the season and, for many people, has its greatest attraction when the leaves are unfolding in the spring and again when they have achieved the brilliant autumnal colors in the fall. At all times of the year, however,

the countryside is a constantly changing scene of interest. (Svenson and Wiley, *The Story of the Landscape* [New York: American Museum of Natural History, 1952], p. 5.)

51. In his 1943 letter to Moore, p. 1, Parr stated: "Of course, since we are directing our efforts primarily on the metropolitan public, their interest would not lie so much in the practical problems of caring for domestic animals as in the general principles which govern economical, sociological, and biological success or failure in this extremely essential and interesting part of human activity."

These displays include "The Rotation of Farm Crops in Dutchess County, New York," "The Apple Orchard in Dutchess County, New York," "Fertilizers in the Soil," and a history of agriculture in New York State.

52. The unidentified author of a short article entitled "Pine Plains Folk View Exhibit Here," which appeared in the *New York Times* on May 15, 1951, notes that inhabitants of Pine Valley were "the most interested spectators at the exhibit" and that they were "highly conscious of the scientific honor" of having their village represented in the hall, but the author does not record any of their personal responses to the way the hall represented their everyday experience of the site.

53. Parr shared his utopian faith in the capacity of storytelling to produce a unified community with Walter Benjamin, yet the differences in their explanations of the relationship between storytelling and the economic structure of the communities they shaped reveals the one-sided nature of Parr's understanding of the practice. In 1936 Benjamin

described storytelling as part of a preindustrial past in which production and consumption were shared equally as experiences: "…the art of storytelling is coming to an end. Less and less frequently do we encounter people with the ability to tell a tale properly. More and more often there is embarrassment all around when the wish to hear a story is expressed. It is as if something that seemed inalienable to us, the securest among our possessions, were taken from us: the ability to exchange experiences. (Walter Benjamin, "The Storyteller," *Illuminations* [New York: Schocken Books, 1969], p. 83).

54. Alfred Parr, "Towards New Horizons," *American Museum of Natural History Annual Report* 78 (July 1946– June 1947), pp. 9–10.

55. F. T. Davison, "Report of the President," *American Museum of Natural History Annual Report* 81 (July 1949– June 1950), n.p.

56. Alfred Parr, "The Museum Explores the World—Report of the Director," *American Museum of Natural History Annual Report* 83 (July 1951– June 1952), pp. 10–11.

57. The *My Weekly Reader* article "U. S. Gives Go Signal for Superjets" contains some evidence of a similar, albeit unacknowledged, slide from national to global concerns. The title represents the competition between the two companies to produce the jets as a national one, yet the article's author uses terms usually reserved for describing the then current international "space race" to portray the stakes involved.

58. Even without the benefit of

extensive research, I can draw some general conclusions concerning *My Weekly Reader's* ideal audience in the 1960s based on the types of subjects consistently represented in the magazine and the manner in which they were addressed: enormous numbers of articles on NASA and technological innovations, generally, studies of rural areas of the United States, and biographical essays on representational painters of the nineteenth century, such as Winslow Homer and contemporary artists, such as Norman Rockwell and the Wyeths. Examples of avant-garde culture, if mentioned at all, were treated as humorous curiosities akin to rare and odd-looking animals from exotic places. Preadolescent girls like me, longing to learn about big cities and looking for images of how cultural life is lived there, particularly by women, could not help but be disappointed.

Susan Buck-Morss

This essay has also been published in *Critical Inquiry* 21, no. 2 (Winter 1995), pp. 434–67. Unless otherwise indicated, all translations are by the author.

1. See Michael J. Piore and Charles F. Sabel, *The Second Industrial Divide: Possibilities for Prosperity* (New York: Basic Books, 1984).

2. Robert B. Reich, *The Work of Nations: Preparing Ourselves for Twenty-First–Century Capitalism* (New York: Vintage Books, 1992). Reich's arguments are controversial among economists, many of whom are critical of his work, but his high-ranking position within the Clinton administration gives them clout.

3. For an economic history of the institution of the U. S. firm and the transformation to "managerial capitalism," see Alfred D. Chandler, Jr., *The Visible Hand: The Managerial Revolution in American Business* (Cambridge, Mass.: Belknap Press, 1977). For a political and social history of the same transformation (to "corporate capitalism"), see Martin J. Sklar, *The Corporate Reconstruction of American Capitalism 1890–1916: The Market, the Law, and Politics* (New York: Cambridge University Press, 1988).

4. Quoted in Reich, p. 48.

5. "To ensure against any return to wartime controls or the seductions of statism and communism, the American business community at midcentury launched a spirited public relations campaign promoting the wonders of the profit system. General Motors produced a full-length Hollywood movie illustrating the advantages of American capitalism. Outdoor billboards erected by the Advertising Council proclaimed the benefits of free enterprise and the evils of government planning" (ibid., p. 43).

In 1953, the chairman of Eisenhower's Council of Economic Advisors pronounced that the "ultimate purpose" of the American economy was "to produce more consumer goods" (quoted, p. 45).

6. See Karl Marx, *Grundrisse: Foundations of the Critique of Political Economy*, trans. M. Nicolaus (London: New Left Review, 1973).

7. See Georg Simmel, *The Philosophy of Money*, trans. Tom Bottomore and David Frisby, 2nd ed. (New York: Routledge, 1990).

8. Ivaylo Ditchev, "Epitaph for Sacrifice, Epitaph for the Left" (forthcoming): "According to the official doctrine of the

Stalin era, the present generation had to be sacrificed for the one to come.... [A Party member was] infinitely indebted ...ready...at any moment to organize, to put into practice, to rouse enthusiasm, to be the avant-garde and the model for the rest[:]...modest...'collectivist'... [without] privacy and selfishness."

9. Reich, p. 64.

10. Still, as Reich notes, it was no "mere coincidence that the Central Intelligence Agency discovered communist plots where America's core corporations possessed, or wished to possess, substantial holdings of natural resources" (ibid., p. 64).

11. Ibid., pp. 4–5, 8.

12. Ibid., p. 3.

13. Ibid., p. 303.

14. It might allow the claim that there is no economy except capitalism (although the latter term had to wait a century for its own discovery, when it was coined by socialists to stigmatize the prevailing economic system). I have had recent discussions with Russian intellectuals who argue that the Soviet system *had* no economy in the modern sense of the term. Before this, the term *economy* meant simply domestic accounts, derived from *oikos* and *nomos*, the ancient Greek words for *house* and *law*, applied to both family and national budgets. Rousseau's 1755 entry "Economy, (Moral and Political)" in the *Encyclopédie* distinguishes between general, or "political" economy, and domestic, or "private" economy. See Jean-Jacques Rousseau, "Economie ou Oeconomie, (Morale et Politique)," in *Encyclopédie ou dictionnaire raisonne des sciences, des arts et des métiers*, ed. Denis

Diderot and Jean Le Rond d'Alembert, vol. 5 (Paris, 1751–72), pp. 337–49. Quesnay was also a contributor to the *Encyclopédie*.

15. See Louis Dumont, *From Mandeville to Marx: The Genesis and Triumph of Economic Ideology* (Chicago: University of Chicago Press, 1977): "It should be obvious that there is nothing like an economy out there, unless and until men construct such an object" (p. 24).

16. See Edward R. Tufte, *The Visual Display of Quantitative Information* (Cheshire, Conn.: Graphics Press, 1983).

17. The term *physiocracy* means "rule of nature." Alfred Marshall traced the origin of the term to Stoic law in the late Roman empire, and to the "sentimental admiration for the 'natural' life of the American Indians, which Rousseau had kindled into flame....Before long they were called Physiocrats or adherents of the rule of Nature." (Alfred Marshall, *Principles of Economics*, vol. 1 [London: Macmillan for the Royal Economic Society, 1961], p. 756 n. 2.) Marshall's own view was far less "sentimental": "'Savage' tribes have proven incapable of keeping themselves long to steady work"; "there seems no reason to doubt that nearly all the chief pioneers of progress have been Aryans" (pp. 723, 724).

18. Quoted in David McNally, *Political Economy and the Rise of Capitalism: A Reinterpretation* (Berkeley: University of California Press, 1988), p. 110.

19. Quesnay went to Versailles as physician of the Marquise de Pompadour and was promoted in 1755 (at age sixty-one) to *le premier medecin ordinaire of the king.* Sir William Petty, John Locke,

and Nicholas Barbon (author of *A Discourse of Trade* in 1690) were all trained in medicine. Petty studied anatomy in Holland and later wrote *The Political Anatomy of Ireland*. Locke joined the household of the Earl of Shaftesbury as a physician.

20. More precisely, landowners were the *classe distributive*, the land cultivators were the *classe productive*. and all those engaged in nonagricultural pursuits were the *classe sterile*.

21. As a result of the enclosure movement of the seventeenth century, peasant farming had to a great extent been replaced by larger farms run as capitalist enterprises. Land owners hired agricultural laborers to work their large holdings with the goal of improved production for commercial gain. "Unprocessed agricultural products as a share of English manufactured exports rose from 4.6 percent in 1700 to 11.8 percent in 1725 and to 22.2 percent by 1750." English agriculture "provided a 100 percent return on advances" (McNally, pp. 14, 146). Quesnay's "science" was in fact a mandate for (capitalist) reform in France, where agricultural production was still largely modeled on the seignorial system and production was comparatively low. "To think of exchange as advantageous to both parties represented a basic change and signaled the advent of economics" (Dumont, p. 35).

22. The teaching of mathematics (applied to commerce) was well established in northern Italy by the quattrocento. Reckoning schools developed in cities along the trade routes. The first printed book of mathematics, *Treviso Arithmetic*, taught addition, subtraction, multiplication, and division in a format that was largely unchanged in the twentieth century. A typical *Treviso* problem: "two merchants wish to barter. The one has cloth at 5 lire a yard, and the other has wool at 18 lire a hundredweight. How much cloth should the first have for 464 hundred-weights of wool?" (quoted in Frank I. Swetz, *Capitalism and Arithmetic: The New Math of the Fifteenth Century, Including the Full Text of the Treviso Arithmetic of 1478*, trans. David Eugene Smith [La Salle, Ill.: Open Court, 1987], p. 151).

23. Quoted in McNally, p. 73.

24. Quoted in Reich, p. 14.

25. Quoted in McNally, pp. 106, 107, 141. Note the metaphor of birth to describe the "fertility schema" of productive labor.

26. Quoted in Jean-François Lyotard, *Libidinal Economy*, trans. Iain Hamilton Grant (Bloomington: Indiana University Press, 1993), pp. 188–89.

27. Ibid., pp. 198–99. I am distorting Lyotard's point somewhat to make a better one.

28. See McNally, pp. 110 and 122. The "universal laws of natural order...appl[ied] equally to the Incas of Peru, the emperor of China, and the king of France" (p. 129).

29. Voltaire was horrified: "that a single man should be proprietor of all the land is a monstrous idea" (quoted in ibid., p. 142).

30. Ibid., p. 102.

31. Ibid., p. 117. (Quesnay's italics). McNally warns against misunderstanding. Quesnay explicitly rejected "monarchial despotism" as a "fantasy" because no single man "could arbitrarily govern

millions of men" (p. 126). "Legal despotism" meant, rather, the rule of the law—not so much a judicial check on the monarch by the *Parlements* as an appeal to Enlightenment principles as the "laws" that ought to guide the action of kings (p. 127).

32. Ibid.

33. Joseph A. Schumpeter, *History of Economic Analysis*, ed. Elizabeth Boody Schumpeter (New York: Oxford University Press, 1986), p. 229.

34. Adam Smith's book achieved general popularity, appealing to an international reading public. The first edition of the book sold out in six months. Between 1779 and 1791 there were four English and two Irish editions; by 1793 there were two French translations, a poor German translation appeared within a year, but a second, excellent translation by Christian Garve (used by Hegel) appeared in 1794–96. The first Russian translation was 1802–06, and editions in Danish, Dutch, and Italian were also forthcoming. See ibid., p. 193.

35. Of course, Smith was indebted to Quesnay for the whole conception of an "economy" of growth through production and exchange. According to Dugald Stewart, who said he was told by Smith himself, the latter intended to dedicate *The Wealth of Nations* to Quesnay: "the Physiocrats are the only group of authors recognized by Smith as operating on the same plane of discourse" (Donald Winch, "Adam Smith's 'Enduring Particular Result': A Political and Cosmopolitan Perspective," in *Wealth and Virtue: The Shaping of Political Economy in the Scottish Enlightenment*, ed. Istvan Hont and Michael Ignatieff [New York: Cambridge University Press, 1983], p. 268).

Quesnay was influenced not only by Petty but by Locke, Shaftesbury, and Hume, so that the difference between Quesnay and Smith was due less to intellectual lineage or even to generations—Smith, born in 1723, was twenty-seven years younger—than it was to context. Agricultural capitalism was well established in England by this time, so that the self-regulation of the market appeared natural and commercial interdependence a fact of life. See the important work of Joyce Oldham Appleby, *Liberalism and Republicanism in the Historical Imagination* (Cambridge, Mass.: Harvard University Press, 1992).

Smith's vision of the new collective body produced by the economy is so out of line with what a social body *ought* to be like that he reverts to quite traditional notions in his political and social theory. These incompatible visions of the collective are the source of ambiguities in his texts.

36. Jean-Jacques Rousseau, "Discourse on Political Economy," *Basic Political Writings*, trans. and ed. Donald A. Cress (Indianapolis: Hackett Publishing Company, 1987), p. 114.

37. Compare Rousseau: "the body politic…is also a moral being which possesses a…general will….The most general will is also always the most just…the voice of the populace is, in effect, the voice of God" (ibid., pp. 114, 115).

38. Quoted in J.G.A. Pocock, *The Machiavellian Moment: Florentine Political Thought and the Atlantic Republican Tradition*

(Princeton: Princeton University Press, 1975), p. 123.

39. This is a significant break from Renaissance tradition in England, which considered commercial Athens "effeminate" in comparison with Sparta's military virtue: "society as an engine for the production and multiplication of goods was inherently hostile to society as the moral foundation of personality" (ibid., p. 501). Smith sustains some of this criticism in *The Theory of Moral Sentiments*; economic activity is not sufficient for the creation of the good society that demands as well civic virtue and moral constraint. But in the limited realm of economics, the predominant passion of egoism *can* be given free reign under the form of self-interest because it produces the good of the whole. See Adam Smith, *The Theory of Moral Sentiments* (New York: Garland Publishing, 1971).

40. Machines do not cause the division of labor but foster this tendency that is itself a "consequence" of human nature: "this division of labour, from which so many advantages are derived, is not originally the effect of any human wisdom, which foresees and intends that general opulence to which it gives occasion. It is the necessary, though very slow and gradual, consequence of a certain propensity in human nature which has in view no such extensive utility; the propensity to truck, barter, and exchange one thing for another." (Adam Smith, *An Inquiry into the Nature and Causes of the Wealth of Nations*, ed. Edwin Cannan [New York: Modern Library, 1993], book I, chap. ii, p. 14.)

41. McNally's book is an excellent corrective of the traditional view of classical economic theory as "a sustained theoretical rationalization for industrial capitalism" (McNally, p. xiii); his scholarly argument that the significance of the Physiocratic tradition in pre-Ricardian theory has been overlooked is convincing. But if Smith were indeed "strongly critical of the values and practices associated with merchants and manufacturers" (p. xiv), if his political and moral theory favored the values of agrarian life, this does not change the fact that it was Smith's theoretical description of nascent industrial society that was absolutely innovative, and that it was this element of his theory that (whether rightly or wrongly interpreted) had a deep and lasting historical effect.

42. Smith, *Wealth of Nations*, book I, chap. i, pp. 4–5.

43. Machines eliminate "sauntering" by the worker from one sort of employment to another and "by making this operation the sole employment of his life, necessarily increases very much the dexterity of the workman" (Smith, *Wealth of Nations*, book I, chap. i, pp. 8, 9).

44. Ibid., Introduction, p. lxi. Against the mercantilist fetishization of money, Smith held "that gold and silver are merely tools, no different from kitchen utensils, and that their import increases the wealth of a country just as little as the multiplication of kitchen utensils provides more food" (Simmel, p. 173).

45. Schumpeter, p. 187. Again, this is a break from the Anglo-Scottish humanist tradition that viewed the division of labor as a "prime cause of corruption" (Pocock, p. 499).

46. Smith writes that language has the same property of a mechanical engine in that it "becomes more simple in its rudiments and principles, just in proportion as it grows more complex in its composition" (quoted in McNally, p. 179).

47. Smith, *Wealth of Nations*, book I, chap. i, pp. 11, 9. "I have seen several boys under twenty years of age who had never exercised any other trade but that of making nails, and who, when they exerted themselves, could make, each of them, upwards of two thousand three hundred nails in a day" (p. 8).

48. Ibid., book V, chap. i, p. 840. The preventative Smith has in mind is a state-funded system of public education. Smith compares the dullness of the industrial worker with the intelligence of members of "barbarous" societies in which the division of labor has not advanced, and every man is competent as a warrior and "in some measure a statesman" (p. 841).

49. Ibid., book I, chap. i, pp. 12–13.

50. Ibid., book I, chap. ii, p. 17.

51. Ibid., p. 18. Of course, Smith quite rightly criticizes the logical "fallacy of composition," that is, the belief that what holds on the composite level is merely an extension of what holds for the individual. But even if the benefits lost to the individual are recouped on the collective level, this does not yet provide philosophical legitimacy for privileging the collective over the individual.

52. See Ludmilla Jordanova, "The Hand," *Visual Anthropology Review* 8 (Fall 1992), pp. 2–7. On natural theology, see John Hedley Brooke, *Science and Religion:*
Some Historical Perspectives (New York: Cambridge University Press, 1991).

53. See Smith, *Wealth of Nations: Introduction*, p. lx; book I, chap. iii, p. 23; book I, chap. i, p. 13; book IV, chap. iii, p. 485.

54. These lectures (1970–84) have not been published, but see Colin Gordon's editorial description of, especially, the 1978 and 1979 lectures on "governmental rationality," in Colin Gordon, "Governmental Rationality: An Introduction," in *The Foucault Effect: Studies in Governmentality*, ed. Graham Burchell, Colin Gordon, and Peter Miller (Chicago: University of Chicago Press, 1991), p. 15.

55. The extent of the division of labor is limited only by "the extent of the market"—the global expansion of which was still in its infancy" (Smith, *Wealth of Nations*, book I, chap. iii, p. 19).

56. Smith, *The Theory of Moral Sentiments*, pp. 14, 39.

57. This idea is new, and it is quintessentially modern—compare the ancient Greeks, who were persistently concerned with hubris, "the boundless desire that unbalances an individual" and thereby "poses a threat to the polis" (Nicholas Xenos, *Scarcity and Modernity* [New York: Routledge, 1989], p. 3).

58. Smith, *The Theory of Moral Sentiments*, p. 348.

59. Ibid., pp. 349–50.

60. See Smith, *Wealth of Nations*, book I, chap. iv, pp. 32–33. Smith recognized this paradox and agreed that the goals of national defense might rightly be placed before considerations of free trade. See Smith, *Wealth of Nations*, book IV, pp. 455–746. This section is a plea for free

trade but it defends the protectionist Navigation Acts. In Germany, where commercial interdependence was in advance of political unity, the tendency of the economy to escape national boundaries was a cause of complaint rather than affirmation. Johann Gottlieb Fichte argued that the state alone unites an indeterminate mass of people into an enclosed whole. See Johann Gottlieb Fichte, *Der geschlossne Handelsstaat* (1800). Friedrich List (1789–1818) founded a nationalist and historicist school of political economy in opposition to Smith's cosmopolitan doctrine, which argued that a customs union of German states could provide the means to the greater goal of national union. He was particularly impressed by the United States economic system. See Friedrich List, *Outlines of American Political Economy* (Philadelphia: S. Parker, 1827).

61. Gordon, "Governmental Rationality," p. 15.

62. Tufte, p. 46.

63. Ibid., p. 47.

64. This conception gained broad acceptance in the nineteenth century. Whereas in "archaic" societies collective consciousness was alleged to be constitutive of society, in modern "civilization" the division of labor was constitutive. See, particularly, the social theories of Herbert Spencer and Emile Durkheim, and Jürgen Habermas's discussion of them in *Lifeworld and Systems: A Critique of Functionalist Reason*, vol. 2 of *The Theory of Communicative Action*, trans. Thomas McCarthy (Boston: Beacon Press, 1984).

65. Manfred Riedel, *Between Tradition and Revolution: The Hegelian Transformation of Political Philosophy*, trans. Walter Wright (New York: Cambridge University Press, 1984), p. 44.

66. The most exhaustive scholarship documenting this influence is Norbert Waszek, *The Scottish Enlightenment and Hegel's Account of "Civil Society"* (Boston: Kluwer Academic Publishers, 1988).

67. Let me explain, relying on Riedel's account, how this differs from previous natural law theory as it is presumed by Hobbes, Locke, or Rousseau. Natural law theory is contract theory (although it claims to be ahistorical). It holds that "societies" are essentially political associations that people (with natural rights) choose to enter contractually as citizens. It is a "union of rational, articulate individual agents" who, "by means of rational discussion," have consented to be bound by a common will that then has the force of law (Riedel, p. 44). Naturally autonomous, "free" individuals willingly submit to the law, which ensures the autonomy of all; this takes place on one topological space, a political space. For Hegel, it is the (depoliticized) system of the economy that produces the social form (see p. 148), and in modernity that form is the division of labor. Society is not a political creation, but an economic one.

68. As he expresses it in fragment twenty-two of the 1803–04 text, "the satisfaction of needs is a general interdependency of all upon one another" (Georg Wilhelm Friedrich Hegel, *Das System der spekulativen Philosophie: Fragmente aus Vorlesungsmanuskripten zur Philosophie der Natur und des Geistes*, vol. 1 of *Jenaer Systementwürfe*, ed. Klaus Düsing and

Heinz Kimmerle [Hamburg: F. Meiner, 1986], p. 229). In stark opposition to natural law theory (autonomous individuals in a state of nature), this is a historically specific anthropology of mutual interdependency: "thus philosophy becomes [self-consciously] the theory of its age" (Riedel, p. 40).

69. Hoffmeister's edition of Hegel's early Jena writings (which he called *Jenenser Realphilosophie I and II*) appeared in 1931–32. These texts were discussed enthusiastically by Georg Lukacs in *Der junge Hegel: Über die Beziehungen von Dialektik und ökonomie* (Berlin, 1948). They figure centrally in the commentaries of Herbert Marcuse, *Reason and Revolution: Hegel and the Rise of Social Theory* (London: Routledge and Kegan Paul, 1941); Shlomo Avineri, *Hegel's Theory of the Modern State* (Cambridge: Cambridge University Press, 1972); Paul Chamley, *Economie politique et Philosophie chez Steuart et Hegel* (Paris: Librairie Dalloz, 1963); and Riedel, *Between Tradition and Revolution*. Riedel writes, "Hegel's assimilation of the most advanced theories of political economy, as found in the classical British thinkers from James Steuart to Adam Smith and (in *The Philosophy of Right* of 1821) David Ricardo, had no parallel in the German idealistic philosophy of his period" (Riedel, p. 108).

70. See Hegel, *Das System der spekulativen Philosophie*, p. 230. Hegel does not quite get Smith's numbers right. In fact, each time in his writings that he refers to Smith's pin factory (1803–04, 1805–06, 1817–18, 1819–20, 1824–25), he makes a new numerical mistake, indicating that it was not the exactness of Smith's new science that intrigued him

but rather its innovative conceptualization. See Waszek, pp. 130–31.

71. Hegel, *Naturphilosophie und Philosophie des Geistes*, vol. 3 of *Jenaer Systementwürfe*, ed. Rolf-Peter Horstmann (1805–06; Hamburg: F. Meiner, 1987), p. 229. See also Hegel, *Das System der Spekulativen Philosophie*, p. 228, and Waszek, p. 229.

72. Hegel, *Naturphilosophie und Philosophie des Geistes*, pp. 222–29. It is the interdependency of the division of labor that gives desire "the right to appear" (p. 205). Fashion, "essential and reasonable," is the manifestation of this insatiability of needs, the limitlessness of which mirrors the division of labor (p. 223). In *The Philosophy of Right* Hegel extends this early analysis of civil society, describing the "system of needs" as a process of subdivision and multiplication that goes on "*ad infinitum*"; the process has "no qualitative limits" (Hegel, *The Philosophy of Right*, trans. and ed. T. M. Knox [New York: Oxford University Press, 1967], pp. 126, 127, 128).

73. Hegel, quoted in Waszek, pp. 152, 150.

74. Hegel, *The Philosophy of Right*, p. 267.

75. Hegel, *Das System der spekulativen Philosophie*, p. 230; compare Hegel, *Naturphilosophie und Philosophie des Geistes*, pp. 223–24.

76. Riedel, p. 125.

77. Hegel, "Fragments of Historical Studies," trans. Clark Butler, Clio 7 (Fall 1977), p. 128; see Waszek, pp. 119–28.

78. Hegel, *Philosophie des Rechts: Die Vorlesung von 1819/20 in einer Nachschrift*, ed. Dieter Henrich (Frankfurt am Main:

Suhrkamp, 1983), p. 282. This is the first publication of the transcript of these lectures, a manuscript recently discovered in the Lilly Library of the University of Indiana.

79. Hegel, letter to Friedrich Immanuel Niethammer, 5 July 1816, *Hegel: The Letters*, trans. Clark Butler and Christiane Seiler, ed. Butler (Bloomington, Ind.: Indiana University Press, 1984), p. 325.

80. The conception of Marx's project for *Capital* was contemporaneous with Minard's graphic. Its brilliance is similar; its critical eloquence is derived from the fact that we are plunged beneath the surface of commodity exchange to the actual level of human suffering—here thousands of factory workers—that was the lived truth of really existing capitalism during the era of industrialization. Marx insisted that the human effects of the economy be made visible and palpable, and this remains his contribution to political economy no matter how often his theories—of crisis, of value, of increasing misery—may be disproved.

81. Schumpeter, p. 576. Marshall "worshipped" Kant and claimed that Hegel's *Philosophy of History* influenced the "substance" of his views (p. 780, n. 19), but there is no Hegelianism in his analysis, and the Kantian influence was more the neo-Kantian concern for grounding social "science" than the critical rationality of Kant's original project.

82. Mary Douglas and Baron Isherwood, *The World of Goods* (New York: Norton, 1979), p. 15.

83. Although there were precedents as early as the 1830s, and although

marginal theory fought an uphill battle before it was accepted at the end of the century (its victory largely due to its power as a counterargument to Marxist critiques of capital), the term "marginal revolution" refers to the nearly simultaneous but completely independent "discovery"—by William Stanley Jevons, Carl Menger, and Leon Walras (in Manchester, Vienna, and Lausanne around 1870)— of the principle of diminishing marginal utility. See Mark Blaug, *Economic Theory in Retrospect* (New York: Cambridge University Press, 1985), p. 309. Marshall synthesized their contributions in *Principles of Economics*. "One of the uncomfortable aspects of utility theory seemed to be the implication that only an egalitarian distribution of income maximizes satisfactions. Most writers after 1870 were extremely critical of the existing inequalities in income distribution and did not hesitate to use utility theory to fortify their critical outlook.... The Marshallian tradition culminated in Pigou's *Wealth and Welfare* (1912), which is virtually a blueprint for the welfare state. The Fabians adopted the utility theory in *Fabian Essays* (1889) to display the systematic inequities of the market mechanism.... It was the Austrian School that was markedly conservative and given over to attacks on socialism and the espousal of laissez-faire" (Blaug, pp. 302–03). F. A. Hayek, a powerful twentieth-century figure at the University of Chicago, worked in this Austrian tradition.

84. "The dominant role of the concept of substitutions at the margin in the new economics accounts for the sudden

appearance of explicitly mathematical reasoning....It is not utility theory but rather marginalism as such that gave mathematics a prominent role in economics after 1870" (Blaug, p. 296).

85. Schumpeter, p. 602.

86. Blaug, p. 309. "An unkind critic might say that neoclassical economics indeed achieved greater generality, but only by asking easier questions" (p. 299).

87. This is Thunen's theory of "symmetrical relations" between labor and capital. See Johann Heinrich von Thunen, *Der isolierte Staat in Beziehung auf Landwirtschaft und Nationalökonomie* (Berlin: Akademie-Verlag, 1990) and *Von Thunen's Isolated State*, trans. Carla M. Wartenberg, ed. Peter Hall (Oxford: Oxford University Press, 1966).

88. Marshall's "theory of the firm" equated economic growth with the expansion of the firm, an organizational model of fertility that dates to the turn of the century. Note that in Marshall's fantasy the firm was organic, with growth followed ultimately by inevitable decline and "senility."

89. Quoted in F. A. Hayek, *The Fatal Conceit: The Errors of Socialism*, vol. 1 of *The Collected Works of F. A. Hayek*, ed. W. W. Bartley III (Chicago: University of Chicago Press, 1988), p. 95.

90. Fredric Jameson, the obvious exception, still presumes that economics provides a base for cultural phenomena rather than being itself a cultural product. Bill Brown has proposed that we "see" the material evidence of the system via the media (rather than Playfair's graphics). This suggests interpreting global images as ciphers for the system, which is today cultural as well as (more importantly than?) economic.

Peter Wollen

1. Hugo Ball, *Flight out of Time: A Dada Diary* (New York: Viking, 1974), p. 104.

2. Rudolph von Laban, *A Life for Dance*, trans. Lisa Ullman (London: Macdonald & Evans Ltd., 1975), pp. 85–86.

3. Ibid., pp. 14, 16.

4. Ibid., pp. 50–51.

5. Ibid., pp. 52–53.

6. Martin Green, *Mountain of Truth: The Counterculture Begins, Ascona 1900–1920* (Hanover, N. H.: University Press of New England, 1986).

7. Martin Bernal, *The Fabrication of Ancient Greece 1785–1985*, vol. 1 of *Black Athena: The Afroasiatic Roots of Classical Civilization* (London: Free Association Books, 1987), p. 212.

8. Green, p. 99.

9. Ibid., p. 101.

10. Ball, p. 104.

11. Quoted in Susan A. Manning, *Ecstacy and the Demon: Feminism and Nationalism in the Dances of Mary Wigman* (Berkeley: University of California Press, 1993), p. 192.

12. Laban, pp. 133–34.

13. Ibid., p. 128.

14. Ibid.

15. Rudolf von Laban and F. C. Lawrence, *Effort: Economy in Body Movement* (Boston: Plays, Inc., 1974), p. 10.

16. Ibid, p. 11.

17. Ibid.

18. *Degenerate "Art,"* exhibition guide, trans. William C. Bunce (Redding, Conn.: Silver Fox Press, 1972), p. 26.

Marina Warner

1. Her full name was Jeanne Bécu, Comtesse du Barry, 1743–93.

2. Ludmilla Jordanova, *Sexual Visions: Images of Gender in Science and Medicine between the Eighteenth and Twentieth Centuries* (Madison: University of Wisconsin Press, 1989), pp. 43–65.

3. John Theodore Tussaud, *The Romance of Madame Tussaud's* (London: Madame Tussaud's, 1920), p. 52.

4. She is depicted at work in a complex tableau in the museum today, next to the scene of Marat's death, beneath shelves filled with heads of heroes past and present.

5. See Edward V. Gatacre and Laura Dru, "Portraiture in Le Cabinet de Cire de Curtius and its Successors," in *La Ceroplastica nella Scienza e nell'arte Atti del 1 Congresso Internazionale, Florence 3–7 June 1975*, vol. 2 (Florence: Leo S. Olschki, 1977), pp. 617–38; Helen E. Hinman, "Jacques-Louis David and Madame Tussaud," *Gazette des Beaux Arts* 66 (December 1965), pp. 331–38.

6. Emilie Desmier d'Archaic, born 1773, married François Louis Barthelemy de Saint Amaranthe aged 16. Died with him on June 1, 1794.

7. *La Guillotine en 1793 d'après des documents inédits des Achives nationales* (Paris: 1908), p. 290.

8. *Biographical and Descriptive Sketches of the Distinguished Characters which Compose the Unrivalled Exhibition of Madame Tussaud's and Sons* (London: Madame Tussaud's, 1850).

9. Charlotte Angeletti, *Gerformtes Wachs Kerzen,Votive,Wachsfiguren* (Munich: Calwey, 1980), Pl. 207.

10. Denis Diderot, *Oeuvres completes,* vol. 2 (Paris: Herman, 1975), p. 822.

11. William Shakespeare, *The Winter's Tale,* ed. Horace H. Furness (New York: American Scholar Publications, 1988), p. 296.

12. René Descartes, *The Philosophical Works of Descartes,* trans. Elizabeth Haldane and G.R.T. Ross, 2 vols. (Cambridge: Cambridge University Press, 1911), pp. 1, 363; Stephen Greenblatt, *Marvelous Possessions: The Wonder of the New World* (Chicago: Chicago University Press, 1991), p. 20.

13. See Angeletti, Pl. 56. A display today shows Jerry Hall being modeled, her blue eyes matched for color with a glass set.

14. See David Freedberg, *The Power of Images: Studies in the History and Theory of Response* (Chicago: University of Chicago Press, 1989).

15. Henry Weekes, *Lectures on Art* (London: Bickers and Son, 1880), p. 159. *The Tinted Venus* is in the Walker Art Gallery, Liverpool.

16. Ibid., p. 169.

17. See for instance, Francesco Solimena, "Sic Transit Gloria Mundi," in *Vanitas II Simbolismo del tempo* (Bergamo: Galleria Lorenzelli, 1981), pp. 280–81.

18. In the Victoria and Albert Museum, London.

19. See Elisabeth Bronfen, *Over Her Dead Body: Death, Femininity, and the Aesthetic* (New York: Routledge, 1992).

20. See Franco Ruggeri, "Il Museo dell'Istituto de Anatomia Umana Normale," in *I Luoghi del conoscere*, vol. 2 of *La Citta del sapere* (Milan: A. Pizzi, 1988); G. Martinotti, *Le Cere anatomiche della Specola* (Florence, 1979); and

Bronfen, pp. 100–01.

21. Rainer Maria Rilke, Rodin and Other Prose Pieces, trans. G. Craig Houston. (London: Quartet Books, 1986), p. 121.

22. A photograph in John Adams Whipple, "Hypnotism (ca. 1845)," in The Waking Dream: Photography's First Century (New York: The Metropolitan Museum of Art, 1993), shows hypnotists at work on four subjects sitting in states of trance (p. 125).

23. See Lewis Carroll, The Complete Sylvie and Bruno (San Francisco: Mercury House, 1991).

24. E.R. Hilgard and J.R. Hilgard, Hypnotism and the Relief of Pain (Los Altos, Calif.: W. Kaufman, 1975); see under "Hypnosis, Experimental," in Oxford Companion to The Mind, ed. Richard L. Gregory and O. L. Zangwill (Oxford: Oxford University Press, 1988), pp. 329–30; see also Alison Winter "'The Island of Mesmeria': The Politics of Mesmerism in Early Victorian Britain" (Ph.D. diss., Cambridge University, 1992).

Ludmilla Jordanova

This paper was revised in March 1995, not long after the release of The Road to Wellville. Although it has not received general critical acclaim, this film can be appreciated as a brilliant commentary on genres of medical display at a particular historical moment when the vogue for health and consumerism came together in a poignantly tragi-comic manner. Some of the research on which this essay is based was funded by the Wellcome Trust, to whom I give my warmest thanks. The themes discussed above have been examined in other publications that include full scholarly apparatus. See "Earth Science and Environmental Medicine: The Synthesis of the Late Enlightenment," in Images of the Earth: Essays in the History of the Environmental Sciences, ed. L. J. Jordanova and Roy S. Porter (Chalfont St. Giles: British Society for the History of Science, 1979), pp. 119–46; "Gender, Generation, and Science: William Hunter's Obstetric Atlas," in William Hunter and the Eighteenth-Century Medical World, ed. W. F. Bynum and Roy Porter (Cambridge: Cambridge University Press, 1985), pp. 385–412; "Museums: Representing the Real?" in Realism and Representation: Essays on the Problem of Realism in Relation to Science, Literature, and Culture, ed. George Levine (Madison, Wisc.: University of Wisconsin Press, 1993), pp. 255–78; "Has the Social History of Medicine Come of Age?," Historical Journal 36 (1993), pp. 437–49; "Melancholy Reflection: Constructing an Identity for Unveilers of Nature," in Frankenstein, Creation, and Monstrosity, ed. Stephen Bann (London: Maxwell Macmillan, 1994) pp. 60–76; "Medical Men: 1780–1820," in Portraiture, ed. J. Woodall (forthcoming).

1. See Steven Shapin and Simon Schaffer, Leviathan and the Air Pump: Hobbes, Boyle, and the Experimental Life (Princeton: Princeton University Press, 1985).

2. William Munk, "1770," The Roll of the Royal College of Physicians of London, vol. 2 (London: The College, Pall Mall East, 1861), p. 289.

3. See Pierre Choderlos de Laclos, Les Liaisons dangereuses, trans. Douglas Parmée (New York: Oxford University Press, 1995).

Lisa Cartwright

1. Diana Phillips Mahoney, "Picture This/RX," Computer Graphics World (September 1992), p. 43.

2. Jeffrey C. Weinreb and Helen C. Redman, Magnetic Resonance Imaging of the Body (Philadelphia: W. B. Saunders Co., 1987), p. 4.

3. See Constance Penley and Andrew Ross, eds., Technoculture (Minneapolis: University of Minnesota Press, 1991).

4. Rosalind Pollack Petchesky, "Fetal Images: The Power of Visual Culture in the Politics of Reproduction," in Reproductive Technologies: Gender, Motherhood, and Medicine, ed. Michelle Stanworth (Minneapolis: University of Minnesota Press, 1987), pp. 57–80.

5. Janelle Sue Taylor, "The Fetus and the Family Car: From Abortion Politics to a Volvo Advertisement," Public Culture 4, no. 2 (Spring 1992), pp. 67–80. See also Carol A. Stabile, "Shooting the Mother: Fetal Photography and the Politics of Disappearance," Camera Obscura 28 (Spring 1992), pp. 179–205.

6. Susan E. Browne, et al., "Sonographic Determination of Fetal Gender," American Journal of Radiology 135 (December 1980), pp. 1161–65.

7. Israel Meizner, "Sonographic Observations of In Utero Fetal 'Masturbation,'" Journal of Ultrasound in Medicine 6 (1987), p. 111.

8. Sigmund Freud, "Some Psychical Consequences of the Anatomical Distinction Between the Sexes," Standard Edition of the Complete Psychological Works of Sigmund Freud, vol. 19 (London: Hogarth Press, 1953), p. 250.

9. See Alessandra Piontelli, From Fetus to Child: An Observational and Psychoanalytic Approach (New York: Routledge, 1992).

9. Donna J. Haraway, Simians, Cyborgs, and Women (New York and London: Routledge, 1991), p. 204.

Eric Santner

1. See Michel Foucault, Preface to Gilles Deleuze and Félix Guattari, Anti-Oedipus, trans. Robert Hurley, Mark Seem, and Helen R. Lane (Minneapolis: University of Minnesota Press, 1983), p. xiii.

2. I am grateful to Elizabeth Bellamy for her lucid reflections on these issues, which she presented at the Modern Language Association's panel mentioned above in a paper entitled "Psychoanalysis and 'The Jews'—or, Can Psychoanalysis Be Postmodern?"

3. Pierre Bourdieu, Language and Symbolic Power, trans. Gino Raymond and Matthew Adamson, ed. John B. Thompson (Cambridge, Mass.: Harvard University Press, 1991), p. 113.

4. Slavoj Žižek, The Sublime Object of Ideology (London: Verso, 1989), p. 115.

5. Slavoj Žižek, Enjoy Your Symptom! Jacques Lacan in Hollywood and Out (New York: Routledge, 1992), p. 56.

6. Ibid., pp. 89–90.

7. Žižek, The Sublime Object of Ideology, pp. 126–27.

8. Slavoj Žižek, For they know not what they do: Enjoyment as a Political Factor (London: Verso, 1991), p. 206. It was precisely Nietzsche's insight into this "truth about the usurpation" that motivated his use of the genealogical—rather than historical—approach to the study of morals. See, in this regard, section 12 of

the second essay in Friedrich Nietzsche, *On the Genealogy of Morals*, trans. Walter Kaufman and R. J. Hollingdale (New York: Vintage Books, 1967), as well as Michel Foucault's important essay on the genealogical method, "Nietzsche, Genealogy, History," in *Michel Foucault: Language, Counter-Memory, Practice: Selected Essays and Interviews*, ed. D. F. Bouchard (Ithaca: Cornell University Press, 1977).

9. On this, Nietzsche's *On the Genealogy of Morals* still remains the crucial text.

10. Slavoj Žižek, "In His Bold Gaze My Ruin is Writ Large," in *Everything You Always Wanted to Know About Lacan (But Were Afraid to Ask Hitchcock)* (London: Verso, 1992).

11. One might be reminded of Christopher Lasch and Richard Sennett as the two most important critics of the "culture of narcissism."

12. In a discussion of Céline, George Steiner put it this way, "As Sartre, a close student of Céline, remarked, there is about the urban Jew something that concentrates to a singular pitch the infirm humanity of man. The Jew is not only human but a touch more human than most. In this murky light, hatred of Jews is the natural distillation of a generalized contempt for the human race" (George Steiner, "Books: Cat Man," *The New Yorker* [24 August 1992], p. 82).

13. Žižek, *The Sublime Object of Ideology*, p. 115.

14. Ibid.

15. Ibid., p. 113.

16. See Wilhelm Dolles's *Das Jüdische und das Christliche als Geistesrichtung* (1921), cited in Yosef Hayim Yerushalmi, *Freud's Moses, Judaism Terminable and Interminable*

(New Haven: Yale University Press, 1991), p. 126. Of particular interest in this context is also a short monograph by Henry Meige called *Le Juif-errant à la Salpêtrière: Etudes sur certains nevropathes*, a study of an ostensibly Jewish psychopathology of ceaseless peregrination based on observations made in Charcot's famous clinic. Meige argues there that Jews are particularly susceptible to nervous disorders and associates this in large part with a pathological restlessness: "There obsession is not absurd in itself; nothing is more legitimate than to go in search of a lucrative job or an effective remedy. What is no longer reasonable is never to be able to continue an occupation undertaken or a treatment initiated, to be always seeking *something else and somewhere else*. What is pathological is not to be able to resist this need to keep moving, which nothing justifies and which may even be detrimental." (Cited in *The Wandering Jew: Essays in the Interpretation of a Christian Legend*, ed. Galit Hasan Rokem and Alan Dudes [Bloomington: University of Indiana Press, 1986], p. 194.) Sander Gilman has done the most to situate the early history of psychoanalysis within the discourses on Jews and women circulating in nineteenth-century medicine and bourgeois European culture in general. See, for example, *Freud, Race, and Gender* (Princeton: Princeton University Press, 1993).

17. In a certain sense, Žižek understands hysteria as a kind of defense against historicism itself, against the idea that a "thick description" of an historical context, understood as a congeries of discourses and practices, is the way to secure knowledge of an historical object.

The hysteric's symptoms are efforts to negate such thick descriptions insofar as they are applied to him or her.

18. Žižek, *The Sublime Object of Ideology*, p. 113.

19. Kaja Silverman has developed this thesis in great detail, at least with regard to the question of gender, in her book *Male Subjectivity at the Margins* (New York: Routledge, 1992). She argues that women have never enjoyed the privilege of being able to disavow, by way of a phantasmatic equation of phallus and penis, the maddening complications of being a speaking subject. Her book is energized by the perhaps utopian cultural project of a more equitable distribution of the burdens of the socio-symbolic condition. Such a redistribution of psycho-semiotic labor "would require that we collectively acknowledge, at the deepest levels of our psyches, that our desires and our identity come to us from the outside, and that they are founded upon a void. It would involve, as Julia Kristeva suggests, interiorizing 'the founding separation of the socio-symbolic contract'—introducing 'its cutting edge into the very interior of every identity.' Renegotiating our relation to the Law of Language would…seem to necessitate, in other words, dismantling the images and undoing the projections and disavowals through which phallic identification is enabled" (pp. 50–51). Much of Silverman's book addresses the ways in which traumatic events such as war periodically shatter male patterns of fetishistic disavowal, serving to refeminize the conditions of male subject formation, to make it impossible for men to project, thanks to fantasy scenarios of phallic

mastery and entitlement, the hysterical structure of subjectivity onto the Other, female, Jewish, or otherwise.

20. In *Moses and Monotheism* (New York: Knopf, 1939), Freud alludes to the presence of such a "monotheistic perverse" when he suggests that in the course of their turbulent history the Jews, unwilling to abandon faith in their God and his promises to them as his chosen people, subjected themselves to ever-more stringent prohibitions, producing the unexpected by-product of perverse enjoyment. Compare in this context, Žižek, *Looking Awry: An Introduction to Jacques Lacan through Popular Culture* (Cambridge, Mass., The MIT Press, 1991): "We should, then, renounce the usual notion of the unconscious as a kind of 'reservoir' of wild, illicit drives: the unconscious is also (one is even tempted to say: above all) fragments of a traumatic, cruel, capricious, 'unintelligible' and 'irrational' law text, a set of prohibitions and injunctions. In other words, we must [citing Freud's *The Ego and the Id*] 'put forward the paradoxical proposition that the normal man is not only far more immoral than he believes but also far more moral than he knows'" (p. 152).

21. Žižek, *For they know not what they do*, p. 272.

22. Ibid., pp. 272–73.

23. Žižek, *The Sublime Object of Ideology*, p. 205.

24. Ibid., p. 205.

25. Ibid., p. 207.

26. Ibid., p. 116. Žižek would no doubt argue that it is precisely this "post-modern" dimension of the partial object, the "little piece of the real," that is missing

from Jean-François Lyotard's analysis of the "post-Holocaust condition" in his essay *Heidegger and "the Jews,"* trans. Andreas Michel (Minneapolis: University of Minnesota Press, 1990). From Žižek's perspective, Lyotard's analysis could be said to remain at the level of the traumatic interpellation, the hystericizing call that deposits in the subject a fundamental disequilibrium: "One can, one must (one cannot not) give it a thousand names: the sexual, castration of the mother, incest taboo, killing of the father, the father as name, debt, law, paralyzing stupor, seduction, and, perhaps, most beautifully: exogamy, if one redirects its meaning toward an unstoppable and uneven pairing between man and woman, but first between child and adult. Whatever the invoked scene might be, in the night of time, of individual or of the species, this scene that has not taken place, that has not had a stage, that has not even *been*, because it is not representable, but which *is*, and is *ex-*, and will remain it whatever representation, qualifications one might make of it, with which one might endow it; this event exists inside, insisting, as what exceeds every imaginative, conceptual, rational synthesis...." (p. 19).

27. See *Looking Awry*: "There is, perhaps an experience in the field of politics that entails a kind of 'identification with the symptom': the well-known pathetic experience 'We are all that!,' the experience of identification when we are confronted with a phenomenon that functions as an intrusion of unbearable truth, as an index of the fact that the social mechanism 'doesn't work.' Let us take, for example, Jew-baiting riots.... We attain an authentic attitude only when we arrive at the experience that— in a sense that is far from being simply metaphorical—'we are all Jews.' And it is the same for all traumatic moments of the intrusion into the social field of some 'impossible' kernel that resists integration: 'We all live in Chernobyl!,' 'We are all boat people!,' and so on. Apropos of these cases, it should also be clear how 'identification with the symptom' is correlated with 'going through the fantasy': by means of such an identification with the (social) symptom, we traverse and subvert the fantasy frame that determines the field of social meaning, the ideological self-understanding of a given society, in particular, the frame within which, precisely, the 'symptom' appears as some alien, disturbing intrusion, and not as the point of eruption of the otherwise hidden truth of the existing social order" (p. 140). I am arguing here that Žižek's Hegelian-Lacanian understanding of the differences between Jewish and Christian monotheism leads him to conclude that this supreme ethical attitude of enjoying or identifying with the social symptom is somehow foreclosed to Jewish theology.

28. Many of these ideas about the differences between Judaic and Christian conceptions of ethics and identificatory practices occupy Elaine Scarry in her breathtaking study of the role of the body, and more particularly, the wounded body, in providing what she calls "analogical substantiation" for the symbolic materials of human culture, *The Body in Pain: The Making and Unmaking of the World* (New York: Oxford University Press,

1985). Much of Scarry's book analyzes the ways in which societies in states of emergency, societies plagued by ideological fatigue, make use of the body in pain to reestablish the efficacy of the dominant fictions governing that society. Scarry is especially interested in the ways that torture and war, by producing this "sheer material factualness of the human body" in the form of wounds, mutilation, and agonizing physical pain, are enlisted in this enterprise of substantiation. Her goal is ultimately to demonstrate "that it is part of the original and ongoing project of civilization to diminish the reliance on (and to find substitutes for) this process of substantiation, and that this project comes in the West to be associated with an increased pressure toward material culture, or material self-expression" (p. 14). In the course of this demonstration, Scarry argues, much as Žižek does, that Jewish monotheism does not go far enough in this project of restructuring the ethical imagination. (See, in particular, pp. 204–05.)

29. See The Sublime Object of Ideology, p. 116, and Enjoy Your Symptom!, p. 57. In this context, Serge Leclaire's theological gloss on the Lacanian concept of the phallus is most interesting: "Let us call the phallus 'God.' It's an old tradition. You don't have to see 'God,' properly speaking, you have no image of him. 'God' (the phallus) is invisible; therefore, the relation to the phallus is marked by a nonformalizable relation, a relation of exclusion. At the same time, everything is in relation to the phallus; everything is in relation to 'God.' Let's suppose that there is a child, Jesus, the son of God, who

serves as mediator. Now, let's replace the 'child Jesus' with the penis, which happens to be the most convenient representative of the phallus. Because man has in his body a relation with his *penis as the representative of the phallus*, schematically, his natural inclination leads him to forget the fact that the phallus ('God') is invisible, unseizable, unnamable. But woman does not have this representative in her body; therefore, her relation to the phallus is less veiled. She is less tempted to forget the fact that the phallus is absent. Consequently, man's and woman's relations to castration are profoundly different. I am referring to castration as the relation to the phallus, to the Invisible, to an unnamable term. In Lacanian language I would say that it is both signifier and object.... In the whole evolution and history of woman, nothing has ever come as a screen between the invisible 'God,' phallus, and the way she speaks. For man, the possession of the penis, which is highly cathected, serves as a screen denying the fundamental character of castration. Man comes to believe that he has not been castrated" (cited in Silverman, Male Subjectivity, p. 43). Žižek's "postmodern" point, here, would be, I think, that Jesus is also available as a kind of partial object or symptom, an identification with which can mobilize an even more radical experience of castration rather than mask it.

30. Žižek, Looking Awry, p. 150.

31. Enjoy Your Symptom!, pp. 79–80.

32. I understand Elaine Scarry to be arguing much the same thing in The Body in Pain, where, for example, she suggests there may be a necessary correlation

between the anti-authoritarian impulse and an emphasis on material culture, an emphasis seen as lacking in the Hebrew scriptures and as figuring quite prominently in the New Testament writings (see especially, pp. 241–42).

33. For an in-depth discussion of Wagner's anti-Semitism in its historical context, see Paul Lawrence Rose, *Wagner, Race, and Revolution* (New Haven: Yale University Press, 1992).

34. Bourdieu, *Language and Symbolic Power*, p. 106. In a later section of the book, Bourdieu cites a contemporary example of liturgical crisis brought on by a certain priest's behavior that could be compared with Amfortas's seduction: "Two years ago an old lady who was a neighbor of mine lay dying, and asked me to fetch the priest. He arrived but without being able to give communion, and, after administering the last rites, kissed her. If, in my last moments on earth, I ask for a priest, it isn't so that he can kiss me, but so that he can bring me what I need to make the journey to eternity. That kiss was an act of paternalism and not of sacred Ministry" (p. 115). To put it in Foucaultian terms, the kiss marks the point where "sexuality" is produced as the by-product of a transgression of traditional authority, of a shift to a different kind of power and mode of "treatment" of the subject.

35. Drawing on an association between Amfortas's wound and the famously repulsive world described by Kafka in his short prose text, "A Country Doctor," Žižek suggests, against all expectation, a deeper, thematic affinity between Wagner's late-Romantic fetish-ization of Germanic legends and Kafka's decidedly post-Romantic explorations of totalitarian bureaucracy: "…if we look closely we perceive that the fundamental problem of *Parsifal* is eminently a bureaucratic one: the incapacity, the incompetence of Amfortas in performing his ritual-bureaucratic duty…In a somewhat perfunctory sociological manner, we could say that Wagner's *Parsifal* is staging the historical fact that the classical Master (Amfortas) is no longer capable of reigning in the conditions of totalitarian bureaucracy and that he must be replaced by a new figure of a Leader (Parsifal)" (Žižek, *The Sublime Object of Ideology*, pp. 76–77.)

36. Slavoj Žižek, "'The Wound is Healed Only by the Spear that Smote You': The Operatic Subject and Its Vicissitudes," in *Opera Through Other Eyes*, ed. David J. Levin (Palo Alto, Calif.: Stanford University Press, 1993), pp. 205–06.

37. Thomas Elsaesser has recently suggested that such a status/condition was precisely what Rainer Werner Fassbinder attempted to embody in his films (public lecture, Dartmouth College, 1 November 1992), which may go a long way in understanding Fassbinder's highly ambiguous relation to women and Jews. For an extended reading of Fassbinder from a similar approach, see Silverman, *Male Subjectivity at the Margins*.

38. Žižek, "'The Wound is Healed Only by the Spear that Smote You,'" p. 218.

39. Žižek has noted that his own approach can seem at times to come close to the perverse scenario. See "The Sublime Theorist of Slovenia:

Peter Canning interviews Slavoj Žižek," *Artforum* 31, no. 7 (March 1993).

40. Žižek's position here is quite close to that taken by Judith Butler in *Gender Trouble: Feminism and the Subversion of Identity* (NewYork: Routledge, 1990). See, in particular, pp. 56–57. Butler's own position in *Gender Trouble* is not that one should or could project oneself beyond the reach of Law into a realm of pre- or postjuridical innocence, but rather that one can, by way of parody, *repeat* the institutions of Law from the perspective of the Law's own inconsistency; and from the point of view of its own aberrant products, its—to use Žižek's phrase —"queer remainders." Such breakdown products of the Law serve to materialize the Law's own vicious circularity, its existence as a set of discursive practices, which produce the realities it claims only to manage. According to Butler, *insofar* as the Law is productive and not merely restrictive or repressive, it necessarily produces more than it wants to. This "more" is what I have called the "monotheistic perverse." In *The Bonds of Love: Psychoanalysis, Feminism, and the Problem of Domination* (NewYork: Pantheon, 1988), Jessica Benjamin, working primarily within an object relations framework informed by the Hegelian-Marxist legacy of the Frankfurt School, proposes a theory of mutual recognition in which we find the same structural paradoxes. In Benjamin's view, the ethical space of intersubjectivity, a space free of domination, is paradoxically dependent upon the perverse remainders of this ethical space. The ethical subject can play with perverse fantasy as a support for recogni-

tion of another human subject, whereas the pervert's only source of connection to the other is in the fantasy scenario of his or her destruction as other. Most importantly, the constitution of a social space free of domination cannot do without the "symptom," the perverse remainder.

Scott Bukatman

I would like to thank the Colloquium der Abteilungen Literatur und Kultur at the Freie Universitat Berlin, John F. Kennedy Institut für Nordamerikastudien for their very helpful comments, questions, and discussion during the summer of 1994.

1. An attempt to situate authorship around the visual designers of the film is progressive in that it displaces the director as the sole "author" of a cinematic text, but it retains a reliance upon the continuity of a single creator as a locus of textual meaning. While this latter position has been roundly criticized in recent years as outmoded in its assumption of a coherent subjectivity, it has produced an undeniably important body of textual interpretation. Authorship remains a valuable critical concept, although it is a tool to be wielded with some caution.

2. Such ontological questions are emphasized when the technologies are *alien* in origin.

3. Jonathan Crary, *Techniques of the Observer: OnVision and Modernity in the Nineteenth Century* (Cambridge, Mass.: The MIT Press, 1990), p. 2.

4. Ibid., p. 9.

5. Ibid., p. 24. The idea that increasing industrialization and rising urban concentration challenges older paradigms

of spatio-visual experience is not new—
Henri Lefebvre wrote in his book
Production of Space, trans. Donald Nicholson
Smith (Oxford: Basil Blackwell, 1991).
"The fact is that around 1910 a certain
space was shattered. It was the space of
common sense, of knowledge, of social
practice, of political power, a space hith-
erto enshrined in everyday discourse, just
as in abstract thought, as the environment
of and channel for communications;
the space, too, of classical perspective
and geometry, developed from the
Renaissance onwards on the basis of the
Greek tradition (Euclid, logic) and bodied forth in Western art and philosophy,
as in the form of the city and town. Such
were the shocks and onslaughts suffered
by this space that today it retains but a
feeble pedagogical reality, and then only
with great difficulty, within a conservative educational system" (p. 25). Their
periodization may be at odds, but Crary
and Lefebvre are concerned with the
same epistemological rupture. Lefebvre
even shares with Crary the sense that this
is not simply a shift within the field of
"representation," but the disappearance
of a particular lived, *bodied* conception
of spatiality.

6. Ibid., p. 136.

7. Ibid., p. 14.

8. Ibid., p. 19.

9. Ibid., p. 103.

10. Ibid., p. 44.

11. See Wolfgang Schivelbusch, *The
Railway Journey: The Industrialization of Time
and Space in the 19th Century* (Berkeley:
The University of California Press, 1986).
Originally published in German in 1977.

12. Crary, p. 24.

13. Ibid., p. 7.

14. Barbara Maria Stafford, *Artful
Science: Enlightenment Entertainment and the
Eclipse of Visual Education* (Cambridge,
Mass.: The MIT Press, 1994), p. 51.

15. Ibid., p. xxii.

16. Ibid., p. 51.

17. Ibid., p. 32.

18. Ibid., p. 3.

19. Barbara Maria Stafford, *Body
Criticism: Imaging the Unseen in Enlightenment
Art and Medicine* (Cambridge, Mass.:
The MIT Press, 1991), p. 343.

20. Susan Buck-Morss, *The Dialectics of
Seeing: Walter Benjamin and the Arcades Project*
(Cambridge, Mass.: The MIT Press, 1989),
p. 91.

21. Ralph Hyde, *Panoramania: The Art
and Entertainment of the "All-Embracing" View*
(London: Trefoil Publications, 1988),
p. 37.

22. Tom Gunning, "The Cinema of
Attractions: Early Film, Its Spectator, and
the Avant-Garde," in *Early Cinema: Space,
Frame, Narrative*, ed. Thomas Elsaesser
(London: British Film Institute, 1990),
p. 57.

23. Miriam Hansen, *Babel & Babylon:
Spectatorship in American Silent Film*
(Cambridge, Mass.: Harvard University
Press, 1991), p. 34.

24. Ibid., p. 83.

25. Gunning, p. 57.

26. See Annette Michelson, "Bodies
in Space: Film as 'Carnal Knowledge,'"
Artforum 8, no. 6 (1969), pp. 54–63.

27. Brooks Landon, *The Aesthetics of
Ambivalence: Rethinking Science Fiction Film in
the Age of Electronic (Re)production* (Westport,
Conn.: Greenwood Press, 1992), p. 94.

28. While this is not the place to

review the entire, complex history of the sublime, a very useful review is provided in Raimonda Modiano, *Coleridge and the Concept of Nature* (Tallahassee: Florida State University Press, 1985), pp. 101–14.

29. *Longinus on the Sublime*, trans. W. R. Roberts (1935), p. 65.

30. See Modiano, p. 106.

31. Joseph Addison, in *The Spectator* (2 July 1712), cited in Andrew Wilton, *Turner and the Sublime* (Chicago: University of Chicago Press, 1980), p. 11.

32. Andrew Wilton argues that this was a careful strategy of Turner's, and finds that a significant progression in his series of marine paintings (1801–10) "is one of gradually increasing involvement of the spectator in the scenes depicted" (Wilton, p. 46).

33. To concentrate solely upon the phallic implications of this movement of penetration seems to me unfairly and uninterestingly reductive (except, I'll admit, in the case of *Star Trek*). Annette Michelson, for example, has linked this cinematic trope to works by Stanley Kubrick, Michael Snow, and Claude Lanzmann, among others. See Michelson, "Bodies in Space."

34. Further, spectatorship is especially pronounced in the films of Steven Spielberg, whose characters spend much of their time staring upwards (or downwards, in the case of *Jaws*, 1975).

35. For some viewers, the *Star Trek* action figures may be an exception.

36. Note the extended sequences during which amplified breathing dominates the soundtrack, an auditory effect that often has a regulatory effect on the spectator's own respiration.

See Michelson, "Bodies in Space."

37. Alan Trachtenberg, *The Incorporation of America: Culture and Society in the Gilded Age* (New York: Hill & Wang, 1982), p. 59.

38. Ralph Waldo Emerson, "Nature," in *Selected Essays, Lectures, and Poems*, ed. Robert D. Richardson (New York: Bantam Books, 1990), pp. 18–19.

39. The connection forged between the Western landscape and American transcendentalism might help explain an odd portion of the Stargate sequence, as the cinephilic spectator suddenly recognizes the spires and pinnacles of Monument Valley. While I assumed that this was simply an obvious and rather pointless homage to John Ford, perhaps there is another explanation. Referring to the furfeit of representations of the American West in the nineteenth century, Barbara Novak has written, "For the vast expansive prairies, the immense extensions of space, the awesome mountains, the forbidding and majestic scale that characterized the varied landscape of the West could only then, as now, be called 'sublime'" (Barbara Novak, *Nature and Culture: American Landscape Painting, 1825–1875* [New York: Oxford University Press, 1980], p. 149). It is at least possible that Clarke and Kubrick's tale of a lone pioneer traveling through the "forbidding and majestic landscapes" that lie "beyond the infinite" might make some reference to these aesthetic forebears.

40. John Wilmerding, ed., *American Light: The Luminist Movement, 1850–1875*, (Washington, D. C.: National Gallery of Art, 1980), p. 98.

41. Earl A. Powell, "Luminism and the American Sublime," in Wilmerding, p. 72.

42. Novak, p. 27.

43. These canvases were indeed large-scale works (Church's *The Heart of the Andes* [1859] measured about 66-by-120 inches), and Barbara Novak has noted that a consideration of these works must involve "a consideration of art as spectacle." She further notes that "this art had a clear twentieth-century heir in the film, which rehearsed many of the nineteenth century's concerns" (ibid., p. 19).

44. Wilton, p. 39 (my emphasis).

45. See David C. Huntington, "Church and Luminism: Light for America's Elect," in Wilmerding, pp. 155–92.

46. Powell, p. 90.

47. Novak, pp. 41–42.

48. Wilmerding, p. 121.

49. Novak, pp. 37 and 29.

50. Mark Seltzer, *Bodies and Machines* (New York: Routledge, 1992), p. 3.

51. See Leo Marx, *The Machine in the Garden: Technology and the Pastoral Ideal in America* (New York: Oxford University Press, 1964).

52. Ibid., p. 206.

53. Novak, p. 4.

54. See Rosalind Williams, *Notes on the Underground: An Essay on Technology, Society, and the Imagination* (Cambridge, Mass.: The MIT Press, 1990).

55. Buck-Morss, p. 70 (my emphasis).

56. Ibid., p. 140.

57. Ibid.

58. This is a trajectory completed in the cyberspace of William Gibson's novel *Neuromancer* (West Bloomfield, Mich.: Phantasia Press, 1986).

59. Thomas Weiskel, *The Romantic Sublime: Studies in the Structure and Psychology of Transcendence* (Baltimore: Johns Hopkins University Press, 1976), p. 6.

60. "His current projects, like *Smoke*, carry the implications of these hazards further, as even in the midst of a gorgeous abstraction of smoke and sky the viewer remembers that chemical pollution from industrial plants poses an unremitting, ongoing health threat that cannot, should not, be ignored. Pfahl does not ask the viewer to indulge in mere passive contemplation, even though it must be admitted that the unbridled beauty of his landscapes is a temptation. Pfahl asks that we think." (Estelle Jussim, "Passionate Observer: The Art of John Pfahl," *A Distanced Land: The Photographs of John Pfahl*, ed. Cheryl Brutvan [University of New Mexico Press, in association with Albright-Knox Gallery, 1990], p. 25.)

61. Wilton, p. 101.

62. Novak, p. 97.

63. Edmund Burke, *On the Sublime and the Beautiful* (Charlottesville, Va.: Ibis Publishing, Facsimile of 1812 Edition), p. 145.

64. Williams, p. 185.

65. Novak, p. 157.

66. Williams, p. 1.

67. On the resistance to progressivism, see T. J. Jackson Lears, *No Place of Grace: Antimodernism and the Transformation of American Culture, 1880–1920* (Chicago: University of Chicago Press, 1994).

68. Weiskel, p. 92.

69. See Patricia Yaeger, "The Language of Blood: Toward a Maternal Sublime," in *Genre: Forms of Discourse and Culture* 25, no. 1 (1992).

70. Harold Bloom, *Agon: Towards a Theory of Revisionism* (New York: Oxford University Press, 1982), p. 12.

71. Ibid., p. 238.

72. Ibid., p. 206.

73. Novak, p. 176.

74. Cited in Richard Slotkin, *Regeneration Through Violence: The Mythology of the American Frontier, 1600–1860* (Middletown, Conn.: Wesleyan University Press, 1973), p. 525.

75. See Vivian Sobchack, "The Virginity of Astronauts: Sex and the Science Fiction Film," *Alien Zone: Cultural Theory and Contemporary Science Fiction Cinema*, ed. Annette Kuhn (London: Verso, 1990), pp. 103–15. This is especially true of *Star Trek: The Motion Picture* (directed by Robert Wise). Sobchack has noted the privileging, in science fiction cinema, of penetration over procreation. Penetration is, in fact, the sole plot device in *Star Trek*, which also features an array of references to the "Creator," "Enterprise" (a fascinating contraction, particularly when someone notes that "Enterprise is barren"), and the "Kirk-unit." This most virginal of virginal astronaut films is actually a screwy masterpiece of sexual displacement.

76. Hansen, p. 112.

CONTRIBUTORS

Edward Ball has been architecture columnist for *The Village Voice* and managing editor of *Lusitania*, a bilingual journal of criticism, and is a contributor to National Public Radio. He is currently writing a book about his family's slave-owning past for Farrar, Straus & Giroux.

Stephen Bann is a cultural historian concerned with the representation of history in museums and collections, as well as a critic of contemporary art. He is Director of the Centre of Modern Cultural Studies at the University of Kent, Canterbury, England. He is also the author of *The True Vine: On Visual Representation and the Western Tradition* (Cambridge University Press, 1989), *Under the Sign: John Bargrave as Traveler, Collector, and Witness* (University of Michigan Press, 1994), and *Romanticism and the Rise of History* (Maxwell Macmillan International, 1995).

Susan Buck-Morss is Professor of Political Philosophy and Social Theory in the Government Department at Cornell University. Her books include *The Origin of Negative Dialectics: Theodor W. Adorno, Walter Benjamin, and the Frankfurt Institute* (Harvester Press, 1977) and *The Dialectics of Seeing: Walter Benjamin and the Arcades Project* (MIT Press, 1989).

Scott Bukatman is Assistant Professor in the Media Arts Program at the University of New Mexico in Albuquerque. He is the author of *Terminal Identity: The Virtual Subject in Postmodern Science Fiction* (Duke University Press, 1993). He is also the coorganizer of "Cine City: Film and Perceptions of Urban Space, 1895–1995" at the Getty Center in Los Angeles.

Lisa Cartwright is Associate Professor of English and Visual Cultural Studies at the University of Rochester. She is the author of *Screening the Body: Tracing Medicine's Visual Culture* (University of Minnesota Press, 1995) and coeditor of *Imaging Technologies, Science and Gender* (Indiana University Press, forthcoming).

Lynne Cooke has been Curator at the Dia Center for the Arts since 1991.
She has published widely on contemporary art, and is coeditor of *Joseph Beuys: Arena — where would I have got if I had been intelligent!* (D.A.P. in association with Dia Center for the Arts, 1994). She has also taught at various institutions including the University of London.

Ludmilla Jordanova has been Professor of Cultural History at the University of York, England, since 1993. Previously she held posts at the Universities of Cambridge, Oxford, and Essex. She is the author of *Sexual Visions: Images of Gender in Science and Medicine between the Eighteenth and Twentieth Centuries* (University of Wisconsin Press, 1989).

Jean-Hubert Martin was Director of the Musée National d'Art Moderne, Centre Georges Pompidou, Paris, from 1987 to 1990. In 1989, he cocurated the exhibition "Magiciens de la Terre." Presently, he is Artistic Director of the Chateau d'Oiron.

Ann Reynolds is Professor of Art History at the University of Texas at Austin. She is completing a book entitled *Robert Smithson: Learning from New Jersey and Elsewhere.*

Ralph Rugoff is a writer and curator in Los Angeles. He writes about art, contemporary visual culture, and popular museums. He is the author of the forthcoming book, *Circus Americanus.*

Eric Santner teaches in the Germanic Languages and Literatures Department at Princeton University. He is the author of *Stranded Objects: Mourning, Memory, and Film in Postwar Germany* (Cornell University Press, 1990).

Susan Stewart is a critic and poet. She is the author of the critical works *Crimes of Writing: Problems in the Containment of Representation* (Oxford University Press, 1991), and *On Longing: Narratives of the Miniature, the Gigantic, the Souvenir, the Collection* (Johns Hopkins University Press, 1984). Her poetry is featured in *The Hive* (University of Georgia Press, 1987) and *The Forest* (University of Chicago Press, 1995).

Marina Warner is a writer, critic, and historian. She is the author of a collection of essays, *Six Myths of Our Time: Little Angels, Little Monsters, Beautiful Beasts, and More* (Vintage, 1995) and the socio-cultural study, *From the Beast to the Blonde: On Fairytales and Their Tellers* (Farrar, Straus & Giroux).

Peter Wollen is Professor of Film in the Critical Studies Program of the Film Department at the University of California, Los Angeles. He is a filmmaker, film theorist, and has written widely on the history of art. His most recent books are *Raiding the Icebox: Reflections on Twentieth-Century Culture* (Indiana University Press, 1993) and *Singin' in the Rain* (BFI Publishing, 1992). He has also curated exhibitions, including "Frida Kahlo and Tina Modotti" and "The Situationists International."

PHOTO CREDITS

Page 8, Photography Collection, Harry Ransom Humanities Research Center, The University of Texas at Austin; page 14, Courtesy The Pierpont Morgan Library, New York; page 17, Christopher Wilson; page 19, courtesy Stephen Bann; page 23, Courtesy Getty Research Center, Resource Collections; page 30, courtesy The Detroit Institute of Arts; Founders Society Purchase, Director's Discretionary Fund; Copyright ©1995 Founders Society Detroit Institute of Arts; page 36, Private Collection; page 39, courtesy Philadelphia Museum of Art, Given by The Barra Foundation, Inc.; page 43, courtesy Philadelphia Museum of Art, The George W. Elkins Collection; page 47, courtesy The Peale Museum, Baltimore City Life Museums; page 48, courtesy The Pennsylvania Academy of the Fine Arts, Philadelphia. Collections Fund; page 50, Collection of The New York Historical Society; page 52, The Pennsylvania Academy of the Fine Arts, Gift of Mrs. Sarah Harrison (The Joseph Harrison, Jr. Collection); pages 54, 60, 62, 63, 64, 65, and 67, courtesy Daniel Spoerri; page 56, Stefan Moses; page 57, courtesy Claes Oldenburg; pages 68, 71, and 81, courtesy Museum of Jurassic Technology, Los Angeles, California; pages 76–77 and 79, courtesy Los Angeles County Sheriff's Museum, Whittier, California; pages 82, 84,

86, and 96, courtesy Ann Reynolds; page 97, Neg. no. 321862A, photo by A. Rota, courtesy Department of Library Services, American Museum of Natural History; page 100, Neg. no. 323965, photo by Rota-Logan, courtesy Department of Library Services, American Museum of Natural History; page 102, Neg no. 321873, photo by A. Rota, courtesy Department of Library Services, American Museum of Natural History; page 104, Neg no. 321867, photo by A. Rota, courtesy Department of Library Services, American Museum of Natural History; page 110, Picture Collection, New York Public Library; pages 112, 114, 117, 125, 129, 130, 135, 138, 140, and 141, courtesy Susan Buck-Morss; pages 142, 144, 145, 146, 149, 150, 152, and 153, courtesy of Edward Ball; page 154, 164, 166–67, and 173, courtesy The Museum of Modern Art, New York; pages 159 and 160, courtesy of the Mary Wigman Archive, Berlin; page 174, courtesy Dr. Mario-Andreas von Lüttichau, Museum Folkwang, Essen; pages 178, 182, 183, 184, 194, 195, 196, and 197, courtesy Madame Tussaud's, London; page 200, courtesy The Prints and Photographs Collection, History of Medicine Division, National Library of Medicine; page 202, Tate Gallery, London/Art Resource, New York, photo by John Webb; pages 204,

Discussions in Contemporary Culture is an award-winning series of books copublished by Dia Center for the Arts, New York City, and Bay Press, Seattle. These volumes offer rich and interactive discourses on a broad range of cultural issues in formats that encourage scrutiny of diverse critical approaches and positions.

Discussions in Contemporary Culture
Edited by Hal Foster

Vision and Visuality
Edited by Hal Foster

The Work of Andy Warhol
Edited by Gary Garrels

Remaking History
Edited by Barbara Kruger
and Philomena Mariani

Democracy
A Project by Group Material
Edited by Brian Wallis

If You Lived Here
The City in Art, Theory, and
Social Activism
A Project by Martha Rosler
Edited by Brian Wallis

Critical Fictions
The Politics of Imaginative Writing
Edited by Philomena Mariani

Black Popular Culture
Edited by Gina Dent

Culture on the Brink
Ideologies of Technology
Edited by Gretchen Bender
and Timothy Druckrey

For information:
Bay Press
115 West Denny Way
Seattle, WA 98119
tel. 206.284.5913
fax. 206.284.1218